FORGING A NEW SWORD

AMERICAN PROJECT SERIES
Center for International Studies
Massachusetts Institute of Technology

FORGING A NEW SWORD

A Study of the Department of Defense

By WILLIAM R. KINTNER

in association with

Joseph I. Coffey *and* Raymond J. Albright

Harper & Brothers, Publishers, New York

Library of Congress catalog card number: 58-7973

CONTENTS

CHARTS

FOREWORD

W. W. ROSTOW

Director, American Project
Center for International Studies
Massachusetts Institute of Technology

The American Project—a Carnegie Corporation-financed venture at the Center for International Studies, M. I. T.—is concerned with the interaction between the United States as a domestic society and its problems and performance on the world scene. The postwar evolution of American military policy and organization is a central issue; a substantial part of the nation's problem in dealing with the world is a military problem. Moreover, for close on to two decades almost every aspect of our life at home has been touched by the scale and character of the military effort required for our survival.

It has been my responsibility to form views on this revolutionary national experience; and these will be presented in another forthcoming book *The United States and the World.* In addition, however, I judged it essential to have prepared and presented an independent analysis focused around certain of the issues of defense organization which are the legitimate concern of every citizen but on which it is difficult for even the well-informed layman to hold confident views.

We were extraordinarily lucky in persuading Colonel William R. Kintner, United States Army, to devote himself to this enterprise in time off-duty in the midst of a busy and responsible career; and he, in turn, exhibited rare qualities of enterprise in mobilizing a distinguished group of colleagues.

Although I share many of the judgments reached by Colonel Kintner and his associates, this book is, of course, wholly theirs. It represents a candid but measured effort to make generally available insights and conclusions which only those living and working within the military establishment could form. Whether and how the military establishment should move toward further unification is, of course, a spiky question, on which men honestly differ. The authors claim nothing sacrosanct for the concrete proposals presented in the final chapters of the book. I can, however, state something with confidence about those proposals: they are in no sense a brief for the position of a single military service. They were developed by the authors out of the living experience of many men, military and civilian, reflecting on that experience as American citizens rather than as soldiers, sailors, airmen, or bureaucrats. One knowledgeable in the history of American military organization will note, for example, that their proposals weave together two great tested principles: the Army principle of strong civilian control, exercised through unified military command, backed by first-class staff work; and the Navy principle of separating command over forces at combat readiness from the administration of training and logistical support.

Aside from the merits of the final recommendations made by Colonel Kintner and his associates, the book is an effort to help break down the barrier between the interested citizen and important aspects of his nation's policies and problems that have remained dangerously remote from public and even Congressional attention. Among hard-pressed Congressmen and Senators, all but a few have traditionally been inclined to leave the problems of defense to the Executive Branch and to hope for the best. Defense matters usually reach public attention only in the form of interservice quarrels and budgetary debates, or on other enflamed or melodramatic occasions, as with the Soviet satellite of October 1957. The deeper and more abiding problems of fashioning and re-fashioning an effective military establishment, loyal to democratic principle and capable of guaranteeing survival in a world of continuing conflict and technological revolution, are not sufficiently discussed or understood. This is a bad thing in a working democracy.

This book is, then, an exercise in expanding the democratic process as well as a constructive contribution to the continuing national debate on defense policy.

PREFACE

The prophecy made by de Tocqueville over a century ago regarding the United States and Russia has been fulfilled: ". . . they have suddenly placed themselves in the front rank among the nations . . . their starting point is different, and their courses are not the same; yet each of them seems marked out by the will of Heaven to sway the destinies of half the globe."

The United States for the first time in its history faces a powerful opponent capable either of making a direct military attack on the United States or of undermining United States security by a gradual takeover of the remaining nonCommunist areas in Europe and Asia. Moreover, the fact that the Communist system is, of its nature, committed to aggression in every dimension has changed the nature of our defense problems. Conflict is no longer limited to military warfare directed by trained military experts. The specific military means must therefore be constantly related to the many other factors on which national security depends.

Illustrations of this interconnection are legion. The fact that some of the American prisoners of war captured in Korea collaborated with their Communist captors shows how vital is sound education to the performance of our troops in battle. The attitude of our citizens toward war itself and to the types of conflicts in which they believe we might engage determines their willingness to contribute their funds and their services to our national defense effort. The kinds of men who can be recruited to enter public life and our methods of training top executives for the government departments have become important factors in the global struggle. In short, we are living in a period when the interplay between military power and the sociological, economic, political, and cultural elements of our society is greater than ever before.

Figuratively speaking, the impact of the Pentagon reaches every

American city, town, and hamlet and every level of American society. Over 10 per cent of our current gross national product is used to support defense activities. Over half the basic and applied research undertaken in the United States is devoted to military purposes. The insatiable demands of our defense industry for trained scientists and engineers have necessitated a critical re-examination of the American educational system. Entire communities have been established because of some specific defense need. Because of its ubiquitous influence on our national life, the Department of Defense has long since ceased to be the sole responsibility of either civilian governmental officials or our trained professional military men. National security today is everybody's business. The existing structure and the future evolution of the Defense Department are of major political and sociological concern.

This book examines the evolution of the Department of Defense in relation to the American society which created it and which it, in turn, serves. It focuses on problems which are the direct responsibility of the Defense Department, but it is set in the context of the reciprocal relations between our defense policies and programs as such and the broader issues of national security. Its subject is in a sense the process whereby human beings work together in a gigantic enterprise: the defense of the United States.

This book is the result of a cooperative effort. The authors have had frequent opportunity to observe the operations of the Defense Department from many vantage points—from beneath and within it, and from positions alongside and above it in other agencies of the United States Government. To all of us the opportunity of exploring the evolving defense structure in a comprehensive way was a provocative and stimulating challenge. Our research has been conducted with the fullest possible freedom of inquiry as to material and to findings. The authors have had no axe to grind. They have searched for no individual heroes or culprits.

My own approach to the problem has been influenced by past associations with men who had to grapple officially with this issue. I acknowledge my indebtedness to several men for the inspiration and guidance which they have given me in the course of my career in governmental operations. Among them are Colonel Kilbourne Johnson, former Director of a principal element in the Central Intelligence Agency, who gave me generously of his rich years of experience on the War Department General Staff, and Brig. General Charles H. Bonesteel, III, former defense member of the National Security Council Planning Board, whose appreciation of the subtleties of the relations existing between the Secretary of Defense and the Joint Chiefs of Staff and of the Armed

Services gave me invaluable insight. During my services on the staff of Nelson A. Rockefeller, Special Assistant to the President, I gained from him and from his principal assistant, Major General Theodore Parker, an appreciation of the dynamic relations among the executive departments at the national level.

My participation in numerous studies conducted at the Operations Research Office of Johns Hopkins University and in the discussions of the Foreign Policy Research Institute of the University of Pennsylvania concerning a wide range of substantive and procedural problems confronting the United States Government added immensely to the background on which I was able to draw in developing this book.

Equally valuable was the contribution made by some of my working-level contemporaries. These include Colonel Frank Elliott, a graduate of the National War College and a member for several years of the Air Force Staff and the International Security Affairs Staff in the Office of the Secretary of Defense; Brig. General Clifton Von Kann, a graduate of the National War College and the Harvard School of Business Administration, who has served in the Comptroller's Office of the Department of the Army; Colonel Cuyler Clarke, a graduate of the National War College, who has served on the Department of Defense Staff on two occasions and also in the Office of the Secretary of the Army.

It is difficult to express adequately my appreciation to those men closely associated with the project who have either contributed to drafting the various chapters or who have participated in the review, criticism, reorganizing, and editing of the work.

The two who have made the greatest individual contributions are my associates: Colonel Joseph I. Coffey and Mr. Raymond J. Albright.

Colonel Joseph Coffey received his doctoral degree in international affairs from Georgetown University, where he is a lecturer in the Graduate School, and has served on both the Army General Staff and in the Department of Defense. He also participated as Assistant Director in the Special Studies Project of the Rockefeller Brothers Fund during the year 1956-1957. Colonel Coffey contributed some of the material in Part II and is in large measure responsible for Parts III and IV of the study, which deal with recommended changes in the Department of Defense. (The line of argument set forth in Part III was developed and focused over a long series of discussions in which many of the persons mentioned above participated.) In addition, Colonel Coffey performed with rare skill the role of *alter ego* in preparing the text for publication. Because of my reassignment to France in the fall of 1957 there fell upon him the burden of final preparation of the book, a task which he performed with care and with competent judgment.

Mr. Raymond J. Albright, a Foreign Affairs Officer in the Office of the Secretary of Defense for the past several years, is currently completing his dissertation for the doctoral degree in political science from Harvard University. Mr. Albright developed the bibliography and bore the major task of research for the initial portions of this study. He also helped in drafting many of the chapters, particularly those in Part II, materially assisted in the coordination and review of individual contributions, and aided Colonel Coffey in preparing the final text.

Others who had a direct hand in either writing or criticism include Dr. John R. Probert, a member of the faculty of the United States Naval Academy at Annapolis, Maryland, who has specialized in studies in the field of organization for National Security Affairs, Lt. Col. Anthony Wermuth, formerly in the Office of the Chief of Staff, United States Army, and Dr. Eli Ginzberg of Columbia University. Officers from the military services and civilians in and out of the Department of Defense have provided valuable advice on portions of this book.

Walt Rostow's confidence in the ultimate outcome of the project and his pointed and illuminating suggestions were helpful throughout the entire undertaking. Other members of the CENIS staff have contributed their time and effort. In particular, the skillful editorial assistance and organizing ability of Mr. Richard W. Hatch were instrumental in putting the material into more readable form.

Whatever merit the book may possess is due to the contributions of all these wise and experienced people. The responsibility for the views and interpretations expressed are solely my own. The final story, however, represents an unusual degree of consensus regarding the evolutionary process which is molding the future Department of Defense.

WILLIAM R. KINTNER
Colonel, United States Army

Part I

BACKGROUND OF
THE PRESENT INQUIRY

One

SOME REASONS
FOR THE PRESENT INQUIRY

Any meaningful inquiry into the present functioning of the Department of Defense proceeds implicitly from the fact that for the first time in its history the United States is faced with a direct threat to its existence. There appears to be little doubt that the Soviet Union is capable of dealing a serious, if not shattering, blow to our political, social, and economic structure—and that it is restrained from such an attack only by the knowledge that the United States is presently capable of delivering an even more shattering retaliatory blow.

Looking ahead, it is evident, since the Soviet stockpile of nuclear weapons is bound to grow and the Soviet system for the delivery of such weapons is bound to improve and increase, that we may soon find ourselves in an era of relative nuclear plenty, when each side will be capable of devastating the other regardless of either defensive measures or the effect of initial attacks upon the striking force of the other. To use the now classic analogy, the United States and the Soviet Union may soon confront each other like scorpions in a bottle, each afraid to sting the other for fear of being killed itself. Such a state of affairs will not necessarily mean that the Soviet scorpion will be deterred from moves against other countries of the Free World or from the initiation of actions which, although short of general nuclear war, may threaten United States security. In fact, an uneasy but definite balance in the field of strategic deterrents may well encourage the Communists to campaign even more actively and freely than during the period of our air-atomic superiority— when they did not hesitate to stage a *coup d'état* in Czechoslovakia, initiate the Berlin Blockade, support the invasion of South Korea, and, even after the death of Stalin, press to a successful conclusion military operations in North Vietnam.

3

THE NATURE OF THE PROBLEM

The basic fact, then, confronting the nation and setting the task for the Department of Defense is that the United States must be prepared not only to deter nuclear attack but also to cope with a wide range of actions short of general war—from subversive efforts and guerilla operations to local aggression in widely separated and distant places.

The strictly military problems posed by this global necessity may be set in three broad contexts. We must develop a comprehensive strategic concept to deal with the whole range of Communist threats—a task which must be accomplished in a period of accelerating technological change which renders dubious, if not invalid, the employment of weapons and tactics which were effectual only yesterday. We must plan for the reorganization, the re-equipment, and possibly the redeployment of United States forces. We must simultaneously consider, and to a degree provide for, the security needs of our Allies while at the same time bearing in mind the contribution to the collective military effort which Allied forces can make.

But these strictly military problems of strategy and tactics, of weapons and organization, are only the first of those confronting the United States in its quest for security. It is now more than ever necessary that our military policy be shaped to conform with national policy, and that our national policy be formulated with due regard for the military facts of life. As a nation, we are confronted with the necessity for reconciling our traditional views on and procedures for civil control of the military with the new requirements imposed by the "age of military revolution." For example, no one will question the necessity for a Presidential decision (and the desirability of Congressional approval) on the use of United States forces; but many a military commander, whose forces can at best have only minutes warning of possible attack, may well ask whether the procedures for obtaining such approval are either foolproof or sufficiently rapid.

We are faced with a number of other equally thorny questions. Are we prepared, in light of the 1957 British White Paper on Defense, to accept—and act on—the fact that the United States is the only nation of the Free World capable of upholding peace with justice—wherever threatened? Have we realized the close interaction between military strategy and foreign policy evidenced by the German reaction in the summer of 1956 to bare rumors of United States troop cuts in Europe? Have we considered the complex interaction of civil and military planning, policies, and personalities in such fields as air defense and industrial mobilization?

In addition to the basic problems of strategy and national policy and inseparably related to them, there are manifold administrative and organizational problems which are of increasing concern to the Depart-ment of Defense. How, for example, can we cut to a minimum our lead time on weapons development and procurement in order to obtain maximum use at least cost of new and rapidly changing weapons systems? The B-52 bomber took seven years to go from drawing board to production; was this fast enough? How can we obtain, and retain, com-petent government and military personnel in the numbers required? What can we do to make more effective use of the monies appropriated for our armed forces, and to offset so far as possible the increasingly astronomical costs of modern weapons systems?[1]

Any search for answers to such questions encounters the primary fact that the rapid advances in the technology and complexity of modern weapons have greatly complicated the problems of decision-making within the defense organization. If new weapons are not to be outdated by newer ones by the time they are integrated into the active military forces, decisions concerning the development, procurement, and strategic employment of weapons must be made with increasing rapidity. More-over, because of their implications for the national security these deci-sions must attain a high level of accuracy and validity. Thus the rapidity of technological advance places prime importance upon our capabilities for innovation to meet constantly changing situations and requirements.

However, the magnitude of the defense organization and the hier-archical nature of its structure tend to frustrate the development of new concepts and ideas. Because of the manifold management tasks which demand their attention, top executives have little time to reflect on old problems, or to take the lead in introducing new concepts.

The Defense Department must employ techniques and organizational patterns which not only foster technical and scientific innovation but also effectively channel these developments into new weapons and assure that they are adequately reflected in new or modified strategic concepts and plans. The Department must be able to adapt flexibly to the demands of both such advances and the continually changing requirements of the "cold war." In order to assure a capability for in-novation and change within defense policies, programs, and organiza-tion, the defense structure must provide an environment which is conducive to the continual development of alternative solutions to continuing problems and of new ideas for resolving novel issues. In addition, the organization must permit balanced, objective analysis of all the alternatives before decisions are made.

The historic boundaries between air, land, and sea warfare have largely disappeared. The military dynamics of this revolutionary change challenge the established limits of responsibility between the branches of our armed forces, making plain that any system of planning geared to the old division of labor between the services is no longer adequate. And yet the services, rather than adjusting to this fact, seem each determined to become omnicompetent and all-powerful.

Under these circumstances it is natural that criticism of the Pentagon has been widespread. In brief, some of the principal criticisms follow. The organizational machinery is not effective. This country is not doing its planning adequately; we have not yet solved the problem of program balance, timing, and coordination. Responsibility for decision-making is diffuse and time-consuming; problem-solving must be freed from the restrictions of service cognizance. We do not know how to handle the problem of planning and management of weapons system technology; we need a streamlined administrative system that can react to technological changes, for technological changes are coming faster than our current decision-making process can deal with them. In our conflict with the Soviet Union, Soviet professionals are stacked up against United States amateurs at the decision-making level. Present organizational structure is influenced by extraneous interests. The ponderousness of the governmental machinery inhibits imaginative thinking. The inflexibility of our annual budgetary process makes long-range planning difficult. Each military service interprets strategic guidance in its own way and in its own favor. There is no over-all group which reviews and analyzes past achievements of our defense organization. Our current military policy neglects giving flexible military support to our total foreign policy. There are major differences regarding strategic concepts which have haunted the Pentagon ever since the formation of the Department of Defense and which are not being resolved. The integration of military and civilian personnel at the higher levels of the decision-making process is not yet satisfactory.

Moreover, there have been public indications of unhappiness with the results of Pentagon decisions as well as with the decision-making apparatus. No one who has glanced even cursorily at the testimony given before the 1956 Symington Committee[2] will fail to note disagreements among the services and to some extent between top military and civilian officials as to strategic concepts, requisite force levels, responsibilities for weapons development, and the adequacy of mechanisms for the funding and procurement of equipment. It can, of course, be argued that these are matters which would be in dispute regardless of organizational structure; but the fact that such controversies have continued so long and have been charged with so much emotion suggests a closer look both at the nature and the causes of some of the problems confronting the Department of Defense.

Even such a bare outline as the above makes it abundantly clear that the Department of Defense, entrusted with the solution of problems so vast and complex, and so central to the nation's safety, must be subjected to continual and searching scrutiny. Moreover, it suggests that the first focus of inquiry should be on the answer to one fundamental question: *How can we best organize and administer the Department of Defense itself?*

In response to this imperative, strenuous efforts have been undertaken to make the Department fully effective, and it has gone through several organizational evolutions since its creation by the passage of the National Security Act of 1947. Over the past four years numerous groups and individuals have studied virtually every aspect of Department of Defense organization and operations. The Rockefeller Commission in 1953 covered over-all organization and procedures, as did the Second Hoover Commission in 1955.[3] In addition, individuals have written on such varied topics as the role of the Department in the formulation and implementation of national security policy,[4] the reciprocal impact of military strategy and organization,[5] and the budgetary process.[6] In no instance has the Department escaped criticism.

The organizational problems implicit in these criticisms must be seen in broad perspective if a sound approach toward their solution is to be made. They are bigger than any of the personalities that have attempted to wrestle with them, and there would be little purpose in criticizing the many wise, dedicated men who have labored prodigiously toward their solution.

ATTITUDES TOWARD DEFENSE ORGANIZATION

Along with the many criticisms and recommendations for improvement of the Defense Department organization, there has been continuing disagreement as to the desirable directions and means for improving it. The two predominant schools either oppose further unification or favor steps toward tighter integration of the Defense Department.

The Navy League publication, *Now Hear This,* for October 1956, in an article entitled "Power and Strategy," stated:

It is to be hoped for the future welfare of our democratic forms of government and for the soundness of our national defense that . . . no further reorganizational plans be attempted.

In November 1956 the same publication took a stronger position by opposing further integration of the armed services for fear that this would result in a "monolithic structure of Prussian type, headed by an almighty chief of staff." Influential Congressmen have similarly viewed further integration of the armed services as being "Prussian and un-American" or have seen danger of an improper encroachment upon Congressional power "to raise and support armies."

As recently as the Defense Department appropriations hearings in May 1957, Secretary of Defense Wilson and Secretary of the Army Brucker went on record against further unification. Secretary of Defense Charles E. Wilson, in a speech given at the graduation exercises of the National War College on June 11, 1957, ably stated his views regarding the adequacy of the existing organization of the Department of Defense. They are so germane to this inquiry that selections from them are set forth below:

> There appears to be general agreement among those that are interested in the matter that some kind of unification of the armed forces is essential for our military as well as our economic security. Past experience as well as current developments make this conclusion self-evident. Not only do the Military Services increasingly supplement each other's striking power, but the demands that they must make upon our industrial and economic capacity—even in peacetime—are such that uncontrolled competition would be ruinous to our country.

> The differences of opinion that arise do not, therefore, deal with the need for unification but center on the form of unification. It is something like the difference between strategy and tactics. . . .

> The problems created by the current international situation and by our rapidly advancing technology require the thorough consideration of all possible points of view and alternative courses of action. Any other course might be fatal to the security of our country and would be contrary to the traditions to which we adhere. . . .

> Our government is a government of checks and balances. The President cannot do certain things without checking with the Congress. Within the Executive Branch, policies are coordinated with all the Departments concerned, and decisions are reached after all have had their say. We follow the same procedure within the Department of Defense. . . .

> The final decision will not always completely satisfy everybody concerned. In an organization composed of people working for a common purpose, decisions are accepted in the knowledge that they were reached after full consideration of all points of view and a realization that the decisions can be reconsidered at any time if new facts are discovered which bear upon the problems.

> I would like to clearly go on record with all of you that I believe the

present organization of the Department of Defense is sound, incorporating as it does the separate Military Services and Military Departments in an organization which is responsive to the President, the Congress, and the American people. I would caution those who recommend radical changes to advocate them only after the most careful thought and when experience has proved that they are necessary.

On the other hand, General Twining, successor to Admiral Radford as Chairman of the Joint Chiefs of Staff, testified before the Symington Committee investigating airpower in June 1956: ". . . I do lean toward a single service . . . I think it would serve to settle them [issues between the services] promptly. I think it would be less expensive than the present organization." A policy statement adopted by the Air Force Association at New Orleans, August 3, 1956, noted that "sweeping revolutions in weapons technology have outmoded our country's traditional approach to national security," and that "the three service system can be tolerated no longer because the system ties military careers to obsolescent weapons and postpones basic decision by piling compromise upon compromise and wasting time, money, and manpower."

In testifying before the Symington Committee in June 1956, Dr. James R. Killian, President of Massachusetts Institute of Technology, when a member of the Science Advisory Committee of the Office of Defense Mobilization made a cogent appeal for further integration of the defense organization:[7]

The military task no longer divides up neatly into three mission areas, defined by the vehicle the fighting man rides in. . . . There are no longer any natural boundaries which cannot be penetrated by comprehensive offense, and our defense against this comprehensive threat does not separate naturally into three parts but requires new, functional-type military organizations to do the job. . . . In my judgment, one of the major problems affecting the security of the United States is our capacity to deal wisely with this problem of integration within the Military Establishment. I do not suggest that this means complete unification of the three services. I do suggest that in dealing with air defense, with intercontinental ballistic missiles, and other great weapons systems we must create the organizational patterns which will make it possible, first, effectively to develop them without wastage of manpower and resources and unprofitable duplication of effort, and, secondly, to manage them in terms of their wholeness as systems. So far we have not been able in the definition of roles and missions of the services to keep pace with evolving weapons-systems technology, and as a consequence we lengthen our lead times, we make more difficult our decision-making processes, we needlessly increase costs, and we find it difficult to avoid friction and duplication of effort.

This appeal reflects many of the complex issues confronting the Department of Defense, but primarily it relates to a core issue, decision-making and execution, including the manifold human problems of obtaining the consensus and cooperation which these terse words imply.

The nearly continuous efforts since its creation to make the Department of Defense truly effective in terms of the revolutionary requirements of the nuclear age have by no means been fruitless. In fact, it is possible to agree in a sense with the statement that "more has been accomplished toward achieving truly effective teamwork for national defense in the past ten years than in the previous one hundred and fifty."[8] Yet there are still questions which press for an answer. Is the Department of Defense as presently established capable of making the correct decisions in time? Is it capable of distinguishing between the decisions which must be made immediately and those which can be deferred? Does it provide special organization and priority allocation of resources for the highest priority projects? Does it insure prompt execution of security programs and timely modifications in them as the conditions relating to them are changing? Does it always make decisions in the proper framework of the problem or does it sometimes make decisions with respect to the wrong problem? Are problem-solving techniques with regard to the major national issues being utilized to the fullest extent possible? Is there a selective process established so that the key problems are identified and given priority treatment?

The present study had its origin in an attempt to answer such questions. Our inquiry proceeded from a full awareness that the present shape of the Department of Defense, set by the National Security Act of 1947, the first Forrestal reorganization, and the Reorganization Plan Six, represents a compromise between two significant forces. The first is the rigidity of the legally defined service structure, which results from both the historical relationship between the military services and Congress and the service views on organization and strategy. The second is the civilian attitude (often reflected through Congress) toward the role of professional military men in the administration of national defense. These two forces more than any others have placed restraints on the timely attainment of an optimum defense structure.

Our inquiry also proceeded from an exercise in firsthand experience which led to the conviction that, despite the constructive changes in governmental organization for national security since the end of World War II, the Defense Department as of today is still designed to cope with problems of the past rather than with the revolutionary challenges posed by the Soviet concept of total war and the accelerating surge of new technology. The basic pattern of division of responsibilities remains much the same as at the conclusion of World War II. The integration of our military forces which is required has not yet taken place.

Our purpose here, then, is three-fold: first, to review the experience the United States has had with the Department of Defense beginning with the National Security Act of 1947; second, to examine the workings of the present mechanism; third, to suggest areas in which the Department of Defense organization might be improved.

Footnotes

1. The Assistant Secretary of Defense (Comptroller) cited the following as examples of increased costs:
A World War II submarine cost $4,700,000; a Korean War submarine, $22,000,-000; the present nuclear submarine, $50,000,000;
A B-36 bomber wing cost $132,000,000; its replacement, the B-52 bomber wing, costs over $500,000,000; an intercontinental ballistic missile wing will probably cost $1,000,000,000. (*The New York Times*, September 29, 1957, p. 28.)

2. Hearings before the Subcommittee on the Air Force of the Committee on Armed Services, United States Senate, 84th Congress, Second Session, *Airpower*, Washington: Government Printing Office, 1956, hereafter referred to as *Symington Committee Hearings on Airpower*.

3. The pertinent reports of these various study groups and committees are as follows:
Rockefeller Committee: *Report of the Rockefeller Committee on Department of Defense Organization*, Committee Print, Senate Committee on Armed Services, 83rd Congress, Washington, 1953, hereafter cited as *Rockefeller Committee Report*.
Commission on Organization of the Executive Branch of Government (Second Hoover Commission), *Report on Business Organization of the Department of Defense*, Washington: G.P.O., 1955, hereafter cited as *Business Organization of the Department of Defense*.

4. Timothy W. Stanley, *American Defense and National Security*, Washington: Public Affairs Press, 1956.

5. Henry A. Kissinger, "Strategy and Organization," *Foreign Affairs*, April 1957.

6. Arthur Smithies, *The Budgetary Process in the United States*, New York: McGraw-Hill, 1955. See also his "Role of Budgetary Process National Policy," an unpublished manuscript prepared for the Special Studies Project, Rockefeller Brothers Fund, Inc.

7. *Symington Committee Hearings on Airpower*, p. 1186.

8. Stanley, *op. cit.*, p. 138.

Two

THE MEASURE OF PERFORMANCE

Before reviewing the evolution of the Department of Defense in terms of organizational proposals, reorganizations effected, and accomplishments from 1947 to 1957, it is essential to establish some criteria by which the progress of its evolution can be measured. It is obviously useless to attempt to define the form, the exact organizational pattern in terms of size and parts and lines of authority, which the Department should take. It is, however, both desirable and possible to set standards for judgment in terms of the functions it must perform—or, put another way, in terms of the Department's responsibilities in the service of the national interest. Accumulated experience under the various organizational structures which have evolved since World War II, and analysis of the requirements arising from the nature of an intermittent "cold war" in a nuclear environment, permit the statement of general, but fairly definitive, characteristics and requirements of an effective defense organization.

This chapter sets forth eight such basic requirements for the operational performance of the Department of Defense. They are not offered as the basis for some specific optimum defense organization; they are submitted as being generally valid requirements which must be fulfilled by any organization of the Department of Defense for the foreseeable future.

If the Department of Defense is to defend a free and vital United States and its fundamental security interests throughout the world, it must operate in accordance with high standards of effectiveness. What follows, then, are performance measures which set the critical rationale of the subsequent discussion. These performance measures are more than theoretical concepts; they are basic organizational factors which have already brought success or failure in actual conflict during the more or less extensive period of modern global war.

CIVILIAN CONTROL

It is fundamental to our political heritage that the military forces of the United States be subordinate to the control of civilian representatives of the people and thus, ultimately, to the people themselves. This concept, cherished by all responsible elements of our society, including the military, has been expressed in various clauses of the Constitution as well as in innumerable legislative acts and resolutions throughout our history. On the basis of these fundamental statutes and their administrative expansion has developed a pattern of civil-military relationships which provides the basic framework for maintaining civilian control over the exercise of our national military power.

Because of their ultimate political responsibility to the people for the development and employment of our military power the politically-appointed top-level civilian officials of the Defense Department should exercise general policy control over all the programs and operations of the Department. This control need not mean actual direct supervision of these manifold, complex Defense Department activities; in fact an attempt to conduct such supervision can detract from the effectiveness of the over-all control. In addition to assuring that policy decisions are made by responsible civilian officials, civilian control should serve three other purposes: authoritative coordination and unified direction of Defense Department operations; effective integration of nonmilitary factors into the predominantly military activities; and achievement of the highest possible levels of economy and efficiency.

According to this pattern for the exercise of civilian control, it remains the proper responsibility of the professional military personnel to advise their civilian superiors on the development and employment of military forces and to conduct the actual military operations under the over-all policy control of the politically responsible civilians. The nature of potential armed conflict today places great strain upon our traditional channels of military responsibility. Our military forces are responsible to civilian secretaries in the Defense Department, to the President as Commander-in-Chief, to the Congress, and to the people. Channels of command must be devised which permit full consideration of expert military advice by the Executive Branch, Congress, and the public in order that our defense policies and programs may be responsive to our security needs and obtain the national support needed to make them effective. Moreover, these command channels must maintain the essential elements of military responsibility yet permit rapid response to any enemy move in order to minimize the effect of surprise, which constitutes such a crucial determinant of current military operations.

The manner in which civilian control is implemented in the future will be a central factor in whatever answer we develop to the problem which has remained with us since our nation's birth: How can we maintain an adequate and soundly organized defense over the long haul without surrendering a wise and proper apprehension of the dangers inherent in maintaining large standing forces over a period of decades? Whatever the organizational answer to this question, it must provide for effective civilian control, for a meaningful role for the military, and for the integration of military and nonmilitary factors in the decision-making process.

PARTICIPATION IN NATIONAL POLICY FORMULATION

The development of policies and programs to maintain the national security in an era of cold war power politics requires the close coordination of the activities of many agencies in order to meet the challenge which simultaneously confronts the nation on many fronts—economic, psychological, and political, in addition to the military. The major military problems of the cold war conflict can rarely be considered in isolation from these political, economic, and ideological aspects; and *vice versa*. Thus the Defense Department is called upon to participate in coordinated planning with several agencies in all these fields. This interagency planning should reflect effective integration of the views of all the agencies concerned.

Since the unified defense establishment represents the merger of three heretofore relatively independent services, organizational patterns must be devised which not only permit consideration within the Defense Department of all alternative points of view on an issue before the Department establishes a policy position, but which also assure that the Department eventually, in its relations with other agencies, speaks with one voice. Channels of communication between the various staff levels within the defense structure and assignments of responsibility must be established in a manner contributing to these ends. The effectiveness of these organizational and procedural patterns can have a real influence upon the degree to which the military factors are adequately reflected in national security policies, as well as upon the timely development of defense programs intended to help put those policies into effect.

The effectiveness of the internal Defense Department organization and procedures in performing the tasks contributing to national policy planning depends to a great extent upon the adequacy of the government-wide planning structure. The strategic concepts and plans of the military forces must be effectively tied into our over-all national strategy as set forth in National Security Council guidance; and the programs to implement Defense Department responsibilities within the national strategy must be geared to general budget policies and to the budgetary cycle. In the final analysis military plans and programs are valid only to the extent that financial means are made available for their implementation.

By means of its control over the purse-strings, through Congressional inquiries, and through direct legislation on program authorizations and defense organization, Congress also exerts a powerful influence upon the Defense Department role in national policy formulation. Inquiries into defense activities conducted to obtain information upon which to base legislation often lead into questions of broad defense policy and strategy and result in changes in programs or priorities. The Defense Department must maintain close cooperation directly with Congress on defense matters, as well as support the broad objective of maintaining satisfactory Executive-Congressional relations, if it is to gain understanding and support for defense programs both from the Congress and from the public which elected it.

Defense organization and procedures are required which, while adequately reflecting the various nonmilitary elements of defense problems and assuring effective patterns of liaison and cooperation with other interested agencies, will enable the Defense Department fully to meet its responsibilities in national policy formation. Such procedures should provide for a close relationship between national policies and the resources devoted to implementing programs, and should enable the presentation to the Congress, as well as to the President, of cohesive and comprehensible recommendations on military policies and programs.

MAXIMUM READINESS

Defense Department organization and procedures meet their ultimate test at that moment in history when enemy action requires active employment of American armed forces. The nature of potential armed conflicts with which we could be confronted today requires that our military power be capable of instantaneous reaction to any enemy attack in a manner characterized by speed, responsiveness, and control. Such instantaneous action requires speed and precision of decision-making and implementing action, not only at the time of the emergency, but also during the earlier build-up period when many decisions determining the overall state of military preparedness are actually made.

During the actual emergency, the defense organization must facilitate the rapid flow of military commands to the active forces and the presentation of up-to-the-minute intelligence from the field to the top command echelons. Moreover, the structure and procedures must themselves be flexible enough and responsive enough to permit rapid and precise implementation of commands and flexibility of action, so that we may inflict upon the enemy, no matter what the nature of his attack, damage sufficient to nullify or defeat his action, without inevitably expanding the conflict into a war of increasingly intensified or widespread destruction. While the desired action may be facilitated by the existence of previously approved plans and strategies, the organizational structure must not be so unwieldy as to preclude the introduction of timely new concepts to meet unforeseen circumstances. Finally, the need to maintain a careful balance of strategic and political factors in any use of nuclear weapons requires that command channels and communications be developed which assure control at the highest level without undermining effective actions in the field.

An organizational structure which, during periods of relative peace, fosters innovation and imagination on the basis of careful analysis of trends is equally important. Failure to conceive in advance the nature of future conflicts or the possibilities of novel alternatives to expected actions may result in such a low state of preparedness in vital weapons and techniques, or such a rigidity in plans and strategies, that we seriously jeopardize our chances for victory. The peacetime structure for planning and decision-making affects the availability of forces on hand and the adequacy of their reaction at the time of an enemy attack. If we develop the right structure and use it properly, we should be successful in anticipating the enemy capabilities and intentions and the trends of modern warfare.

In short, the organization of the Department of Defense must be such as to enable it to take immediate and responsible action in the event that the use of armed force is required. The satisfaction of these two requirements will necessitate effective channels of command and communication between military commanders and their civilian superiors, and procedures enabling speedy decisions by these responsible civilian officials.

SOUND STRATEGIC DOCTRINE

Military strategic concepts and plans provide the means for translating our over-all national security policy into implementing tasks and missions for the armed forces. However, the strategic planners must contribute to the development of our over-all national security policy, in order that this policy adequately reflect expert military appraisals of the nature of potential military conflicts in which we might become involved. Beyond generalized alternatives, the nature of a future enemy attack is difficult to anticipate during the contemporary "cold war" conflict. The range of possible actions reaches from incitement and encouragement of insurrections, through open intervention in civil wars, through overt aggression on a limited scale, through nuclear conflict restricted in area and magnitude, to general thermonuclear war. Genuine security demands that we be prepared to meet an attack in any of these major forms with flexible forces capable of a broad range of military actions.

The Department of Defense must be able to meet its basic responsibility for formulating sound strategic doctrine. This strategy should maximize the functional contribution which each of the services might make toward a unified concept for the application of military power. It will involve critical decisions on the priority of effort to be assigned to the major functions of strategic attack, air defense, tactical forces for territorial defense, etc. It will also involve progressive and rational "unbalancing of forces" as changes in technology alter the weight that should be given the various functions which comprise a comprehensive strategic posture. The gradual erosion of boundaries between rigidly defined service roles necessitates the development of strategic doctrine which will enlist the strong organizational motivation of the services behind an integrating concept of mutually supporting operations. Such a concept would induce cooperation rather than generate the kind of sterile competition which so often characterizes "organizational" conflicts.

Beyond this requirement of harmonizing distinctive service roles, the Defense Department has the equally difficult task of formulating strategic concepts which will be compatible with the political obligations of a global alliance system. Collaboration with allied nations for mutual security requires that our strategic concepts be geared to the attainment of military objectives mutually acceptable to our allies. In addition, the United States must bear the responsibility of leadership in formulating strategic concepts to maintain the security of ourselves and our allies, since United States military power is the principal deterrent to Communist aggression in the world today. Moreover, the effectiveness of our military assistance to allies depends upon the degree to which it is designed to support a sound strategic doctrine.

In this era of rapid technological advance strategic concepts require constant review and modification to reflect the implications of new weapons. Organizational patterns and procedures play a significant role in integrating technological and scientific advance into strategic and tactical planning. Even major advances in weapons technology will be of little value to the ultimate military striking power unless their potential utilization has been adequately reflected in strategic and tactical concepts. In the desirable course of events, however, innovations in strategic and tactical thinking should guide weapons development or modification. The success of the defense organization in integrating scientific advance and strategic planning has a major impact on over-all national security policies and programs, and may in fact determine whether or not some programs are feasible in terms of our military or financial capabilities.

Thus the Defense Department must be capable of developing strategic doctrine compatible both with our national interests and with the political obligations imposed by our collective security efforts, of altering that doctrine in accordance with changes in the political situation and in military technology, and of integrating service capabilities into one cohesive pattern which supports this strategic doctrine.

ORDERLY INNOVATIONS

The impact of the current technological revolution is felt throughout the Department of Defense. The urgency of keeping abreast with the rapid advances of the Soviet Bloc in military technology and the steadily increasing costs of developing and producing new weapons demand that our defense organization assure maximum development and application, with minimum duplication and waste, of available scientific resources. Organization and procedures must not only facilitate the integration of technological "breakthroughs" into new weapons and strategic concepts for their employment, but must foster conditions through the Department which assure that the implications of these scientific advances are reflected in orderly innovation in all defense policies and programs.

The limited supply of highly qualified scientific and truly creative manpower requires careful organization of this invaluable resource. Within the governmental structure, but particularly within the Defense Department, means must be found to combine advanced scientific thinking, most often found among civilian scientists, with that of the highest caliber of military strategic thinking, usually found among experienced, professional military officers. In addition, mutual cross-fertilization of scientific and strategic innovations and understanding of their political and economic implications should be facilitated at all levels.

Military implications inherent in technological development extend in many instances through the entire cycle of research and development, from basic research to the procurement of new weapons and their introduction into ready military forces. Further along in the process, new weapons in the prototype stage, and technological innovations at advanced stages of development, must be carefully evaluated as to their probable effectiveness in some anticipated future role in the armed forces before decisions regarding procurement and training, which involve the commitment of large sums of money, can be made.

Any system of organization must reduce the time-lag between the discovery of novel principles and techniques or the development of new weapons and their full utilization by the armed forces. With weapons increasingly complex in mechanical and electronic components, the cycle from drawing board, through development, to mass production often covers such a long period of time that aircraft, for example, are outdated by aircraft of higher performance just as they enter the supply line to the armed forces. The Defense Department organizational structure and procedures must be such as to foster a decision-making process, including a cycle of research and development, which assures the timely introduction of the most scientific advances into modern armed forces and their weaponry, but in a planned, smooth transition which avoids disrupting the effectiveness and readiness of forces already maintained.

Particularly important to American success in the technological competition with potential enemies is the degree to which the defense organization and procedures permit or foster free analysis, criticism, and innovation. For example, decisions, regarding anticipated roles for aircraft and missiles of various capabilities and characteristics require critical evaluation both of the available items and of the trends of future conflict. Moreover, new organizational patterns may be necessary for directing the most rapid possible development of certain new weapons, such as missiles, and ultimately for their operation. Department of Defense organization can be a determining factor as to whether novel alternatives will be forthcoming to resolve the impending issues and whether such alternatives will receive adequate weight in the decision-making process.

In brief, the ideal Defense Department research development organization should not only minimize duplication efforts and speed up the cycle from drawing-board to production line but also assure that technological developments are interrelated with strategic planning. Perhaps most importantly, it should foster innovation, enable free criticism of both weapons and procedures, and provide maximum scope for scientific talent.

FLEXIBLE ADJUSTMENTS IN MISSIONS

In addition to making the best use of technological advances and of devising advanced strategies, it is obviously essential to organize and train forces of the correct type to realize the strategies and to use the weapons to maximum advantage. Current strategic concepts must be adequately reflected in the assignment of functional military missions throughout the military structure; as strategies evolve, appropriate adjustments must be made in the functions of the armed forces. Forces required to carry out such functional military missions as anti-aircraft defense, strategic bombing, and protection of sea communications, or integrated striking teams of combined army and supporting air forces, for example, must be anticipated during the actual development of new strategic concepts in order to be organized for ready action when the strategic plans go into effect.

Rapidly changing world conditions and revolutionary technological advances dictate constant revision of strategic concepts with concomitant rapid readjustments in military tasks and missions. One measure of success as an effective defense organization will be the Defense Department's ability to realize flexibility in readjustment of missions, without jeopardizing the effectiveness of the available forces which may be called upon at any time for instantaneous reaction to enemy attack.

In order to meet this requirement, our Defense Department organization must feasibly provide not only for adjustments in service roles and missions but also for the formation and development of multiservice task forces. In earmarking forces and weapons systems for the performance of specified missions, provisions should be made for a comparable allocation of resources in a meaningful order of priority. The procedures developed for this purpose must be such as to guide the military services in the development of the necessary forces, weapons and resources, and to relate these directly to the military tasks and missions imposed by national security policy.

MAXIMUM COST EFFICIENCY

In an era of continuing crisis, demanding a sustained high level of military preparedness, the economic resources of the country are subjected to continuing heavy exploitation in order to satisfy the defense requirements. Pressure upon the national economy is aggravated by the steadily increasing costs of weapons and equipment. The technological race simultaneously increases the complexity—and hence, the cost—of weaponry and intensifies the need to develop more and more new weapons in order to avoid falling behind the enemy and granting him a degree of superiority prejudicial to our national security. Accordingly, defense organization and procedures are faced with steadily increasing pressures from all sides to achieve maximum cost efficiency and to gain the optimum defense capabilities from the dollar expenditures available.

The main principles are clear. Budgetary procedures establishing standards and guides for the development of uniform programs and indicating clear priorities for the allocation of resources require constant review and improvement. Efficient business organization and management can release resources from wasteful or low-priority programs for increased application to essential high-priority programs.

Careful alignment of functions and close integration of the budget cycle with policy and program development are essential. Duplication must be eliminated not only to cut down waste but also to permit more accurate estimation of budgetary requirements for specific military tasks and missions. Closely gearing the budget cycle to major policy and program determinations will permit more realistic planning for military requirements and will help assure the availability and allocation of resources for their achievement.

However, a note of warning must be sounded. While budget, accounting and other financial tools are invaluable to the responsible defense officials, they should not be regarded as decisive in the formulation of defense policy. Other criteria stem from military strategic plans and advice, political appraisals of domestic and international conditions, and technical and scientific evaluations. In many situations these will, or should be, overriding.

The governing fact here is that, if certain military courses are decided upon, the wherewithal to pursue those courses must be provided. Organizational patterns and procedures relating to fiscal accountability and management controls must be devised to assure that available resources are properly allocated as well as to produce maximum efficiency within the business organization of the Department of Defense, particularly in fields such as procurement, distribution, maintenance, and transportation.

MOTIVATION AND MORALE

Perhaps the most vital element in a defense organization is the manpower within it. The adequacy with which the Defense Department functions in fulfilling its task of enhancing the national security depends ultimately upon the quality, motivation, and morale of the civilian and military personnel who wield the nation's sword. Policies, plans, and weapons are meaningless when separated from the human beings who develop and utilize them.

The defense organization must be so designed as to attract and retain sufficient qualified manpower. The basic requirements for fulfilling this objective are common to both the Civil Service and the military profession. The defense establishment must offer adequate financial compensation, opportunity for career advancement, the chance to perform meaningful work, and recognition of personal effort. If the Department is to obtain the quality of leadership required by our gigantic, complex defense activities, similar incentives must be available for personnel offered political appointments to responsible defense positions.

Certain personnel problems peculiar to the Defense Department staff arise from the fact that it combines two separate career services, the professional military and the Civil Service. Effective operations depend upon close cooperation between these two professional staffs based on mutual respect and confidence. The intimate relationships between them at the working level result in constant comparisons of competence, responsibility, authority, and opportunities in their respective careers. If the civilian or military professional finds the competence of his counterpart to be below the standards of his own career service in comparable positions, or, and especially, if these counterparts seem consistently to enjoy positions of higher authority and responsibility or greater compensation and opportunities for advancement, effective collaboration can easily be undermined.

In a broader sense the morale and motivation of those serving in the Defense Department is conditioned by events occurring both within and outside the Department. Interservice conflicts, whether over strategic concepts or over defense policies, not only inhibit effective joint planning and action but also fragment and narrow loyalties and damage the common and shared basis of morale which must underlie an effective military establishment. The additional layers of civilian staffs which have been superimposed upon the military staffs by unification tend further and further to separate the professional fighting men from the top civilian defense authorities in terms of flow of command and information and in terms of the mutual confidence essential to the effective development of a successful defense establishment. The recurrent confusion concerning economy and austerity generated by drives to economize at the expense of the people in the service inevitably weakens morale at every level. In large measure the morale of those serving within the Department of Defense is dependent upon outside factors; however, there is much that those in charge of the Department can and should do to improve morale and motivation.

If it is to perform its mission effectively, the Defense Department must attract and retain the highest quality personnel, civilian and military. Within its own sphere, there is much that the Department can do to enhance the loyalty and the sense of purpose of individuals serving therein, and any new organization must decrease, rather than increase, the number of key people dissatisfied with their lot.

The set of requirements we have briefly outlined applies to all the tasks assigned to our military services. How well the Department of Defense performs those tasks is a measure of the welfare and security of the nation. In turn, how well the Department of Defense performs those tasks will depend to a large extent on the logic and clarity of its organizational structure. We turn first, then, to examine the principal organizational developments within the Department of Defense over the years that have passed since the armed forces were "unified" under the National Security Act of 1947.

Three

EVOLUTION AND PERFORMANCE: 1947 TO THE 1949 AMENDMENTS

The Department of Defense was created by the National Security Act of 1947, signed by President Truman on July 26 of that year. That act contained the following basic elements: (1) creation of a separate Air Force as an equal service with the Army and Navy; (2) establishment of three equal military departments, each with a civilian secretary; (3) creation of a National Military Establishment under a civilian Secretary of Defense with "general authority, direction, and control" over the three military departments; (4) provision of legislative authority and a charter for the Joint Chiefs of Staff; (5) creation of a Munitions Board and a Research and Development Board within the National Military Establishment to coordinate interservice activities in these fields; (6) creation of the interagency policy coordinating organs on which the National Military Establishment was to be one of the represented agencies: the National Security Council and the National Security Resources Board; (7) creation of the Central Intelligence Agency.

The unification of the military departments achieved under the National Security Act was more a reconciliation of divergent views than an ideal form of defense organization. The structure established by the Act revealed a compromise between the Army's traditional preference for a tightly organized staff operation and the Navy's historical tendency toward the committee system for reaching military-political decisions. It also reflected a partial compromise between Forrestal's strong anti-centralization bias and the Army proposals for an integrated military staff reporting to a single civilian secretary of a unified Department of the Armed Forces. Moreover, the terms of the Act aimed at directly contradictory objectives. While unification was the over-all goal, the objective of civilian control was to be achieved by establishing strong civilian authority at the head of each military department in addition to the civilian authority at the level of the secretary of the

ORGANIZATION FOR NATIONAL SECURITY, 1947

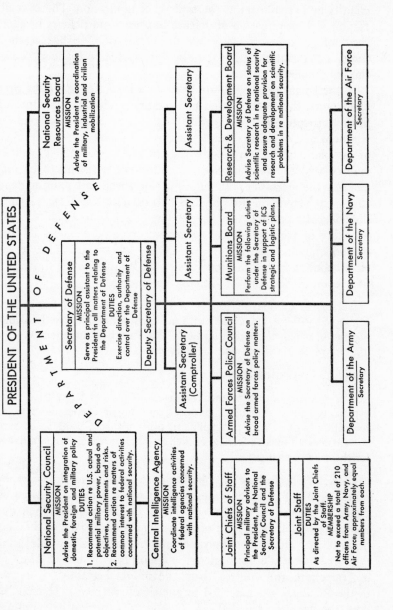

unified military establishment. This, in effect, strengthened service identity and separatism at the expense of unification. The over-all integration and coordination of defense programs and policies by these two levels of civilian secretaries was, by implication, to be accomplished through cooperation rather than by directives from top-level civilians to the three military services.

In the language of Secretary Forrestal's *First Report of the Secretary of Defense*, the initial period of operation under the structure of unification (September 1947 through December 1948) was one "of experiment and of laying foundations on which subsequent development of the National Military Establishment can be based."[1] Forrestal fully realized that the central issues of unification were still to be resolved, and that the success or failure in achieving a workable solution depended to a great extent on how he chose to exercise the "general authority, direction, and control" over the military establishment granted to him as Secretary of Defense. He chose to proceed at the outset by methods of cooperation, negotiation, conference, and compromise to achieve close coordination of the activities of the military establishment. In his first report as Secretary of Defense he observed:

Differences of opinion can be reconciled by free and frank discussion conducted without rancor and with an open mind. That is the democratic process on which the Government of this country is founded. With all its limitations, it is a sound and sane process.[2]

Again, in his diaries, he wrote:

I have gone somewhat slowly because, . . . as you know from your own experience, this is a complex business, and morale and confidence are easy to destroy but not easy to rebuild. In other words, I want to be sure that any changes we make are changes that accomplish something and not merely for the sake of change.[3]

Forrestal's technique of obtaining cooperation and action by the mutual consent of all concerned was as much a necessity as an elected choice. The authority of the Secretary of Defense was then open to considerable debate in light of the ambiguous language of the National Security Act (for which Forrestal was primarily responsible), and the military services did not neglect the opportunity to test it. The "authority, direction, and control" over the military establishment provided to the Secretary was preceded by the significant word "general." Moreover, the Act provided that the three services were to be "administered as individual Executive Departments," and that powers not conferred upon the Secretary of Defense were reserved to the secretaries of the military departments. The confederation of executive departments over which the Secretary of Defense was to exercise his general authority was given the name "establishment" rather than "department." In addition, the three military departments were granted the express right of appeal to the President and the Bureau of the Budget over the head of the Secretary of Defense.

The basic procedures of doing business were also influenced by the establishment of such statutory coordinating bodies as the Munitions Board, the Research and Development Board, and the War Council. The members of these organs consisted of representatives from the three services, thus emphasizing the technique of negotiating mutual cooperation among the services rather than reaching solutions on the basis of decision by the independent authority of the Secretary of Defense. Under such conditions, cooperation by mutual consent was almost a practical necessity.

ACHIEVEMENTS AND DEFICIENCIES

Allowing for the intensity of the unification battle and the compromise structure which had evolved, considerable progress was made in Defense Department organization during the first two years following passage of the National Security Act of 1947. Among the principal achievements was a definition of the roles and missions of the Army, Navy, and Air Force after extensive consideration of the problem by the Joint Chiefs of Staff and by two special conferences held at Key West, March 12-14, and at Newport, Rhode Island, August 20-22, 1948.

The *First Report of the Secretary of Defense* viewed the service agreements on roles and missions as providing "a firm basis for future planning and the reconciliation of many of their differences."[4] The same report recognized the important role of the Joint Chiefs of Staff in the reconciliation of divergent service positions and in reaching agreed solutions to some of the most pressing military problems of the early unification period. In fact, it called the Joint Chiefs of Staff organization the "nerve center of unification."[5] It is doubtful whether the initial National Military Establishment could have functioned at all had not the JCS continued to operate along cooperative lines similar to those followed during World War II.

Other major internal accomplishments during the first two years of unification included: (1) the formulation of long- and short-range strategic plans by the JCS; (2) the formulation and submission to the Bureau of the Budget of the Fiscal Year (1950) budget for the entire National Military Establishment on an integrated basis for the first time; (3) the development of techniques under which an annual legislative program for the National Military Establishment as a whole would be prepared on the basis of centralized control in the Office of the Secretary of Defense and decentralized development in the military departments; (4) closer coordination of Army, Navy, and Air Force procurement and mobilization planning by the Munitions Board; (5) the consolidation of the Naval Air Transport Service and the Air Transport Service and the Air Transport Command into the Military Air Transport Service (MATS); (6) the creation of additional unified command in overseas theaters, thus extending the concept of placing the forces of all three services in a theater under a single commander; (7) the reorganization of the Military Liaison Committee to the Atomic Energy Commission to improve working arrangements with the AEC and to reflect the organizational modifications of unification (this committee consisted of a civilian chairman, who would also serve as an assistant to the Secretary of Defense for all atomic energy matters, and two representatives from each service); (8) the completion of studies and recommendations for forming a comprehensive plan for the reserve components of the three services, for improving military pay levels and retirement benefits, for improving the civil defense structure, and for developing a uniform code of military justice; (9) the formation of a Personnel Policy Board to develop integrated policies for the administration of military and civilian personnel programs throughout the establishment; (10) the consolidation and standardization of transportation, communication, administrative, and service functions and the establishment of joint use procedures in order to produce savings and eliminate duplication; (11) steps toward coordination into an integrated research and development program by the Research and Development Board of some 13,000 projects under way in the three military services in order to reduce duplication, increase exchange of information, and make optimum use of existing facilities; and (12) establishment of a Weapons System Evaluation Group (WSEG) to provide independent technical and operational evaluation and analysis of present and future weapons systems on an interservice basis.

In a sense it is impossible to evaluate the over-all performance of the defense organization during the first two years of unification, in part since this was a relatively short period in which the major transition had to be made but more because the ultimate test of any military system is its effectiveness when actually waging war. At this point, however, we can make some judgments as to what extent the efforts of the first two years under the National Military Establishment organization created a structure which could meet the requirements of an effective defense.

In general, the emphasis during the first two years was on procedural matters, involving organizational techniques, directives, and charters, which established definitions of responsibilities and lines of authority. In the absence of adequate centralized authority, stemming from the built-in contradictions of the National Security Act, there was such a multiplication of interservice coordinating boards and committees that it became necessary, between January and June 1949, to abolish more than 100 coordinating boards and committees as obsolete or useless because of duplication of functions. The most significant progress achieved during the first two years of unification was in the initial steps to develop a system for joint military planning which more closely related strategic concepts to research and development, the budget process, and the assignment of roles and missions.

In the field of strategic planning the "Key West Agreement"[6] provided that the Joint Chiefs of Staff were to prepare strategic plans, joint logistic plans, integrated military mobilization plans, and policies for joint operations and joint training. To implement these plans the JCS were charged, in the original Key West Agreement, with the "general direction of all combat operations." They also had the function of designating one of their members as their executive agent for unified commands and certain other operations. In addition to these specified functions, the Joint Chiefs of Staff were to develop long- and short-range plans to meet possible emergencies and a constantly reviewed list of actions to be taken in the event of emergency.

To judge the extent to which the strategic plans developed in the first years of unification actually achieved their objective, one must turn to the experience of the Korean conflict. Both the delineation by the Secretary of State early in 1950 of a defense perimeter in the Far East—which significantly excluded Korea—and the limited United States military capability in the area implied a reliance upon the strategic application of nuclear weapons to an extent which seriously jeopardized our ability to meet aggression in more limited forms. During his testimony in the MacArthur hearings, General Bradley revealed the restricted nature of our strategic plans and the military capabilities developed to implement them when he stated that it was the opinion of the JCS that enlargement of the Korean conflict against Communist China "would involve us in the wrong war, at the wrong place, at the wrong time, and with the wrong enemy."[7] This view of the possibilities as being either carefully limited war, or general war with the application of nuclear weapons only in massive retaliation, ignored such potential alternatives as graduated employment of force and the tactical use of nuclear weapons. It may also have reflected an underestimation of the effect of our nuclear capabilities in restraining Soviet moves.

On the credit side, the Joint Chiefs of Staff and the Research and Development Board, partly as the result of the discussion regarding roles and missions and in recognition of the need for a close relationship between strategic planning and the development of new weapons systems, with concurrence of the Secretary of Defense established the Weapons Systems Evaluation Group on February 21, 1949. The mission of the group, as defined in the second report of the Secretary of Defense, was to provide, at the request of the Secretary of Defense, the Joint Chiefs of Staff, or the Research and Development Board, "rigorous, unprejudiced and independent analyses and evaluations of present and future weapons systems under probable future combat conditions."[8]

This significant organizational step indicated an effort to integrate technological developments into strategic planning. However, the National Military Establishment did not reveal a similar organizational effort at this time to deal with the other side of the coin; namely, the techniques for deciding when to initiate the development and subsequent procurement of new weapons and for integrating them on a continuing basis into ready military forces with least possible disruption to their efficiency. The Research and Development Board did take a first but faltering step in this direction by developing a "master plan." This plan was to guide the Research and Development Board effort on new weapons in rough priorities according to estimated development schedules and Joint Chiefs of Staff strategic planning requirements.

The determination of roles and missions in the Key West Agreement of April 21, 1948, which was further refined at Newport, laid a basis for reconciling divergencies among the approaches of the three military services to unification. The Joint Chiefs of Staff were made the avenue for recommending to the Secretary of Defense any further assignments or modifications of assignments of functions among the services. This ruling clarified, organizationally at least, the process for making adjustments in roles and missions as technological and strategic developments might require.

The Key West Agreement also assigned to the Joint Chiefs of Staff a significant function in the budgetary process. They were "to prepare and submit to the Secretary of Defense, for his information and consideration in furnishing guidance to the Departments for preparation of their annual budgetary estimates and in coordinating these budgets, a statement of military requirements which is based upon agreed strategic considerations, joint war plans, and current national security commitments." This constituted a big organizational step toward achieving a coordinated military program in place of several programs based upon uncorrelated individual service requirements. In practice, this link between strategic planning and the budget process was applied for the first time to the development of the fiscal year 1950 budget. However, the practice did not conform to the process as conceived in the Key West terminology. According to the *Second Report of the Secretary of Defense*, the Joint Chiefs of Staff were largely restricted to recommending allocations to the services within the President's established ceiling for the fiscal year 1950 budget.[9]

Despite the often declared objective of achieving many and considerable savings through more efficient business practices and organization in the defense establishment, the first two years following unification did not reveal any greater efficiency. Actions were taken to eliminate duplication and to effect consolidation and standardization; but the major benefits of the Munitions Board in the fields of increased coordination in procurement and mobilization planning were yet to be realized. In fact, there were certain trends toward triplication reflecting the Air Force endeavor to "own" its full support structure. In his first report Secretary of Defense Forrestal pointed out that there might be delay in achieving some of the expected economies:

During my testimony before the committees of the House and Senate which drafted the National Security Act of 1947 I consistently maintained that there were no great economies which would flow automatically from the Unification Act. Such economies, I held, would be achieved only after a substantial period of careful examination and vigorous prosecution of the methods of economy and efficiency.[10]

Regarding the requirement to maintain the confidence of the American people in the defense establishment as well as the morale and *esprit de corps* of the armed forces, the first two years of unification were a difficult period for the military establishment. Elements of the respective services continued to harbor major doubts as to the value of unification, and fires of controversy smoldered under the debates regarding the authority of the Secretary of Defense and the definition of roles and missions. These burst forth again in the "revolt of the admirals" which began when Secretary of Defense Louis A. Johnson cancelled further work on the aircraft super-carrier *United States* shortly after taking office in April 1949. Secretary of the Navy John L. Sullivan resigned in protest and it was revealed that the Chief of Naval Operations disagreed with the other members of the JCS in their recommendations concerning the super-carrier. In the summer and fall of 1949 Congressional hearings were held to examine alleged political influence motivating the procurement of the B-36 bomber and to determine its adequacy as a weapon. The testimony in this inquiry, which also delved into broad questions of unification and strategy, revealed that unification and its implications for service roles and missions were still emotional and controversial issues in the Pentagon.

The strong civilian authority at the head of each military department spelled out in the National Security Act, ostensibly as further assurance of civilian control, in effect undermined the ability of the Secretary of Defense to combine civilian control with the desired unification goals of authoritative coordination and unified direction of the armed forces.

While the National Security Council, established by the National Security Act, offered a promising means for more effective interagency collaboration in the formulation of basic national security policies, participation by the National Military Establishment was hampered by its confused internal lines of authority, stemming from the language of the "Unification Act." Because the secretaries of the military departments, in addition to the Secretary of Defense, were members of the National Security Council, and the Joint Chiefs of Staff could advise the NSC directly, contradictory defense views could easily be introduced into Council deliberations. The Secretary of Defense had no control over these independent channels to the NSC.

Whereas the need for a capability for instantaneous reaction was recognized, disputes over the authority of the Secretary of Defense and the independent lines of authority from the service secretaries and the Joint Chiefs of Staff to the President left some doubt as to the clarity of the command lines in time of emergency. This in turn affected the over-all speed and precision of the decision-making and implementation processes.

The creation of the Research and Development Board, its organizational link to the Joint Chiefs of Staff through the Weapons Systems Evaluation Group, and its "master plan" were organizational and procedural steps toward meeting the requirement for timely decisions concerning the development of new weapons and integrating them into strategic concepts and ready forces. However, the test of Korea revealed that the United States forces did not fully apply the potentialities of available technology to the demands of prevailing strategic requirements.

The general assignments concerning roles and missions and the organizational channel, through the Joint Chiefs of Staff, for their readjustment to fit changes in future requirements still took the form of mutual service agreements regarding details of the tasks assigned. The B-36 controversy and the "revolt of the admirals" indicated difficulty in future readjustments.

The Munitions Board and new budgetary procedures were established to enhance optimum defense capabilities from the available dollar resources, but Forrestal himself indicated that any real benefits in economy would evolve only slowly over time.

The emotional display of service disagreements in the "revolt of the admirals" and the B-36 inquiry did little to increase the internal *esprit de corps* of military personnel in terms of their support for a unified defense operation, and service loyalties were perpetuated by the National Security Act itself which carefully retained strong independent authority to each military department. Nevertheless, the capability for effective joint action demonstrated by the dramatic Berlin airlift served to increase the confidence of both Defense Department personnel and the American public in the unified defense structure.

In all fairness it must be pointed out that in this first period of transition the Department was mostly limited to perfecting its organization through the normal course of establishing administrative procedures. Any further fundamental or drastic changes could be achieved only through legislative clarification or modification of the Unification Act. This was now to be undertaken.

THE 1949 REVISION

In his *First Report of the Secretary of Defense*, covering the period through December 1948, Forrestal outlined his recommendations for legislative action in a list of fourteen points. During 1948 the National Military Establishment was also studied by a task force of the Hoover Commission (Commission on Organization of the Executive Branch of the Government, created in 1947), which was examining the over-all national security organization. The recommendations of the task force were submitted to the Commission in January 1949, and the first Commission report to the Congress was forwarded in February of that year. The Hoover Commission reports and the Forrestal recommendations dealt with several common basic issues.

The task force, under the chairmanship of Ferdinand Eberstadt, recommended strengthening the national security organization in six major fields, four of which dealt directly with the defense establishment. Its report called for clarification and strengthening of the central authority of the Secretary of Defense, and for clarifying and improving the organization for research and development, including a closer relationship between military research and development programs and strategic plans. The Hoover Commission report to the Congress generally supported the task force recommendations with particular emphasis upon strengthening the authority and staff of the Secretary and improved budget techniques.

Specifically, the Hoover Commission recommended legislation which would: make the Secretary of Defense the sole member of the National Security Council from the military establishment; create an Under Secretary of Defense to lighten the burden on the Secretary; create a Chairman of the Joint Chiefs of Staff, appointed by the Secretary of Defense, to be his principal military assistant and to improve Joint Chiefs of Staff operations; provide increased powers to the chairmen of the Research and Development Board and Munitions Board to enable more effective accomplishment of their responsibilities; and create boards or staff agencies in the Office of the Secretary of Defense headed by persons with clear authority to assist the Secretary in coordinating and providing central policy guidance to the services in such fields as budget, personnel, public relations, legislation, and medical services.

Forrestal's recommendations revealed a major change in his attitudes toward the organization of the defense establishment. As Secretary of the Navy, and at the outset of his role as Secretary of Defense, he had opposed close integration of the armed forces and a strong central authority for the Secretary of Defense. He had also favored as small a staff as possible in the Office of the Secretary. But after two years in office he proposed the following steps toward increased integration and centralization of authority: changing the National Military Establishment to a regular executive department by eliminating the provision that the services be administered as individual executive departments; eliminating the statutory right of appeal by the military departments direct to the President and the Bureau of the Budget; eliminating the word "general" in the section of the 1947 act granting the Secretary "general authority, direction, and control" over the establishment; eliminating the clause reserving to the military departments all powers not given specifically to the Secretary of Defense; and making the Secretary the only defense representative on the National Security Council.

Forrestal's positive recommendations for an expanded role for the Office of the Secretary of Defense included: transferring the functions of the Munitions Board and the Research and Development Board to the Secretary and giving him the power to appoint their chairmen; providing for three assistant secretaries in addition to the special assistants required to support the Secretary in the performance of his responsibilities; and giving the Secretary power to fix compensation for civilian personnel of the Department except for those in the military departments. He also proposed transferring certain functions of the Joint Chiefs of Staff to the Secretary of Defense, with the Joint Chiefs of Staff "assisting the Secretary" in implementing them, and giving the

Secretary of Defense the power to appoint the Director of the Joint Staff.*

The fourteen recommendations concerning reorganization in the *First Report of the Secretary of Defense* were submitted to Congress as part of the National Military Establishment legislative program in early 1949. Senate approval was completed by the end of May, but House action was delayed by the opening of the investigation of the B-36 bomber program. The House finally passed a bill in July which dealt only with fiscal management in the defense establishment. This was combined with the Senate bill in conference and the resulting amendments to the National Security Act finally passed both houses on August 2, 1949. (The chart on the following page indicates these changes.)

The 1949 amendments strengthened the authority of the Secretary of Defense by making Forrestal's requested statutory changes regarding the removal of the word "general" from "direction, authority, and control." They eliminated the concept of powers "reserved" to the services, thus changing the National Military Establishment to the executive Department of Defense and changing the service departments from executive to military departments. They made the Secretary of Defense the sole defense representative on the National Security Council, and they eliminated the clause permitting direct appeal by the military departments to the President or Bureau of the Budget over the head of the Secretary of Defense—although any service secretary or member of the Joint Chiefs of Staff could make recommendations to Congress on his own initiative after so informing the Secretary of Defense. At the same time that the authority of the Secretary was strengthened by these modifications, it was also limited by the specific provisions that the armed services were still to be "separately administered," that the Secretary was prohibited from transferring or consolidating any combatant functions (e.g., dissolving the Marines or consolidating naval aviation with the Air Force), and that any transfers of noncombatant functions were to be reported to Congress.

The amendments made possible the exercise of expanded responsibility by the Secretary of Defense by providing for a Deputy Secretary of Defense and three Assistant Secretaries of Defense to perform such duties as the Secretary might prescribe in assisting him to perform his tasks. They also empowered the Secretary to appoint and fix the compensation of civilian personnel needed by the Department. The legis-

---

* The Joint Staff provides staff support to the Joint Chiefs of Staff and is composed of personnel detailed from the three services. Service representatives also sit on the coordinating committee which form part of the structure of the Joint Staff.

lation did not permit the recommended transfer of functions of the Munitions and Research and Development Boards to the Secretary; nor did it provide for any transfer of functions to the Secretary from the Joint Chiefs of Staff. The position of the Chairman of the Joint Chiefs of Staff was created with specific provisos that he "shall have no vote"

AFTER NATIONAL SECURITY ACT AMENDMENT OF 1949

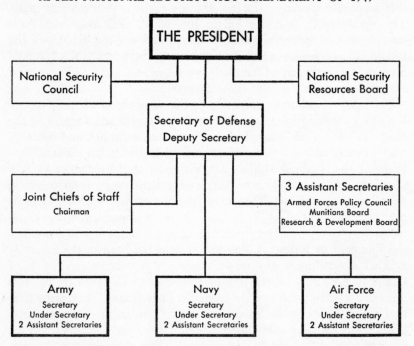

1. Secretary of Defense became principal assistant to the President on national defense, and was given:
    a. a Deputy Secretary and 3 Assistant Secretaries.
    b. direction, authority and control over the Department of Defense.
    c. control of the budget and of funds.
2. Service department secretaries no longer had cabinet status.
3. A non-voting Chairman of the Joint Chiefs of Staff was established.

and "shall not exercise command"; and the power to appoint the Director of the Joint Staff was retained by the Joint Chiefs of Staff rather than being transferred to the Secretary of Defense.

As the result of the House bill on financial management and the strong Hoover Commission recommendations underlying it, a new Title IV was added to the National Security Act, entitled "Promotion of Economy and Efficiency through Establishment of Uniform Budgetary and Fiscal Procedures and Organizations." Title IV spelled out in considerable detail the nature of fiscal and budgetary procedures to be developed within the Defense Department, emphasizing the "performance budget" and providing that a comptroller be added to each of the three military departments and that one of three newly created Assistant Secretaries of Defense assume this function for the Department as a whole.

It is significant that the philosophy of coordination by mutual cooperation and consent which had been put into practice during the first two years of unification was substantially modified after the passage of the 1949 amendments in keeping with the expanded central authority of the Secretary of Defense. Even before the legislative amendments had been completed, the second Secretary of Defense, Louis A. Johnson, took actions which portended a faster shift toward increased central policy direction by the Office of the Secretary of Defense and less reliance upon coordination by mutual consent. Johnson personally cancelled further work on the construction of the $188,000,000 super-carrier *United States* in April 1949 after considering the split Joint Chiefs of Staff views on the problem and consulting with the President. He also made particular efforts to cut down the number of part-time coordinating boards and committees which had evolved to implement the coordination "by cooperation" of the early unification period. Following approval of the 1949 amendments there was an increased trend toward granting expanded authority to the chairman and staffs of the coordinating bodies in the Office of the Secretary, from the level of the statutory Munitions and Research and Development Boards down through their subsidiary formal and informal boards and committees.[11]

Footnotes

1. *First Report of the Secretary of Defense*, Washington: G.P.O., 1949, p. 2.
2. *Ibid.*, p. 7.
3. W. Millis, Ed., *The Forrestal Diaries*, New York: Viking Press, 1951, pp. 334-335.
4. *Op. cit.*, p. 9.
5. *Ibid.*
6. The "Key West Agreement" was promulgated as a Secretary of Defense Memorandum 21 April 1948. It was revised 1 October 1953 and embodied in Department of Defense Directive No. 5100, 1, 16 March 1954, "Functions of the Armed Forces and the Joint Chiefs of Staff." For ready reference the "Key West Agreement" can be found as an appendix in Stanley, *op. cit.*, p. 176.
7. *Military Situation in the Far East*, Hearings before the Senate Committees on Armed Services and Foreign Relations, 82nd Congress, 1st Session, pp. 731-732.
8. *Second Report of the Secretary of Defense*, Washington: G.P.O., 1950, p. 143.
9. *Op. cit.*, p. 36.
10. *Op. cit.*, p. 17.
11. For expansion of this point, see R. E. McClendon, *Unification of the Armed Forces*, Air University Documentary Research Study, Maxwell Air Force Base, Alabama, 1950, pp. 72-74.

Four

EVOLUTION AND PERFORMANCE: FROM THE KOREAN WAR TO THE REORGANIZATION PLAN OF 1953

Within a year after passage of the 1949 amendments to the National Security Act, the first real test of the effectiveness of both defense organization and policy came in the form of the Korean War.

The nature of the conflict, characterized by conventional warfare similar to World War II, did little to test the adequacy of defense organization and policies relating to advanced research and development programs and their integration with strategic planning. The fact that the conflict remained limited in area and conventional and non-nuclear in nature had a dual meaning for the roles and missions as they had been assigned to the respective services. While the effectiveness of these assignments was not tested as they would be in a major general conflict, the Korean War revealed that a "limited" war can require a considerable effort in terms of men, money, and material even though it results only in "partial mobilization." We also learned that the misisons of the services must permit flexible applications of land, naval, and air-power to meet a wide range of potential warfare—from limited conventional conflict to general nuclear war. The conduct of "limited" wars must henceforth be considered in terms of the larger context—the delicate global balance of nuclear armed might.

Once the decision had been made to use United States forces in Korea, the defense structure revealed a capability to react quickly with the available forces. Whether those forces were sufficiently trained and prepared or large enough to meet the kind of attack which the enemy launched is another question.

The early stages of the Korean War proved to be an embarrassing and frightening experience for the United States. Initial reverses nearly pushed the United Nations Army, consisting primarily of Republic of Korea and United States forces, off the Korean peninsula. The North Korean success revealed a state of military unpreparedness within the United States defense establishment which undermined our political prestige and power position and revealed serious defects in our capability to meet even a limited overt challenge by force to our national security interests. Because of the unsatisfactory military developments in Korea during the summer of 1950, Secretary of Defense Johnson was unable to remain in office. To restore morale, so seriously jeopardized by the Korean shortcomings, General George C. Marshall was named Secretary in September 1950. The return of this mature and respected World War II leader from retirement was as crucial to restoring confidence in the competence of the military establishment as it was to guiding the new military build-up.

The most serious weakness in the Defense Department exposed by the reverses suffered in the Korean War was the lack of sufficient ready army and tactical air forces. This shortcoming revealed a failure to correlate adequately strategic requirements, the budget process, and costs. The necessary balance between economy of operation and optimum readiness of essential forces had not been achieved.

Although that failure indicated ineffective operation of the defense organization, it could also be attributed to incorrect policy decisions by the responsible political authorities of the government, not merely in the Pentagon but in the entire Executive Branch and in Congress as well. Reliance on strategic airpower and massive nuclear weapons as the primary expression of American military power had led to the neglect of conventional military forces. Further, an economy-minded administration had fixed the fiscal year 1950 ceilings, under which the Joint Chiefs of Staff could merely recommend allocations to the services of what was available, and Congress had deemed a $14 billion fiscal year 1950 defense budget fully adequate.

The efforts of the Office of the Secretary of Defense to achieve maximum efficiency through close policy control in the management of men, money, and materials fell in the area in which Congress expected unification to produce the greatest benefits. Rapid growth of the armed forces to meet the needs of the Korean War provided a major test of the business organization of the unified Defense Department.

Defense appropriations rose from the $14 billion level for the fiscal year 1950 to $48.2 billion for 1951, $60.4 billion for 1952, and $47 billion for 1953—all for rearmament alone and excluding military assistance programs. From the outbreak of the Korean War to the end of fiscal year 1952 the Army grew from 10 divisions and 11 regimental combat teams (all at less than peacetime manning levels and without operational support units) to 20 divisions and 18 regimental combat teams—an increase in military personnel of roughly one million men. The Navy expanded its personnel from 400,000 to 800,000 and its in-commission warships from 200 to 400, doubling the number of carriers and adding seven carrier groups to its air arm. The Marine Corps increased from 75,000 men to 230,000, organized into three divisions and three air wings. The Air Force grew from 48 groups to 95 wings with a planned goal of 143 wings and increased its military personnel from 400,000 to 980,000.[1]

The problems of managing efficiently the rapid increase in men, money, and materiel were complicated by the fact that the build-up could not be designed solely around the war in Korea. The United States realized that its over-all preparedness effort had to be expanded as a result of the unmistakable revelation of Communist capabilities and intentions. Manpower not only had to be mobilized and trained but also had to be returned to the United States after gaining experience and completing tours of duty in accordance with the rotational policy designed to lighten the burden of those who bore the brunt of the fighting. Presumably the rotation policy also increased the pool of experienced manpower available in the form of reserves after active duty was completed. In actual fact this gain was scarcely realized since little effort was made to enforce the legal obligation of Korean War veterans to participate in the reserve program.

In the production field, partial mobilization was necessary to produce equipment for immediate needs while simultaneously developing an expandable mobilization base for potential future needs. Improved weapons were constantly being developed to replace those in use. The rapid technological advances in the weapons field made it particularly difficult to judge whether or not large procurement orders should be placed for materiel when newer weapons coming off the experimental lines might make such items obsolescent, or even obsolete, by the time they were available in quantity.

These tasks also provided a good test as to whether the Munitions Board and the Research and Development Board were effective means for achieving the coordination and central policy control necessary for the efficient direction of the build-up program. While major accomplishments were achieved, as revealed in the magnitude and rapidity of the rearmament effort, the question remained: At what cost?

During 1951 and 1952 Congress gave this question considerable attention. The Senate Armed Services Committee established Preparedness Investigating Subcommittees, similar to the Truman Committee of World War II, which issued seven reports during 1952 criticizing Defense Department waste in manpower utilization, extravagance in overseas base construction, and shortages in critical kinds of ammunition in Korea. House investigations into procurement and supply operations revealed such differences between military services and resulting waste from ineffective unification that the Defense Cataloging and Standardization Act was passed in June 1952 to remedy blatant deficiencies. Throughout these various reports and investigations the Munitions Board and Research and Development Board were criticized as inefficient and unwieldy. One Preparedness Subcommittee report in July 1952 even called for drastic reorganization of the armed services.

The Semiannual Report of the Secretary of Defense for the period ending June 30, 1952 reviewed the experience of the rearmament effort and pointed out the need for change in the procedures for relating combat requirements to mobilization, procurement, and supply. It recommended improvements in organization and clarification of responsibilities which involved elements of the Office of the Secretary of Defense, the military departments, the Joint Chiefs of Staff, and the Munitions and Research and Development Boards.

In this report Robert A. Lovett, who had succeeded General Marshall as Secretary of Defense, analyzed the problems as ranging from excessive rigidity in the National Security Act, particularly in regard to the composition and functions of the Munitions Board, to purely administrative problems of minor organizational significance. He stressed the need for organizational flexibility in order to be able to meet rapidly changing conditions. One of the principal problems of the Munitions Board, a fault recognized in the Research and Development Board and the Joint Chiefs of Staff as well, was the fact that each member, except for the chairman, was both a claimant and a judge of his own requests. The fact that these three statutory agencies were composed of top civilian or military officials of the three military departments made satisfactory operation "extremely difficult, if not impossible"[2] at times of serious shortages in manpower and material. Accordingly, Secretary Lovett saw the need for both legislative and administrative action to improve the defense organization.

In a letter to President Truman on November 18, 1952 Secretary Lovett described the major problem areas of defense organization as the authority of the Secretary of Defense, the Joint Chiefs of Staff, the Munitions Board, and the organization of the military departments. Lovett stressed the need for strong authority at the top of the defense organization capable of bringing about necessary modifications despite resistance from the military services. This was further revelation of a continuing trend in the evolution of the defense organization favoring increased centralized civilian authority.

Any judgment of the performances of the Defense Department in this period comes to three conclusions. First, the fact that military forces available were barely adequate to accomplish the task revealed a level of preparedness below the actual requirements of cold war conditions. Second, the Korean reverses revealed inadequacies in strategic planning. Third, the organization and procedures of the Defense Department were inadequate for the task at hand.

THE REORGANIZATION PLAN OF 1953

The urgent need for further improvement in the defense organization was recognized by the new administration under President Eisenhower, and a study was conducted early in 1953 by the Rockefeller Committee on Defense Organization, whose recommendations, implemented by Reorganization Plan No. 6, constituted a third major stage in the evolution of the Department of Defense. Under the chairmanship of Nelson A. Rockefeller, the committee included Dr. Milton S. Eisenhower, Dr. Arthur S. Fleming, Robert A. Lovett, David Sarnoff, Dr. Vannevar Bush, and General Omar N. Bradley. General George C. Marshall, Admiral Chester W. Nimitz, and General Carl Spaatz served as military advisors. After extensive hearings and study the committee transmitted its report on April 11, 1953, to the Secretary of Defense, who forwarded it with his full approval to the President.

The Rockefeller report made recommendations in five major areas. First, it recognized the need to provide the Secretary of Defense with clear authority to carry out complete and effective control over the entire Defense Department. The committee adopted and appended to its report a legal opinion which argued that previous challenges to the Secretary's authority, based on the phrase that required military departments to be "separately administered," had no basis in statute or in legislative history. Second, the committee recommended that the civilian secretaries of the military departments be the responsible operating and managing heads of both the civilian and military aspects of their respective departments in order to "have a single channel of command or line of administrative responsibility within the Department of Defense and each of the military department." Third, it was recommended that the Munitions and Research and Development Boards be abolished as unwieldy and their functions transferred to assistant secretaries of defense; for which purpose the committee proposed the creation of additional assistant secretaries and a general counsel with the rank of assistant secretary. Fourth, in order to free military officers detailed to the Office of the Secretary of Defense from service influences, it was recommended that their efficiency reports be completed by their civilian superiors in the Office of the Secretary of Defense rather than by their superior officers in the respective services.

Fifth, the committee made certain recommendations regarding the Joint Chiefs of Staff. The report recognized the difficulties caused by the double role of the service chiefs as members of the Joint Chiefs of Staff and military chiefs of their respective services, but it opposed creating a single general staff or chief of staff or giving the chairman the power to resolve disagreements among the chiefs. Instead, the committee recommended closer adherence than had been the practice to the intent of the National Security Act, which was to emphasize the planning and advisory role of the Joint Chiefs of Staff. To this end it proposed, first, revision of the Key West Agreement to remove the command functions of the Joint Chiefs of Staff and, second, the assignment of executive responsibility for unified commands by the Secretary of Defense rather than the Joint Chiefs of Staff. To facilitate the planning and advisory activities of the Joint Chiefs of Staff, it proposed giving the chairman the responsibility of organizing the structure of the Joint Chiefs of Staff and the Joint Staff and recommended the increased delegation of administrative duties by the chiefs to their respective service deputies on the one hand and to the Joint Staff on the other. Finally, the report stressed the need for close working relationships between the Joint Chiefs of Staff and the Office of the Secretary of Defense and between the individual chiefs and their respective service secretaries.

The proposals of the Rockefeller Committee provided the basis for the President's Reorganization Plan No. 6, submitted to the Congress on April 30, 1953. In his message transmitting the plan[3] the President cited three basic objectives to guide organization of the defense structure: (1) "There must be clear and unchallenged civilian responsibility . . . not only to maintain democratic institutions but also to protect the integrity of the military profession." (2) "Effectiveness with economy must be made the watchwords of our defense effort." (3) "We must develop the best possible military plans. They must incorporate the most competent and considered thinking from every point of view— military, scientific, industrial, and economic."

More specifically, in order to clarify lines of authority so as to strengthen civilian responsibility, the President's message outlined the basic channels of responsibility as running from the President through the Secretary of Defense and the secretaries of the military departments, who were to be responsible "for all aspects of the respective military departments." In the President's words: "No function in any part of the Department of Defense or in any of its component agencies is to be performed independent of the direction, authority, and control of the Secretary of Defense."

The message also called for revision of the Key West Agreement to provide that the Secretary of Defense, on the advice of the Joint Chiefs of Staff, should designate a military department to serve as the executive agency for a unified command rather than the Joint Chiefs of Staff designating one of their members the agent as had been the procedure. Under this arrangement the channel of responsibility and authority to a commander of a unified command ran clearly from the President to the Secretary of Defense to the designated civilian secretary of a military department to the unified command. However, the message clearly pointed out that "for the strategic direction and operational control of forces and for the conduct of combat operations the military chief of the designated military department will be authorized by the Secretary of Defense to receive and transmit reports and orders and to act for that department in its executive agency capacity."

As a means to achieve effectiveness with economy the President's message emphasized decentralization of operations "under flexible and effective direction and control from the center" and relying upon the secretaries of the military departments as the principal agents of the Secretary of Defense for the management and direction of the entire defense enterprise. To assure the necessary flexibility and effectiveness in the direction and control emanating from the Office of the Secretary of Defense, Reorganization Plan No. 6 provided for abolition of the Munitions and the Research and Development Boards, the Defense Supply Management Agency, and the Office of the Director of Installations; transfer of their functions to the Secretary of Defense; and establishment of six additional assistant secretaries of defense. These assistant secretaries were to provide their staff support to the Secretary "without imposing themselves in the direct lines of responsibility and authority between the Secretary and the Secretaries of the three military departments."

The Presidential message also called for study and improvement of the internal organization of the military departments, study and reorganization of procurement and supply procedures and machinery in the defense organization, study and development of policies for attracting and holding competent career civilian and military personnel in the Defense Department, and necessary orders to carry out the Rockefeller

Committee recommendations regarding preparation of efficiency reports on military officers assigned to the Office of the Secretary of Defense.

The President's message also closely followed the Rockefeller Committee proposals in regard to improving the machinery for strategic planning. Calling for improved organization and procedures of the Joint Staff so that the chiefs might better perform their roles as strategic planners and military advisers, it stated specifically that the Joint Chiefs of Staff "are not a command body, but are the principal military advisers to the President, the National Security Council, and the Secretary of Defense."

The Reorganization Plan placed upon the Chairman of the Joint Chiefs the responsibility for organizing and directing the staff activities supporting the Joint Chiefs of Staff, and specifically for managing the work of the Joint Staff and approving the assignment of its member officers. The Joint Staff was described as "a study and reporting body serving the Joint Chiefs of Staff," and the tenure of the Director of the Joint Staff was to be subject to Secretary of Defense approval. The message also cited the need for introducing more diversified and expert skills in such fields as budget, research, engineering, manpower, and supply through staff collaboration in the early stages of staff work in problems before the Joint Chiefs of Staff.

The Secretary of Defense was called upon to "direct the Chairman of the Joint Chiefs of Staff to arrange for the fullest cooperation of the Joint Staff and the subcommittees of the Joint Chiefs of Staff with other parts of the Office of the Secretary of Defense." As a further means for attaining broader and more effective staff contributions to strategic planning the message recommended the addition of competent civilian scientists and engineers to the substructure of the Joint Chiefs of Staff to assure that the implications of new scientific developments and weapons systems were adequately integrated into the strategic plans.

Reorganization Plan No. 6 went into effect on June 30, 1953, and on the same day the Secretary of Defense approved a reorganization which designated the following fields of responsibility within his office: *Assistant Secretary (Comptroller)*—to be the principal assistant and adviser on all budgetary and fiscal management functions and for implementation of Title IV of the National Security Act;* *Assistant Secretary (International Security Affairs)*—to be responsible for the development of Department of Defense views and positions relating to all international affairs involving the armed forces, including coordination of activities in such political-military areas as military assistance, NATO (North Atlantic Treaty Organization), UN (United Nations) affairs,

* See Chapter Nine.

and National Security actions; *Assistant Secretary (Manpower and Personnel)*—to be responsible for the establishment of efficient manpower and personnel programs, the formation of domestic security policies, and the internal administration of the Office of the Secretary of Defense; *Assistant Secretary (Supply and Logistics)*—to provide advice and assistance in most of the areas formerly assigned to the Munitions Board, including the areas of production planning, procurement, distribution, and transportation; *Assistant Secretary (Research and Development)*—to be responsible for evaluating and coordinating integrated programs of military research and development in order to secure the best possible weapons and to correct deficiencies and duplications (the function formerly carried out by the Research and Development Board); *Assistant Secretary (Applications Engineering)*—to be responsible for maximum adaptation of new weapons and equipment resulting from military research and development to existing production facilities and for evaluation of such equipment as to production feasibility; *Assistant Secretary (Properties and Installations)*—to be responsible for the development of effective programs relating to the investment in buildings, posts, bases, and other facilities acquired by the armed forces (functions formerly carried out by the Office of the Director of Installations); *Assistant Secretary (Health and Medical)*—to plan and direct development of efficient programs for maintaining high health standards among personnel of the armed forces and for effective management of medical installations; *Assistant Secretary (Legislative and Public Affairs)*—to coordinate legislative recommendations of all agencies of the Department of Defense prior to their submission to Congress and to supervise all public information activities of the Department, including acting as a central office for providing prompt information requested by Congress; *General Counsel*—(bearing rank of Assistant Secretary) as chief legal officer of the Department, to be responsible for developing authoritative opinions and interpretations for the Secretary; *Assistant to the Secretary (Atomic Energy)*—to be the principal adviser to the Secretary on all atomic energy matters and to act as Chairman, Military Liaison Committee, which advises the Atomic Energy Commission on military applications of atomic energy. (The structure of the Defense Department at that time is shown on the opposite page.)

In addition to this reorganization of the Office of the Secretary of Defense, most of the other provisions of Reorganization Plan No. 6 and the President's message accompanying it were implemented during 1953.

The Key West Agreement of 1948 was revised by a directive dated October 1, 1953, which did not modify the roles and missions of the three services but implemented the President's recommendations regarding the executive agent responsibilities for unified commands. While a military department rather than a member of the Joint Chiefs was now to act as executive agency, clarifying the lines of responsibility from the Secretary of Defense to the civilian secretary of a designated military

AFTER REORGANIZATION PLAN NO. 6, 1953

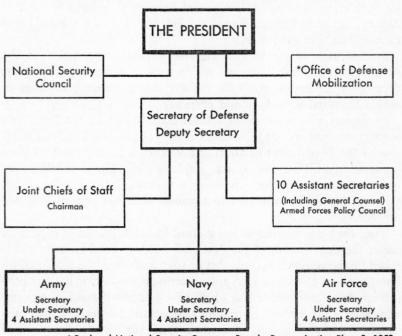

* Replaced National Security Resources Board—Reorganization Plan 3, 1953.

1. The number of Assistant Secretaries of Defense clearly established as staff executives was tripled.
2. Munitions Board and Research and Development Board were replaced.
3. Primary planning role of Joint Chiefs of Staff was strengthened.
4. Chairman of Joint Chiefs of Staff was given administrative authority over the Joint Staff (serving the Joint Chiefs of Staff).
5. The number of assistant secretaries in the departments was doubled.

department, that civilian secretary was to authorize "forthwith" the military chief of his department "to act for such department in its executive agency capacity" for the strategic direction and conduct of combat operations in emergency and wartime situations.[4] The military chief was required to keep his department secretary, the Secretary of Defense, and the Joint Chiefs of Staff fully informed of decisions and actions taken under such authority. The Chairman of the Joint Chiefs of Staff was also authorized to take action with respect to the reorganization and strengthening of the Joint Staff.

In order to implement the President's proposals for decentralization of operational responsibility from the Office of the Secretary of Defense to the secretaries of the military departments, operational responsibility was reassigned from the Office of the Secretary to military departments for such joint agencies as the Armed Services Petroleum Purchasing Agency, the Armed Forces Explosives Safety Board, and the Industrial Employment Review Board.

Studies were begun to examine the internal organization of the Army, Navy, and Air Force and the financial procedures of the entire department in accordance with the President's message in order to obtain increased economies and efficiency.

In general, this summary of actions taken following the President's message of April 30, 1953, brings us up to the present. The basic structure of the Department of Defense has remained fairly constant since Reorganization Plan No. 6 was implemented. Minor modifications have been made to meet changing situations, but these have been achieved mainly by administrative readjustments in organization and procedures.*

Thus the present structure has evolved from the lessons of experience under the organization of the National Military Establishment established by the National Security Act of 1947 and under the modifications brought about under the 1949 amendments to the Act. It has not been subjected to the ultimate test of its effectiveness—the ability to wage war—as was the earlier organizational structure. However, it has been in effect during five years of intense "cold war" which has required maintaining maximum preparedness and effectiveness in the defense organization to implement effective "cold war" policies while simultaneously being ready at any moment for the transition to open conflict in any form. It would seem, therefore, an appropriate time to examine

---

* Within the Office of the Secretary of Defense, the Assistant Secretary of Defense (Manpower and Personnel) now lists his responsibilities as (Manpower, Personnel, and Reserve). Early in 1957 the activities of the Assistant Secretary of Defense (Legislative and Public Affairs) were divided in three ways. The Office of Legislative Liaison (i.e., with Congress) now reports to the Secretary of Defense through a special assistant. The Office of Legislative Programs (responsible for coordination of the preparation of defense legislation) was transferred to the General Counsel. The Assistant Secretary of Defense (Public Affairs) is responsible solely for public information activities. Also early in 1957, the offices of two Assistant Secretaries of Defense (Research and Development and Applications Engineering) were merged under an Assistant Secretary for Research and Engineering. This merely merged activities somewhat artificially divided originally and which had worked increasingly as one function.

the over-all state of organizational effectiveness of the present Department of Defense by focusing on its attempts to solve some of the continuing central issues and basic problem areas involved in maintaining the security of the United States.

THE PRESIDENT AND THE NATIONAL SECURITY COUNCIL STRUCTURE

Before making any assessment of Department of Defense accomplishments it is important to note the relationship between the defense structure and the Presidency; for the President, as Commander-in-Chief, plays a significant role in many defense matters, a role which often places both substantive and procedural limitations upon Defense Department decision-making on contemporary problems.

The office of the Presidency is at the top of the national security organization pyramid. The President has direct command authority over the heads of the individual executive departments and also of the corporate body on which some of them serve—the National Security Council.

A brief description of the National Security Council structure (see chart, p. 50) will help clarify the relation of the Defense Department to that organ. The National Security Act of 1947, with subsequent amendments, provides the legal foundation for the National Security Council, the Department of Defense, the Joint Chiefs of Staff and the Central Intelligence Agency. In enacting this legislation, it was "the intent of Congress to provide a comprehensive program for the future security of the United States; to provide for the establishment of integrated policies and procedures for the departments agencies, and functions of the Government relating to the national security; to provide for three military departments, separately administered . . ."*

The Act established the National Security Council and stated that

the President of the United States shall preside over meetings of the Council: Provided, That in his absence he may designate a member of the Council to preside in his place.
The function of the Council shall be to advise the President with respect to the intergration of domestic, foreign, and military policies relating to the national security so as to enable the military services and the other departments and agencies of the Government to cooperate more effectively in matters involving the national security.[5]

In addition to the Council itself there are within the NSC structure the following agencies: the NSC Planning Board, the Operations Co-

* Sec. 2, National Security Act, 1947, as amended.

ordinating Board, the NSC Staff, and the OCB Staff.

The statutory members of the Council include the President, the Vice President, Secretary of State, Secretary of Defense, and the

NATIONAL SECURITY COUNCIL RELATIONSHIPS

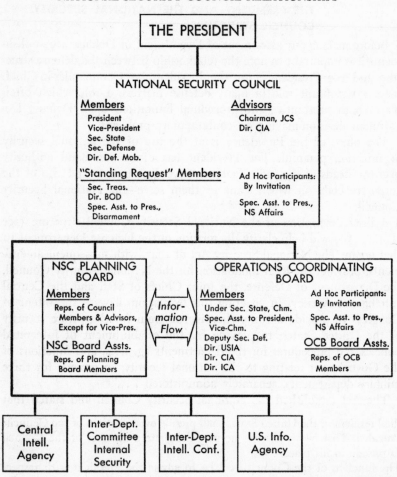

Director of the Office of Defense Mobilization. The Secretary of the Treasury and the Director of the Bureau of the Budget have standing invitations to participate in Council meetings, while such officials as the Chairman of the Atomic Energy Commission are invited when agenda items of interest to them are discussed. Finally the Council is served by two advisers, the Chairman of the Joint Chiefs of Staff and the Director of the Central Intelligence Agency.

In accordance with the current concept of its functioning the Council deals only with issues affecting the national security; advises the President in determining national security policy and the departments in implementing national security policy; assists in integrating domestic, foreign, and military policies, assists in coordinating policies and functions of agencies relating to national security; is concerned with both our actual and potential military power; and is not limited to areas of agency agreement but on its own initiative can seek out areas of agency conflict or omission and act to present alternative or new courses of action.

The Council relies heavily on its Planning Board for the formulation of draft statements of policy for its consideration. As the key forum for the preparation of policy recommendations the NSC Planning Board "anticipates and identifies problems and situations affecting security objectives, commitments and risks of the US and initiates action to provide the required analyses and draft policy statements for consideration by the NSC."

It is also charged with facilitating "formulation of policies during drafting of recommendations by marshalling resources of respective departments, identifying alternatives, seeking acceptable agreements, discussing differences, [and] reducing differences to clearly defined areas prior to reference to the NSC." In its functioning the Planning Board is presided over by a Special Assistant to the President for National Security Affairs.

The Operations Coordinating Board was originally established by Executive Order of the President on September 2, 1953, to improve inter-agency reports to the National Security Council on policy implementation. The same agencies which are represented on the National Security Council also comprise the Operations Coordinating Board, except that the JCS do not advise the OCB as they do the NSC. In addition the United States Information Agency and the International Cooperation Agency are members of this Board. There is also a Presidential Assistant for Security Operations Coordination who acts as vice-chairman and participates in meetings "in close collaboration with" the Under Secretary of State, who is the chairman of the Operations Coordinating Board.

Under Executive Order No. 10700, issued February 25, 1957, the President formally placed the Board within the structure of the National Security Council. This was done to provide a still closer relation between the formulation and the implementation of security policies. According to this Executive Order, the functions of the OCB are as follows:

The President having approved any national security policy after receiving the advice of the National Security Council thereon, the Board shall (1) whenever the President shall hereafter so direct, advise with the agencies concerned as to (a) their detailed operational planning responsibilities respecting such policy, (b) the coordination of the interdepartmental aspects of the detailed operational plans developed by the agencies to carry out such policy, (c) the timely and coordinated execution of such policy and plans, and (d) the execution of each security action or project so that it shall make its full contribution to the attainment of national security objectives and to the particular climate of opinion the United States is seeking to achieve in the world, and (2) initiate new proposals for action within the framework of national security policies in response to opportunity and changes in the situation. The Board shall perform such other advisory functions as the President may assign to it and shall from time to time make reports to the National Security Council with respect to the carrying out of this order.

Both the Council and the NSC Planning Board are set up to be corporate bodies in which the members advise or recommend in their own individual right rather than as representatives of departments or agencies. The solutions they propose are presumably not merely compromises acceptable to all agencies. In actuality, because of inherent limitations of composition and structure, the President's staff agencies in the field of national security affairs do not always function in the manner contemplated. Chiefly because the NSC and OCB are composed of personnel associated with operating agencies, there is a tendency for decisions to reflect the minimum upon which all agencies can agree rather than the cohesive total which may be required to advance United States interests. The recommendations finally agreed upon and presented to higher authority are often so vague and general that each agency can, at least with minor change, fit them to its own self-endorsed policy.

In addition to being part of the National Security Council structure the Defense Department is also directly responsive to the President's command authority. The Presidency first took on the characteristics which it now possesses with the creation in the 1939 Reorganization Act of the Executive Office of the President. This office is now a complex structure, including, as most directly concerned with the Defense Department and military matters, the President's immediate office and staff, the Bureau of the Budget, and the Office of Defense Mobilization. Included in the President's immediate White House office, a very flexible structure, are perhaps a half-dozen or more close civilian advisors to the President on various military or quasi-military matters who comprise a personal presidential staff in contrast to the formal military staff which the President possesses in the Joint Chiefs of Staff, the secretaries and their military departments. Such individuals as the Special Assistant to the President for National Security Affairs, the Special Assistant to the President for Disarmament, the Special Assistant to the President for Security Operations Coordination are included in this number.

Since the Director of the Bureau of the Budget is the President's right-hand man in drawing up the annual budget, he is a key personage in scrutinizing the military estimates and in helping to decide on the allocation of funds to the military. The principal responsibilities of the Office of Defense Mobilization which are of concern to the military are the determination of the proper size of the military base we should maintain against the possibility of war, and decisions as to the allocation of manpower and materials for military purposes in the event of mobilization.

In the national security area the Presidency looms much larger than the foregoing outline would indicate. As Commander-in-Chief, the President has numerous, strong, and detailed powers over the military establishment and military policy. Although he cannot declare war, he may bring it about by his conduct of foreign policy. With the onset of war, his military powers expand. The only limits upon the power of the President in the military area are, generally speaking, the same checks and balances which limit him in his other roles—those vested primarily in Congress. In exercising his military powers the President may actually employ not only the machinery outlined above but practically the entire Executive Branch. Correspondingly, he is the only official of government who can make, or who can authorize others to make, decisions involving the use of United States forces or the manner of their employment. Lastly, it is relevant to note certain effects of the current relationship of the Presidency to specific military problems.

Since World War II, professional military personnel, and, in fact, the military departments themselves, have been successively downgraded in the Executive Branch hierarchy. This is not to say that the professional military voice is unrepresented in or by the Executive Branch in the councils of government. But, whereas prior to World War II the individual military departments and both their military and civilian leaders had access directly and individually to the President, the

Secretary of Defense and a thickening layer of assistants now intervenes. While by law the Joint Chiefs of Staff as a body are the military advisers to the President, the Chairman of the Joint Chiefs is in fact the only one of the group who has ready access to him. Hence, since only one civilian head and one military head now represent the military establishment to the President instead of the two from each military department who represented it before and during World War II, the influence of the professional military may be said to have declined, relatively speaking.

The military budget has been an Executive responsibility since the Budget and Accounting Act of 1921. Certain current aspects of budget-making procedures appear to work a disadvantage upon military planning and performance; for the annual preparation of the budget necessitated under present law and practice militates against the type of long-range planning and flexible expenditure of funds which are required to keep our defense forces ahead of, or at least abreast of, any potential major enemy.* Moreover, there is an additional phase of budget procedure which appears to vitiate military policy in a substantive manner. In the late 1940's the practice of placing a ceiling on military budgets was reinstituted. To do so is undeniably a Presidential prerogative. Yet, should the limit imposed by the President be based primarily on the recommendations of his Budget Director or on those of his military advisers, or should it be the result of reconciliation by the President himself of the divergent recommendations of both?

It is clear that the relationship between the Chief Executive and the military, and, specifically, the effect of that relationship on the capacity of the Department of Defense to act in fulfillment of its responsibilities, must be borne in mind as we undertake an examination of the performance of the Department of Defense after its 1953 reorganization.

Footnotes

1. *Semiannual Report of the Secretary of Defense*, January 1 to June 30, 1952, Washington: G.P.O., 1952, pp. 2-3.
2. *Ibid.*, p. 66.
3. *Message from the President of the United States Transmitting Reorganization Plan No. 6 of 1953, Relating to the Department of Defense*, House of Representatives Document No. 136, 83rd Congress, 1st Session, April 30, 1953.
4. Text of revised Key West Agreement can be found in Stanley, *op. cit.*, p. 176.
5. Sec. 101 (a), *ibid.*
* See Chapter Nine, Part 1.

Part II

THE PRESENT
DEFENSE ORGANIZATION

INTRODUCTION

We turn now to an examination of the effectiveness and adequacy as well as the stresses and strains of the present Defense Department organization and procedures, which are based upon the concepts of the 1953 Reorganization Plan No. 6.

In moving from an analysis of the history of the Department of Defense to an examination of that vast and complex structure, it is well to set forth in advance that there is no simple or single-track approach to a systematic evaluation. Thus, in the examination and evaluation which we now propose to undertake, we must exercise a certain selectivity as to the areas of coverage and the detail with which these areas are treated. In general, we have attempted to treat those difficulties which relate most directly to the criteria developed in Chapter Two, and to do so only in such detail as is necessary to give clarity and concreteness to our views.

Two principal considerations underlie the selection of material for discussion. One is the basic and pervasive nature of the shortcomings pointed out. The other is the susceptibility of the selected shortcomings to correction by available and feasible means. This does not mean that we have consciously evaded the difficult issues; nor has it precluded proposals which may now seem unfeasible but which may, under altered circumstances, be eminently practicable. It does mean that we have formed our judgments in terms of the here and now rather than taking as a standard for criticism an ideal (but improbable) defense organization.

We would emphasize that the interlocking nature of Defense Department functions and activities makes it impossible simply to set against each other on the one hand a set of functions and on the other a set of criteria applying exclusively to one or more functions. For example, the development of strategic doctrine is of necessity closely allied both with orderly technological innovation and with the establishment of service roles and missions. In the following evaluation, therefore, the heading under which a given set of shortcomings is discussed does not necessarily mean that those shortcomings affect only one portion of our yardstick or are themselves subject to judgment only on one account. The evaluation cuts across all strata of departmental activities and indicates neither the order of importance of the problems nor the order of priority in which they should be solved. It represents simply one way—and we hope a logical way—of focusing attention on the implications of present defects in the organization of the Defense Department.

The basis for the development of this part is the "yardstick" set down in Chapter Two. This critical rationale can be summarized as follows: however organized, the Department of Defense during the foreseeable future should be able to:

1. Provide for the authoritative coordination and unified direction of the armed forces under civilian control.

2. Participate effectively in the formulation and implementation of national policy.

3. React instantaneously with all essential force and with utmost efficiency against any enemy military attack.

4. Formulate strategic military concepts which keep pace with dynamic and shifting weapons technology, and yet remain compatible with national policy objectives.

5. Make timely progress with new weapons, from original conception of the idea through mass production, and integrate them, with minimum disruption of efficiency, into the ready military forces.

6. Anticipate timely adjustments that will have to be made in the functional military missions of the various types of armed forces, in order to prevent wasteful duplication of functions.

7. Achieve maximum cost efficiency, or optimum defense capabilities, from dollar expenditures.

8. Attract and retain sufficient qualified manpower, and maintain the motivation and morale of the civilian and military personnel who wield the nation's sword—its military establishment.

Five

CIVILIAN CONTROL

MILITARY RESPONSIBILITY TO CIVILIAN AUTHORITY

Many Americans—civilian and military, interested or disinterested, ignorant or informed, penetrating or superficial—have discussed civilian control, some at great length. Some have known only the military aspects, some only the civilian. Some regard civilian control as a simple matter of precluding the possibility of military dictatorship. A few have passed over the deep edge of prejudice and regard civilian control as being essential for national safety because of some supposed moral and intellectual superiority of the civilian.

Military force, created by and maintained in the midst of any particular society, is always relatively powerful—usually powerful enough to take over physical control of the society if its efforts are so directed. The nature of military force makes it *possible* for a large part of such a force to be developed along lines of loyalty to its own leaders rather than to the national leaders. Therefore every intelligent society develops safeguards to ensure that the leaders of the military force are so trained and so regulated that they will utilize these forces against their nation's enemies and not against their own nation or their nation's leaders.

This is not to say, as some proponents of civilian control believe, that there is some innate superiority in being a civilian, some inherent virtue in not being a military man. The soldier is a citizen of his country quite as much as the civilian. Dependent upon his personal qualities, either a civilian or a soldier may prove more competent in the management of great affairs. The soldier is no more likely than the civilian to possess either admirable or reprehensible qualities of mind or spirit. It does no service to the understanding of civilian control to make comparisons that turn out, whether intended or not, to be contrasts between good civilians and bad soldiers; nor does it serve understanding to compare good soldiers with bad civilians. In any event, the fact that a citizen is a military man does not indicate that he cannot be safely trusted with control of military forces.

Nevertheless, laws, regulations, and organizational procedures rightfully are prescribed that make certain, as much as such things can, that the military forces, despite their daily obedience to their leaders, would obey the elected heads of the government if a disagreement should ever develop between the civilian heads of government and military leaders. This is the valid basis and necessity for the concept of *control* of the armed forces by civilians which, in our view, means that the persons to whom command of our military forces is entrusted must in turn be unquestionably responsive to the duly elected representatives of the people.

The Constitutional provisions for civilian control of the armed forces establish a divided responsibility which, while it provides checks and balances, also serves to bring to the civilian-military problem the same confusion that divided responsibility brings to any other problem. This is a fundamental dilemma the ramifications of which are implicit throughout the discussions in this study. Although the national tradition of maintaining civilian control over the armed forces is firmly imbedded in military and civilians alike, the unique constitutional separation of powers in the United States Government and existing legislation governing Defense Department organization have raised certain real problems in the implementation of civilian control, one of them being the nature of military responsibility to civilian authority.

The Constitution names the President as the Commander-in-Chief of the armed forces.[1] The National Security Act of 1947, as amended, established the Secretary of Defense as "the principal assistant to the President in all matters relating to the Department of Defense," and further declared that "under the direction of the President, . . . he shall have direction, authority and control over the Department of Defense."[2] Thus the present command line runs from the President to the Secretary of Defense to the secretaries of the military departments to the military chiefs of the respective services. However, the 1947 National Security Act also established the Joint Chiefs of Staff as the "principal military advisers to the President, the National Security Council, and the Secretary of Defense."[3] The chiefs of the military services thus have two different relationships to their civilian superiors. As the responsible operating chiefs of their respective military services they must follow the command line up through their respective departmental secretaries, but in their corporate responsibility as the Joint Chiefs of Staff they may advise directly the President and the National Security Council as well as the Secretary of Defense.

The professional military are also responsible to the civilian Congress, as is made clear by both the Constitution and the 1947 National Security Act. By the Constitution Congress is "empowered to make rules for the government and regulation of the land and naval forces," "to raise and support armies," and "to provide and maintain a navy."[4] The National Security Act specifically provides that the secretary or military chief of a military department, on his own initiative, and after informing the Secretary of Defense, may present to Congress any recommendation concerning the Department of Defense he may deem proper.[5] This responsibility to Congress is made tangible by the Congressional power over the military purse through its control of annual appropriations.

With such diversified responsibility to civilian control, the professional military man can encounter real conflicts in determining the priority of his responsibility to civilian authority. Take, for example, the situation, which has arisen on more than one occasion, when the military chief of a service believes that certain decisions of his superiors on a crucial issue with deep political-military implications for the nation are politically, economically, psychologically, or, especially, militarily unsound. He has expressed his views before the decision is made, but the decision is made adversely by his civilian superiors in the executive branch, whether by his service secretary, the Secretary of Defense, the President, or one of the "assistants" to these officials. Should that settle the matter because he has received orders from his civilian superiors?

In furtherance of its duty to legislate on the basis of the best obtainable knowledge and advice, Congress may call on him for his opinions of these planned military programs. The chief of staff's superiors have already given Congress their evaluations and opinions, but he may disagree with many of their evaluations. Is he free to say so to Congress? If he does speak his honest disagreement, should he be castigated or relieved of his position because he is allegedly "disloyal"? The question would be, disloyal to whom: To the civilian Secretary of Defense? To the civilian President? To the Administration? To civilian control? To the civilian Congress? To the Constitution? To the American people? Or is it his essential duty to so testify, whatever be the opinion of his executive branch superiors?

These are questions to be resolved by the individual concerned, of course. Perhaps at such a point, if his views are still fundamentally divergent, a military leader should resign. But resignation has many drawbacks. Certainly no top military leader will resign very willingly when he views an issue with great concern. He would prefer to remain where he can best exert his influence over the course of its resolution.

THE NATURE OF CIVILIAN CONTROL

The concept of civilian control *per se* has been well established in principle and in fact. What is of concern is the way in which that control is exercised, and the resultant impact upon Defense Department organization, procedures, and operations.

There has been some tendency to judge effective civilian control in terms of the number of civilian officials in top level positions and the extent of their activities. Thus, one advocate of Reorganization Plan No. 6 argued that, in order to make the "centralized policy versus decentralized operations" delineation effective, the responsible civilian secretaries (Secretary and Deputy Secretary of Defense and the three service secretaries) should exercise "active" rather than "passive" civilian control over all the military functions. To exercise "active" control, the civilian secretaries were to have staffs which would enable them not only to review and coordinate but also to initiate and control broad basic plans and policies in all the major fields of Defense Department activity, thus ensuring that the three military services prepared and executed their plans and programs in an efficient and coordinated manner. This concept of an "active" approach would seem to require the staffs supporting the top civilian officials to enter increasingly into operational control of military activities. Such intervention into operations would not only prejudice the speed and precision of the operation but also involve top-level civilian officials in increasingly detailed matters while decreasing the time and staff guidance available for consideration of those broad issues of defense policy with which they are centrally concerned. The result would be an overload imposed on top-level decision-makers and an infringement of the operating responsibilities of the implementing agencies.

Instead, the stated aim of the President, in recommending the adoption of Reorganization Plan No. 6, was to combine effective civilian policy control with decentralization of operations. The problem arises from the fact that the areas of interest and responsibility of the military staffs cover the same fields as those covered by the staffs of the civilian secretaries. The military staffs had long been responsible for over-all direction of the armed forces. As subsequent modifications in the defense structure thrust civilian secretaries into operations, well beyond their "policy" roles, duplication developed. While there has been a general effort to keep the Office of the Secretary of Defense at the minimum possible personnel levels, all staff officials responsible for central policy review and control face the continuing problem of effectively carrying out their responsibilities without violating the principle of decentralized operations and without encroaching upon the line of command.

The Office of the Secretary of Defense today consists of more than a big room and a small anteroom. It comprises several thousand people, organized into many levels and agencies, including the staffs of nine assistant secretaries and several special assistants. It provides staff support for the Secretary, the Deputy Secretary, the Assistant Secretaries, and comparable officials. The philosophy underlying its operations is that, although the "Office" should provide the Secretary and Deputy Secretary with the capability for maintaining central policy control over the Department's far-flung activities, the administration of actual operations is to be conducted on a decentralized basis by the three military departments. Civilian-military balance is achieved by the fact that the Office of the Secretary of Defense (OSD) includes the Joint Chiefs of Staff and utilizes both professional military and civilian personnel. At the next level down, civilian control over decentralized defense operations, which are of predominantly military nature, is maintained by the civilian service secretaries and their staffs in the respective military departments. However, this general scheme is subject to the many pressures of personalities, changing workload, and the demands of emergency situations. In present practice within the Defense Department the line between centralized policy control and decentralized administration of operations is seldom clear.*

Moreover, the observation has been made that the current organization is so strongly oriented toward assuring civilian control through civilian supervision that it has tended to undermine the proper position of the military and to alter the desired balance between civilian and military roles in the Department of Defense. The concern that the military voice may be detrimentally muted derives from the way in which civilian control is exercised, and particularly from trends in operating relationships between the military services and the civilian secretaries.

The President's message accompanying Reorganization Plan No. 6 pointed out the need to maintain a careful civilian-military balance both to maintain at all times basic United States democratic institutions and principles and to guarantee the integrity of the professional

---

* For example, note the directive of the Secretary of Defense on penalties for the leakage of information. The general counsel of the Defense Department (who has no direct connection with the service judge advocates) was charged with overseeing the implementation of this part of the directive, and with insuring uniformity of treatment among the three services. It is difficult to see how this can be done without the general counsel's reviewing the decisions of the service judge advocates and/or requiring reports on cases tried—in effect establishing operational control over the administration of justice within the services.

military forces necessary for effective military action whenever required. In the words of the message: "Basic decisions relating to the military forces must be made by politically accountable civilian officials. Conversely, professional military leaders must not be thrust into the political arena to become the prey of partisan politics."[7] Thus true civilian control consists not in detailed civilian supervision over the armed forces but in the exercise of ultimate authority by civilian officials who are in turn held accountable for the manner in which they perform their functions.

CIVILIAN AND MILITARY ROLES

In one sense the principal issues of civilian control stem from the central problem of determining the appropriate, or optimum, roles for the military officer and the civilian. Within this problem are contained such issues as determining whether positions not governed by statute shall be filled by civilian or military personnel; whether certain activities and responsibilities shall be predominantly military or civilian; and whether functions and positions, especially the top level of the Department of Defense, can be defined as being "civilian" or "military" in nature. According to the Hoover Commission report of 1955,[8] much remains to be accomplished in reducing over-staffing by duplicating civilian and military positions in support activities, use of military personnel in civilian-type positions, and the tendency to over-supervise by both military and civilian personnel.

The present defense structure reveals some effort to differentiate functions by giving civilian secretariats principal responsibility for the support, supply, and business management of the armed forces and assigning military staffs the responsibility for planning and directing military operations. The Joint Chiefs of Staff are responsible for the development of strategic and operational plans for the employment of the armed forces; the assistant secretaries of defense act as civilian vice-presidents in broad fields of "producer logistics," such as budget and fiscal control, supply and logistics, personnel, properties and installations, and research and engineering. In the military departments, civilian secretariats are concerned with similar broad fields of "producer logistics," and the military staffs are responsible for the "consumer logistics" involved in actual military operations and direct logistic support of combat units.

It is recognized in the present defense organization that policy development requires an effective and balanced blending of civilian and military voices if realistic and valid decisions are to be made. We have noted previously that the Office of the Secretary of Defense is staffed by both civilian and professional military personnel. Moreover, procedures at this policy-making level are marked by frequent formal and informal consultation and coordination with the military staffs and civilian secretariats of the military departments. At the highest level, the Armed Forces Policy Council, composed of the Secretary and Deputy Secretary of Defense, the secretaries of the military departments, the military chiefs of staff, and the Chairman of the Joint Chiefs of Staff, meets regularly on broad policy questions.

Although the current organization provides formal and informal procedures for blending civilian and military thinking, it often obstructs the optimum use of civilian and professional military talent by unclear division of their respective responsibilities. In actual practice the civilian-military functional distinctions do not fit the over-simplified pattern of "producer" versus "consumer" logistics. For example, in the Army and Air Force the comptroller function is under the military chief of staff, but in the Navy it is retained in the executive office of the civilian secretary. Thus the Army and Air Force utilize professional military men directly in such matters as budget and fiscal controls to a greater extent than the Navy. The involvement of professional military talent in areas theoretically well suited to civilian responsibility appears again in the logistics field throughout all the military services, particularly the Army. Although the military must control the direct logistic support of military operations and need, therefore, be acquainted with the full spectrum of these problems, this need does not justify the military pervading the entire procurement, production, and supply operation.

The current organization has particularly obscured the division of responsibilities between the Joint Chiefs of Staff and offices of the Assistant Secretaries of Defense. The JCS prepare logistics plans to support their strategic plans. However, the committee nature of the JCS structure which emphasizes the importance of reaching unanimous agreement on conclusions and plans, has resulted in compromised and delayed military plans because of differences in service views. Moreover, although the JCS review major material and personnel requirements of the military forces, they do not review the budget as a whole.[9] Consequently, each service develops its own strategic and logistics plans for annual programs which are not subject to an over-all review outside of the staffs of the Assistant Secretaries of Defense. Thus the predominantly civilian staffs in the Office of the Secretary of Defense must arbitrarily make basic decisions to "settle" divergent service strategic and logistic concepts in order to come up with defense programs that can be fitted into a unified budget. Under such conditions civilians, primarily qualified in such fields as budget and fiscal control and procurement and supply management, are indirectly making military decisions—for which professional service personnel should be better qualified.

A foggy admixture of civilian and military functions further weakens decision-making in the current defense organization by increasing the frequency with which civilian patterns of decision-making are erroneously applied to problems more effectively resolved by established military procedures and vice versa. Notwithstanding the spread of the committee system within the Pentagon, professional military men are still trained in the command pattern of decision-making, which requires clear-cut decisions regarding alternative courses of action. Top-level civilian officials, especially political appointees, are accustomed to reaching solutions by response to pressure or by compromise reflecting a consensus acceptable to the majority. Extension of the compromise-committee pattern of decision-making into the area of military operations has proved detrimental to speed and precision. On the other hand, it is equally upsetting to defense programs and policies for military professionals to attempt to deal with the delicate political-military-economic relationships of high-level national security policy in terms of over-simplified alternatives in order to obtain clear-cut decisions.

In sum, although it is essential to differentiate civilian and military functions in certain areas for optimum performance in the Defense Department, it is noteworthy that present organization and procedures are not based upon a clear, effective concept for separating and blending those respective functions and responsibilities.

CIVILIAN SUPERVISION OF OPERATIONS

Whatever the differing arguments and concepts concerning the proper organization and exercise of civilian control, a basic fact which emerges from an examination of the present Defense Department is that it is characterized by an increasing tendency to multiply both the number of civilian policy-making officials and the extent of their involvement in directing operations. This tendency can form a vicious circle, for increased civilian intervention in operational control of military activities requires an expansion of civilian staffs to exercise such control, and multiplication of civilian staffs permits—in fact, encourages—increased intervention in operational details. Such tendencies, in opposition to the philosophy of centralized policy control and decentralized operations, inhibit the organization in fulfilling the following necessary conditions for the exercise of effective central policy control: expressing policy with clarity and precision, establishing firm and familiar channels for command and communication, and generating loyal observance and support of decisions by those who implement the policies.

The multiplicity of civilian staff offices springs in part from statutory provisions, such as the National Security Act, which established two levels of civilian control, the Office of the Secretary of Defense and the respective military department secretariats, and the 1949 amendments and Reorganization Plan No. 6, which reinforced the tendency by providing for additional assistant secretaries at both levels. The multiplicity of offices also springs from the tendency to interpret civilian control to mean not only civilian policy direction but also civilian operation, administration, and detailed direction of the three services.

So long as an assistant secretary of a military department, or one in the Office of the Secretary of Defense, is charged with an independent responsibility for overseeing the performance of a particular function by one or several services he will maintain a special staff to discharge that responsibility, thereby adding one layer to the many-tiered edifice. Although he may attempt to perform his supervisory function through policy control alone, the pressures of being answerable to the service secretary, the Secretary of Defense, or the Congress lead him to direct operational control whenever the multiplicity of policy staff levels and confused communications channels tend to jeopardize his personal reputation for effectiveness.

A current example is the Office of the Assistant Secretary of Defense (International Security Affairs), which has been drawn increasingly into operational control of military assistance programs and overseas weapons deliveries in order to deal more directly with problems of foreign aid where accountability to Congress and timing may be crucial. In fact, experience has revealed that decisions have been so fragmented and command lines so diverse under the present military assistance program that policy decisions at the top have often been negated by the timing of actual deliveries. There have been instances when high-level policy decisions to suspend aid have filtered through the structure so slowly that when deliveries were terminated changes in the world scene had led to a policy of resuming deliveries.

Moreover, most civilian staffs have their counterparts on the service level—although the counterparts are not necessarily grouped in the same fashion in each service. For example, the Navy has no Assistant Secretary for Research and Development; the Air Force does; and the Army, until recently, combined the functions of Logistics with Research and

Development under one Assistant Secretary. On the other hand, the Army, which has certain unique responsibilities, has an Assistant Secretary for Civil-Military Relations, which none of the other services has.

Thus, depending on which particular aspect of a many-sided problem each service deemed important, a directive concerning that problem— say, new weapons for NATO—addressed from the Office of the Assistant Secretary of Defense (International Security Affairs) to the service secretaries might be referred in the Navy to the Assistant Secretary for Material, and in the Air Force to the Assistant Secretary for Research and Development. In Army staff channels alone it might be sent to the Chief of Staff and the Deputy Chief for Military Operations (for military implementation), or to the Deputy Chief for Logistics and the Assistant Secretary for Logistics (for consideration of procurement problems), or to the Army Comptroller (for funding). Similarly, the reply from any one of these offices might go back to the Office of the Assistant Secretary of Defense (International Security Affairs) via another of the assistant secretaries, or it might go to the Secretary of Defense himself.

There are two things of which one can be reasonably sure. No two problems ever traverse the same channel. Those from each service will independently follow different routes.

This situation described above is compounded by the fact that the personal office of the Secretary of Defense is neither organized nor staffed to provide adequate coordination of the flow of papers, studies, and recommendations, much less to analyze the implications of all the related policy proposals and decisions. As of September 1957, the Secretary of Defense had on his personal staff one Marine Corps Brigadier General and two civilians. Fourteen major staff sections, including the Joint Chiefs of Staff, reported directly to the Secretary or his Deputy, as did the three services and eight unified or specified commands. In addition, the Secretary was chairman of two major committees in the Pentagon which bring together the highest officials of the three military departments regularly (the Armed Forces Policy Council and the Joint Secretaries). He also represented the Department of Defense both on the National Security Council and in the Cabinet. Many of his subordinates have far larger office staffs than does the Secretary himself. The absence of an adequate Secretariat within the Defense Department seems to be a major organizational deficiency.

The distinct divisions within the Office of the Secretary of Defense and the lack of an adequate personal staff for the Secretary combine to produce two significant results. First of all, it is difficult for the Secretary to obtain staff advice in a cohesive and comprehensive manner.

Decision-making is fragmented; too many issues are resolved in isolated offices rather than in a broad unified context. Consequently, the policies promulgated to guide operations may suffer in terms of scope, clarity, or precision. Secondly, these shortcomings in policy formation increase the propensity of the staffs to intervene in operations in order to exercise central control on a case-by-case basis. Moreover, it becomes organizationally difficult for the Secretary of Defense in time of emergency to make rational strategic decisions and to direct the defense machine with the speed and precision required.

Present Defense Department channels of communication and command are clogged by the multiplicity of staffs and diversity of organization not only at the level of the Office of the Secretary of Defense and the secretariats of the military departments but also all the way down to the service echelons charged with specific operations. It is inevitable that any unclear policy guidance should lead to confusion in actual operations—even though lower commands are attempting, faithfully and loyally, to implement instructions and commands.

Imprecise policy guidance from the top fosters diverse interpretations at intermediate levels. Incompatible or even contradictory instructions may be issued to guide the same operation by several intermediate-level staffs, each of which may be interpreting differently the same basic policy guidelines received from topside. When the operations concerned constitute a particularly delicate project or program in which service rivalries may be involved, such as in the research and development field, advantage may be taken of vague instructions so as to favor one possible interpretation over another. Such conditions only increase the tendency of the politically responsible top-level civilian officials to delve into the area of operational control in order to assure implementation in accordance with the policies they have established.

In such matters as those within the responsibility of the Assistant Secretary of Defense for International Security Affairs a certain amount of operational authority is probably necessary if the Defense Department is to speak with a single voice. In other areas, such as Research and Development or the activities of the Comptroller, a certain amount of centralization may be required to overcome the very complexity of the problems or the resistance developed as the result of service rivalries. On the whole, however, the fragmentation of responsibilities causes grave difficulties in developing clear and precise policy to guide decentralized operations. Excessive fragmentation of decisions among many offices within the Office of the Secretary of Defense makes coordination both difficult and time-consuming, particularly in such closely related areas as Research and Development, Properties and Installations, Supply and Logistics, and the activities of the Comptroller. For example, to establish a new rocket test area may require comprehensive study and approval by all the offices mentioned as well as by the Assistant Secretary for Manpower, Personnel, and Reserve Forces.

It is evident that the current Defense Department organization reveals weakness in three characteristics for exercising effective central policy control: namely, clarity and precision of guidance, clear channels of communication, and precision of implementation. Failure to maintain effective control through policy has led to intervention in the direction of operations. New and better efforts seem needed to revitalize an effective balance of centralized policy control and decentralized operations.

CIVILIAN LEADERSHIP

It goes without saying that a critical requirement for the national security is leadership which can improve the organization of the national effort, inspire others to acquire the qualities and assume the responsibilities of leaders, and earn the confidence which encourages the people, without abandoning their basic values, to support whatever national efforts may be required. The Defense Department is uniquely dependent upon such leadership.

There are currently nearly forty positions in the category of secretary through assistant secretary in the Office of the Secretary of Defense and the military departments which are filled by politically appointed civilian officials. Their deputies and special assistants are also largely political appointees and predominantly civilian. If civilian control over the world's largest business is to be exercised in a manner which produces realistic and effective decisions on the crucial issues of defense policy, it is mandatory that these top civilian positions be filled with capable and qualified officials. In practice it has proved difficult to procure enough of such men.

Experience has revealed that it has been difficult both to secure for top political positions in the Defense Department civilians who have adequate experience and knowledge and to retain them in office long enough for them fully to comprehend the problems at hand and to follow through on policies and programs which they initiate. A committee studying Army reorganization in 1953 noted that only two of six Assistant Secretaries of the Army for Logistics during the period 1947-1953 had been qualified for the position by experience. The fact that there were six different individuals holding this office in six years in itself underlines the problem of tenure.[10] With notable exceptions, such as Secretary Wilson, who was Secretary of Defense longer than any of his predecessors, and Assistant Secretary of Defense (Comptroller) McNeil, who has been with the Defense establishment since 1947, the average tenure of top civilian political officials has been about eighteen months.

This condition of affairs was commented on quite critically in a private discussion held several years ago. The speaker, who shall be anonymous, said in effect, "Do you realize how important the Pentagon is to your whole economy, to your business picture? Here is perhaps the most important corporation in America, and look at what you have for executives. Compare its system with the way you select and bring up your executives in any other big American corporation. You certainly don't have people come in with no experience, little experience, or some experience of several years back. Nor do they stay for six or twelve months, receive a letter stating what a wonderful contribution and great sacrifice they have made, and then leave and let somebody else come in. How nonsensical that type of thing would be in any big business corporation.

"Take one service as of some years ago," the speaker continued. "You had among the civilian leaders a former school prexy; you had a small furniture company president; you had another small company president; you had a banker from a little midwest town; you had a playboy from the West Coast, independently wealthy but pretty much of a dilettante; and you had a small town lawyer. This group was running what was in fact the largest business in the world. These represent part of a long line of a hundred, at least, that have passed through the Pentagon since unification was adopted in 1947."

He went on to point out that each of the hundred whom we have seen go made decisions that still rest with us today—although as individuals they have now no responsibility or obligation to live with those decisions, which, by virtue of their short-term responsibility, may have been made lightly or at least in relative ignorance. He emphasized that the capacity of the appointive officials to undertake the serious and responsible duties assigned them presents a problem of extreme gravity to the ultimate security of our country. He noted the great paradox in the fact that the military constantly discharges or puts in retirement senior officers whom industry seems to find qualified as presidents of corporations or as board chairmen, the great incongruity in the fact that the Defense Department "corporation" was getting rid of the very top-notch executives it had trouble replacing.

The motivations which prompt executives to come to the Pentagon are varied. Some are induced to accept appointment by virtue of patriotic inclinations. Others have become bored with their business or have had perhaps a wartime assignment in a Washington post—have the wine in their blood, so to speak, and come to town for the excitement. Those so motivated tend to seek out the more sensational and enchanting activities and may neglect the more humdrum aspects of their broad responsibility. Others are inclined to keep an eye cocked over their shoulders at the business that they left, and conduct their affairs in Washington in such a way as to prepare themselves for further progress at home. Then there are the obvious prestige factors. There are the people coming from the small town to the big city who like the pre-requisites of office and play the game for what it is worth—the trips overseas, the protocol, the prerogatives of office such as liveried chauffeurs, and so on.

These considerations are of vital importance in the context of a concept of civilian control which envisages that the individual brought in to be the civilian chief will bring to the task a breadth of judgment and wisdom greater than that which can be encountered in the military services.

Lack of experience and qualifications among civilians expected to perform the tasks of civilian control not only jeopardizes the appropriate exercise of this control but also dilutes the quality of the decisions made. The ability of the military service structures to develop military men with top executive talent is recognized by both the business world and government. Accordingly, inability to attract and hold qualified top civilians has increased the influence and leverage of the professional military personnel trained and experienced in the various ramifications of defense policies and programs. The inadequate backgrounds of appointed civilians tend to cause personality conflicts, to disrupt the civilian-military balance in decision-making by making the civilian either the "captive" of, or resentful of, his highly experienced military advisers. Especially at the top, where the blending of political and military aspects of defense policy must be accomplished, personality conflicts and im-balance in the weight given to the various alternatives concerned can have serious repercussions.

A problem which confronts both the politically appointed civilian officials and military professional personnel at the Office of the Secretary of Defense level is how to maintain objectivity in viewpoint when one has been closely associated with some relatively specialized activity and had lengthy experience in a particular business or military organization. Background and experience inevitably mold the phi-losophy, attitudes, and procedures of an executive. The functions of the Office of the Secretary of Defense, whose responsibility it is to coordinate the over-all operations of the military departments within the framework of a government-wide national security policy, demand a high degree of objectivity and adaptability in order to successfully resolve the urgent and novel problems involved. The political appointee often requires six months or more before he fully comprehends the problems, organization, and procedures and becomes really productive. On the basis of the average eighteen-month tenure, this leaves barely a year of productive work, the last months of which are at reduced effectiveness because he is engaged in looking toward his future position and locating and briefing his successor.

The military professional assigned to the Office of the Secretary of Defense encounters the dual problem of carefully avoiding bias in favor of his particular service (to which he must return in two or three years) and of developing a broad outlook toward national security as a whole rather than maintaining the viewpoint of his particular training. The development of an objective comprehensive outlook on broad security problems is also required of the career civilian professional at this level.

Perhaps the best brief summary of the problem of civilian control is to note that, to put the case most moderately, the Office of the Secretary of Defense has experienced difficulty in obtaining sufficient career and civilian personnel with adequate qualifications, and that, as pointed out by the Cordiner Committee,[11] the broader opportunities and higher financial returns of private industry have contributed to an extraordinary exodus of highly qualified career military and civilian professionals from the Defense Department.

Footnotes

1. Article II, Sec. 2, paragraph 1.
2. Section 202 (b).
3. Section 211 (a).
4. Article I, Section 8, paragraphs 12, 13, 14.
5. Section 202 (c), (6).
6. *Message from the President of the United States Transmitting Reorganization Plan No. 6 of 1953*, pp. 3 & 5.
7. *Ibid.*, p. 2.
8. *Business Organization of the Department of Defense*, pp. 59-65.
9. *Symington Committee Hearings on Airpower*, p. 1449.
10. *Report of the Advisory Committee on Army Organization* (Davies Comittee), December 18, 1953, p. 45. Of course, tenure of military officials is also a problem, although for different reasons.
11. *Report of the Defense Advisory Committee on Professional and Technical Compensation*, Vol. I, Military Personnel; Vol. II, Civilian Personnel, Washington: G.P.O., 1957. See Chapter Ten for a more detailed discussion of the Cordiner Committee findings and their implications.

Six

PLANNING:
NATIONAL POLICY AND STRATEGY

Defense Department planning both derives from and has an impact upon the whole government-wide process of national policy formulation. Since defense programs consume by far the largest portion of the national budget and cut across a broad range of national, domestic, and foreign policies, it is particularly important that they be correlated with national security policy. The Defense Department has two broad responsibilities in this area. First of all, Defense Department planning must adequately reflect national policies; and the Department must speak with one voice, representing the coordinated views of all its elements, when it expresses its views during formulation of over-all national policies. Secondly, within that over-all responsibility, and as its basic contribution to national security, the Defense Department must develop a sound strategic doctrine upon which to base the design and employment of the armed forces.

In Chapter Four we have briefly described the powers of the President as Commander-in-Chief, the impact upon the military establishment of procedures and policies emanating from the Executive Office of the President, and the position of the Defense Department in the National Security Council and its related structure. Now we shall consider the problems stemming both from shortcomings in the government-wide planning process and those resulting from the internal organism of the Defense Department.

THE DEVELOPMENT OF NATIONAL
SECURITY PROGRAMS

At the core of national planning is the process of budgeting the nation's resources. The need for appropriate balance between defense requirements and domestic economic and political conditions is now widely recognized, but opinions as to what constitutes appropriate balance continue to vary considerably. The organization and techniques for coordinating these views into agreed national policies, and particularly Defense Department policies and programs, are of crucial importance to national survival.

Defense programs are derived basically from development of valid military requirements by the Defense Department addressing itself, first, to the threat to the United States and, second, to the framework of budgetary guidelines set forth by the judgments of political leaders at the highest level. These judgments are ultimately expressed in terms of budgetary ceilings.

One of the most important factors which should enter into these judgments is, of course, the intelligence estimates of the military capabilities of potentially hostile powers. The National Security Act recognized the crucial value of intelligence in creating the Central Intelligence Agency. The CIA, as it is popularly known, is charged with presenting to the President and to the National Security Council an integrated picture of the world situation through the medium of "National Intelligence Estimates." These provide the intelligence foundation for national policy decisions.

The CIA has other functions with respect to intelligence. First, it is charged with the collection of a certain specialized kind of information which does not fall within the province of other agencies. Second, it is responsible for coordinating the over-all activities and estimates of the intelligence community in Washington. This "community" is composed of the National Security Agency, the Federal Bureau of Investigation, and the Intelligence Divisions of the Department of State, of the Joint Chiefs of Staff, Army, Navy and Air Force, and of the Atomic Energy Commission. Within the Defense Department the Joint Intelligence Committee performs a comparable function for the JCS and the Secretary of Defense with regard to the intelligence arms of the military services. None of the intelligence agencies except the CIA, however, is charged with developing the over-all picture.

Under this system it can be seen that each agency of government has the responsibility for developing intelligence relating to its own mission (for instance, Army attachés abroad would be interested in new tank developments while a Naval attaché would be concerned with submarines). The fact that all of the intelligence agencies within the Department of Defense (Office of Naval Intelligence, Air Force Office of Intelligence, the Army's Assistant Chief of Staff for Intelligence, and the Joint Intelligence Group) participate independently on the IAC (Intelligence Advisory Committee under the NSC) makes it difficult to get timely agreement on intelligence estimates within the Department and thus complicates the decision-making process.

The problem of introducing sound, comprehensive, and accurate intelligence estimates into the United States decision-making system is a complex one and has been ably covered by other authors.[1] Consequently, we shall merely point out some of the vagaries which enter into the system. First, any American intelligence agency must contend with the national characteristic which leads our operationally-minded executives to make their own intelligence estimates rather than rely upon their specialists. This tendency was notable among Defense executives recruited from industry, some of whom had difficulty believing the reports presented to them with increasing frequency after 1954 concerning the accelerating technological advances within the USSR. Another problem inherent in our system is the difficulty of integrating the individual estimates of the armed services and other agencies into a composite picture. Each service tends to draw its opposing Soviet force on a very large canvas. Those responsible for putting all these individual estimates together often found that they added up to a total Soviet capability beyond even that of the United States. When this was realized some top officials began to adopt a deprecatory attitude toward intelligence in general. These two factors together have contributed to judgments which progressively underrated Soviet capabilities.

Budgetary guidelines also influence national security programs particularly when they reflect judgments on such major problems as the extent to which nuclear weapons will be relied upon to conduct various types of warfare. Such an evaluation carries broad military, political, and economic implications which will have profound effects on the nature of the military and other resources required. Should the United States, for example, increasingly rely upon nuclear weapons so as to reduce the costs of attaining fire-power from conventional weapons and large standing armed forces? On the other hand, would our reliance on such weapons result in greater likelihood of comparable weapons being used against us and result in far greater destruction and greater costs in money, not to mention the greater cost in death and agony, than would result from the use of conventional weapons and forces?

The difficulties in making such decisions are manifold. Top-level guidance on such issues is necessary for effective and realistic budgetary planning in the Defense Department.

But the techniques for imposing on the respective government departments top-level decisions concerning budgetary guidelines vary with each administration and are intimately related to politics and personalities. Accordingly, the guidance provided may also vary considerably in form and content. More important, although the National Security Council is supposedly the responsible organ for integrating over-all national security policies at the highest government level, it does not develop specific basic budgetary guidance to the respective departments for the development of national security programs. Although NSC policy papers contain financial annexes estimating the general costs of implementing proposed policies, only the general implications of the projected national budget are considered in NSC deliberations.

Thus it is inevitable that current organization and procedures for formulating national security policies dangerously separate the development of national security objectives from consideration of the ways and means by which resources can be budgeted to attain these objectives. This parallels within the Executive Branch the Defense Department experience when Congress has, on occasion, authorized military programs but has later failed to appropriate money needed to implement them. The President and the various departments participate through the National Security Council in the formulation of national security policies and objectives. The same agencies carry on the annual budgetary process simultaneously but by different staffs and independently of the NSC deliberations. Failure to combine the dual processes step by step during their respective development results in a gap between the required military forces and the resources made available to support them.

Moreover, divergencies between goals and means are inevitably more difficult to reconcile as the two processes finalize. Compromise solutions to these divergencies not only are difficult and time-consuming to achieve but also result in stop-and-go planning. Consistency in over-all national security programs and national economic planning are difficult to achieve when programs developed on the basis of agreed national security policies must continually be revised in light of a separately determined budget.

In this context, the magnitude of the Defense Department programs makes them particularly difficult to reconcile with budget planning. The Department must present through one channel its views as to national security objectives and requirements, and through another channel its views on what the ways and means should be to achieve the objectives. In this process the Defense Department is only one of many voices; but it must then defend before Congress the compromise solutions reached in the executive branch. In turn, Congress usually makes further modifications in the resources to be made available, necessitating further readjustment in the original military plans and programs.

At this point, Congress, besides exercising its power of the purse, exerts a real influence upon Defense Department national security planning by legislation regarding organization, by legislative specifications concerning programs, and through investigation. Appropriations are the ultimate determinant of the means available for operating the armed forces, and thus have a direct impact upon their composition and upon strategic concepts for employing those forces. Legislation on organization, such as the National Security Act of 1947, established the basic strategic planning function of the Joint Chiefs of Staff and the strong role of the comptroller organization in defense planning. Defense planning must also be conducted on programs established through legislation, such as the military assistance program. In order to develop legislation in these areas, Congress conducts investigations to gather information. Such investigations, often beginning with inquiries into economy and efficiency of operations, have led to examinations of policy directing those operations and their strategic politico-military basis.

Despite this urgent Congressional need for adequate information, one of the two most important problem areas in Defense Department-Congressional relations today that deeply affects defense planning is the deficiency in the conditions under which professional military opinion and defense information reaches and is evaluated by Congress. Perhaps the second most critical problem in Defense Department operations stemming from its relation to Congress is the repeated discrepancy between approved national defense policy and the supporting military appropriations.

Let us consider the conditions under which the Defense Department deals with Congress. The armed forces of the United States, as represented through their respective Departments and the Department of Defense, are unlike many of the other departments of the government in that they have no clientele outside of the government to lobby for them in a direct or overt fashion; and ours is a system of government in which, especially in the legislative branch, pressure groups hold considerable sway. With no specific lobby of its own, in fact with lobbying proscribed by law so far as the military and other government agencies are concerned, the defense establishment advances its military interests in a welter of competing claims on the tax dollar.

It would be inaccurate to claim that the military as a professional group is wholly unrepresented on "the Hill"—even though in matters affecting the personal status and welfare of the professional military man such a statement is largely true. The views of the military are not completely unknown to Congress, since liaison is maintained by staffs of considerable size. At any rate, it is a fact that continuous cultivation by the Defense Department of particular measures which should be enacted for the advancement of our vital national defense interests is not normally possible. Although Congressmen feel a special responsibility for preserving the national security, the country's foremost experts on things military have not always been successful in presenting the facts to Congress.

In this connection it must be pointed out that Congressmen encounter real difficulties in comprehending the highly technical and complex issues of defense policy and then developing the best possible legislation. Even when the necessary information is available, and the competent staffs serving the Senate and House committees dealing with the armed services have analyzed and digested it for the Congress, there are other inhibiting factors. Congressmen are often too busy with the demands of constituents, pressure groups, and other legislation to evaluate the international scene and to determine the size and armament of necessary military forces in terms of legislation. Local interests of constituents often get more attention than the national interest because of the pressure for re-election. Moreover, the very pattern of Congressional action inhibits passing legislation in the form desired by the Defense establishment. Individual committees and their members of long tenure exert powerful independent influence, the preservation of which is sometimes regarded as more important than a crucial issue posed by the Executive Branch. Complex issues of military preparedness, subject to rapid change, are difficult to explain and generalize into broad programs amenable to legislation, and can be easily misunderstood and unjustly attacked. Specific legislation on such issues may greatly complicate the executive or tie its hands in program administration.

A last significant factor in the environment in which the Defense Department must correlate its programs to national planning is that here it encounters, especially in an indirect but powerful form as it operates through Congress, the force of public opinion.

Under present organizational arrangements the public gets only sporadic and incomplete glimpses of military views on defense problems. At best the voice of the military comes through either muffled and distorted (in the sense that only "approved" views reach the public) or in confusing and contradictory form. Separate military departments separately administered; the right of appeal to Congress by the service secretaries and the members of the Joint Chiefs of Staff; the duality of the role of the Joint Chiefs of Staff as advisers to the President, Secretary of Defense, and the National Security Council on the one hand, and as military heads of their own individual services on the other; and the profoundly variant strategic philosophies expressed by spokesmen for the different services—all these tend to divide the military voice and to confuse both the people and their Congress.

In fact, the professional military are placed in a position where it is almost necessary to capitalize on differences of opinion to make their sincere interests heard. The Secretary of Defense is forced to take a position publicly and thereby must argue for one and against another of the disagreeing professional military elements. Under such conditions, the possibility of gaining popular support of a comprehensive defense policy is limited. The public, perfectly capable of choosing among broad policy alternatives, has difficulty in selecting the correct highly technical and complex solutions amidst the welter of claims and counterclaims by the professional military leaders.

NATIONAL SECURITY PLANNING IN THE DEPARTMENT OF DEFENSE

In addition to the basic difficulty of reconciling defense programs with national security policies, the Department of Defense encounters other difficulties as well. Serious problems in Defense Department planning stem first from inadequacies in the National Security Council structure and second from organizational and procedural arrangements for national security planning within the Department of Defense itself.

Although the National Security Council must be recognized as a significant instrument for integrating the political, military, economic, and other elements of national security policies, in practice it has revealed certain shortcomings which magnify planning problems within the various government agencies. As has already been indicated, the National Security Council is essentially a collegial body of advisers to the President, who alone makes the decisions on matters before the Council. Unlike the cabinet in a parliamentary system it has no collective responsibility for making and implementing decisions. Policy papers are developed in the Planning Board, which is composed of representatives of agencies with seats on the Council. The committee nature of the Board, which seeks to obtain the greatest possible consensus, often produces policy papers that give only general guidance expressed in vaguely worded textual compromises. In implementing such policy guidance each agency seeks to maintain as much freedom of action as possible in matters it believes to be within its principal jurisdiction. This jurisdic-tionalism, combined with vague, general policy guidance, inhibits pre-cise and effective planning for policy implementation.

Policy papers considered by the National Security Council and approved by the President are usually assigned to the Operations Coor-dinating Board (OCB) to coordinate implementation by the respective agencies. However, the OCB is also a collegial body set up on a committee structure and has no power of direction. It attempts to develop more detailed courses of action for implementing approved national security policies, but jurisdictional resistance and textual com-promises to attain unanimity dilute the guidance and interpretation of the operational plans it develops.

The net result of the present system is that planning to implement national security policies in the Defense Department proceeds with limited policy guidance from either the NSC or the OCB. Like other agencies, the Defense Department must plan and resolve unanswered issues of broad import on a relatively independent basis, although this undermines the necessary close correlation between political and mili-tary affairs required for the most effective conduct of our national security policies.

The focal point for achieving necessary correlation between the National Security Council structure and Defense Department planning is the Office of the Assistant Secretary of Defense (International Se-curity Affairs). This staff agency operates as the liaison channel to the National Security Council and the Operations Coordinating Board, as well as to other government agencies dealing with international affairs. Other staffs in the Office of the Secretary of Defense and the military departments inevitably become involved in planning which contributes to or derives from national security policies. However, the Assistant Secretary of Defense (International Security Affairs) is the principal advisor to the Secretary and Deputy Secretary of Defense on matters coming before the National Security Council (NSC) and the Operations Coordinating Board (OCB), the organs principally involved in national security policy planning, and as such he serves as the Defense Department member of the NSC Planning Board and as its alternate representative on the OCB.

One of the basic problems encountered by the staff of the Assistant Secretary of Defense (ISA) in correlating Defense Department planning with over-all national security policies is the relationship with the Joint Chiefs of Staff (JCS) and the military departments. As shown on page 82, while the Secretary of Defense is the defense representative on the National Security Council, the Chairman of the JCS also attends as a statutory adviser to the NSC, and a JCS adviser also sits on the NSC Planning Board, although there is no JCS adviser with the OCB. Thus the military services have two intermediate channels by which to express their views to the NSC and the NSC Planning Board, through the Assistant Secretary of Defense (ISA), and through the Joint Chiefs of Staff. These two approaches do not necessarily conflict;

NATIONAL SECURITY ORGANIZATION WITHIN
DEPARTMENT OF DEFENSE

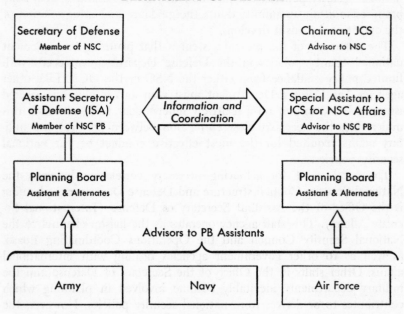

but if the military chiefs of the services feel their views are not adequately voiced through one channel they can turn, as has been done, to the other to exert their influence.

While great effort is made by the Assistant Secretary of Defense (ISA)to reconcile divergent Defense Department views before taking a position at the NSC Planning Board or advising the Secretary of Defense on a national security policy, he is not always successful. He may take a position at the Planning Board to which there is considerable opposition by one or more military services, which may be able to influence the Joint Chiefs of Staff Planning Board adviser to withhold his support or even undermine the supposedly agreed Defense position. The possibility of a service influencing the JCS adviser is enhanced by the fact that there is no firm JCS view on an issue until the members have adopted a corporate position. This complicates the process of achieving agreed Defense views on National Security Council policy papers at various stages of their development before they reach the nearly final form wherein the service chiefs usually consider them.

On the other hand, it is worth recording that the NSC Planning Board and the National Security Council are the highest government-wide forums to which the military services can legally express their corporate views. It is perhaps for this reason that Admiral Radford, former Chairman of the JCS, stated that the principal function of the Joint Chiefs of Staff was "their role as Military Advisers to the Secretary of Defense, the National Security Council and the President."[2]

The expression of different Defense views at an interdepartmental committee, such as the NSC Planning Board, vitiates the impact of Defense advice on the problems at hand, thus weakening the national security policy planning process. Moreover, if the Joint Chiefs of Staff should oppose policy proposals being considered by the National Security Council, to which the Assistant Secretary of Defense (ISA) has indicated Defense approval consistently during their development in the Planning Board, the Secretary of Defense is placed in an ambiguous position. If the Secretary argues in opposition to the Joint Chiefs of Staff views at the National Security Council, the Chairman of the JCS is at liberty under the 1947 National Security Act to give contrary advice direct to the President and the NSC. If he supports the JCS he undermines the influence of the Assistant Secretary of Defense (ISA) both within Defense and as a spokesman for the Department. Regardless of the Secretary's action, the open revelation of split Defense Department views on an issue, resulting from distinctive organizational responsibilities, detracts from effective integration of defense considerations into over-all national security policies.

THE DEVELOPMENT OF STRATEGIC DOCTRINE

To understand Defense Department responsibilities in the formulating of sound strategic doctrine, it must be realized that in substantive content strategic concepts must keep pace with dynamic and shifting weapons technology, be closely integrated with over-all policy objectives, and fulfill the demands of a broad range of military tasks confronting the United States armed forces today. We shall therefore consider this range of military functions before turning to some of the Defense Department organizational problems inhibiting effective strategic planning to meet them.

As one of the pre-eminent protagonists in the arena of international affairs currently characterized by "competitive coexistence," the United States is engaged in a conflict which could become total so quickly that the prevention of this possibility requires the most effective possible utilization of American resources. As part of this effort, American military power must be developed and organized so as to be ready to perform a broad range of tasks, from forceful action in support of the political, economic, and ideological maneuverings of cold-war power politics to complete and instantaneous participation in an all-out global nuclear war. Between these extremes there exists an extensive range of military functions which must be performed. These range from the manning of the distant early warning line in the Arctic to support in the form of training and equipment to our allies to further their internal security or to deter peripheral aggression. This broad range of functions obviously requires armed forces so organized and equipped as to be capable of undertaking a variety of actions with a variety of weapons; and each set of circumstances requiring military action must be carefully assessed in order to select that combination of forces and weapons which will most effectively serve our national objectives.

The military alternatives for which the United States armed forces must be prepared today can be broken down, therefore, into requirements for three basic capabilities: maintaining the highest possible capability for both strategic defense and strategic attack; maintaining sea supremacy; and maintaining the integrity of overseas security positions.

Preserving the territory of the United States secure from attack dictates consideration of defense and strategic strike as two interrelated elements of the same deterrent capability. Maintaining a strategic defensive base requires both passive and active programs. The development of an early warning network around the continent and the establishment of active defenses against hostile aircraft and missiles are designed to blunt the attack of an enemy. Missile defenses, supplemented by interceptors, are set up to defend key industrial and population centers and protect the strategic striking forces which constitute the United States offensive power.

Strategic striking forces, maintained at a high level of readiness for instantaneous retaliation, provide a deterrent to hostile attack, the degree of deterrence depending upon how much damage the potential enemy estimates would be inflicted on his own country by such counterattacking forces. Such strategic striking forces may be composed of strategic air forces; highly mobile joint task forces of land, sea, and air units; and intermediate range and intercontinental ballistics missiles (IRBM and ICBM).

The capability to maintain sea supremacy is associated closely with both the "strategic defense—strategic strike" capability and with the capability to maintain overseas operating bases. One of the vital links in an effective warning system is an outpost network maintained as far as possible from our shores. Such a warning system becomes increasingly critical now that submarines can be made capable of delivering missiles in strategic attacks. Sea supremacy also is essential to the employment of mobile task forces composed of naval, air, and land units as an element of our strategic striking forces. Missiles and aircraft in such task forces can be utilized for long-range strategic retaliation if these task forces are appropriately deployed. Moreover, they constitute a means, when combined with the air lift of land forces, of executing a rapid strategic offensive to follow up the initial exchange of nuclear blows in the event of general war.

The sea lanes also constitute vital communications and supply links to allied countries and to hard-pressed nations requiring support in the event of peripheral aggression. If sea supremacy is maintained, joint mobile task forces can be rapidly deployed to specific areas to meet aggression with appropriate land, sea, and air forces and either conventional or nuclear weapons.

Such flexibility of reaction is essential in discharging the third major military task: to deter either small or large aggressions and to bolster our alliances by being obviously able to back up our commitments. This kind of flexibility also most effectively guarantees security without automatically involving the world in general nuclear war. In the event of enemy aggression against an allied nation, we must be capable of providing military assistance adequate to meet our commitments. Although our action might involve us in a general nuclear conflict, it might, on the other hand, limit any conflict in area and/or weapons. The possibilities are numerous. Our part may consist simply of providing military equipment and training to friendly states in order to improve their ability to maintain their own internal security, or of deploying military units as a show of force to exert influence in our national security interests. The situation may even require actual employment of United States forces to repel aggression, such as in the Korean "police action."

The United States capability for various types of flexible action to maintain our overseas security interests is essential to maintaining the faith of our allies in our intention to meet our commitments. It also contributes to their willingness to permit establishment of bases in their territory from which we would be able to execute strategic strikes and operate joint mobile task forces backed up by adequate supply lines. Our allies recognize that in the present world situation an effective deterrent to possible hostile attack depends almost entirely on the capability and readiness of American armed forces to perform these missions.

As the principal organ charged with strategic planning to perform those tasks the Joint Chiefs of Staff have evolved a highly organized system for the development of the requisite plans to guide operations, logistics, and mobilization plans and programs. However, fundamental obstacles exist which tend to frustrate and vitiate the organization and procedures for strategic planning within the JCS and, consequently, throughout the Department of Defense. At the center of the difficulty are the broad problems of *weapons-roles-missions* and *service cognizance*.

Because of the newness of various weapons systems and the failure to develop theories for their integrated use; because each service has concentrated on the development of certain systems; and because there has been honest disagreement as to effectiveness of some weapons and the circumstances under which they could and should be used, there has been no real agreement on strategic concepts. Each service supports a concept which enables it to claim a decisive role, and each seeks to control weapons and elements which will enable it to carry out that role virtually independently of the other services. The Air Force, Army, and Navy all cite the need for weapons systems capable of striking targets deep in enemy territory—and these may be the same or adjacent targets.

Under current procedures each of the three forces is basically responsible for conducting operations against its enemy counterpart. Thus the Army is to defeat enemy land forces and seize, occupy, and defend land areas; the Navy, in addition to destroying enemy naval forces, maintaining general sea supremacy, and protecting vital sea lines of communication, is to conduct air and land operations essential to the prosecution of a naval campaign; and the Air Force is to gain and maintain general air supremacy to defeat enemy air forces, to control vital air areas, and, with exceptions, to establish local air superiority.[3] Under these circumstances it is inevitable that each of the three services, confronted with essentially different and fragmented tasks, should develop a strategic concept distinctly different from that of its sister services. As one student of strategy remarked, this in effect gives "each service a claim to develop a capability for total war,"[4] since the successful execution of the primary mission of one service requires that it carry out tasks inseparable from the primary mission of the other services.*

One of the most notable results of the dichotomy of assigned missions

* The effect of service rivalries on the determination of roles and missions is discussed at greater length in Chapter Seven.

is failure to develop an integrated strategic concept which will relate the plans and preparations of one service to those of another. The Air Force strategy for general war, and its assessment of the probable results of a strategic interchange of nuclear weapons, is incompatible both with the Army's plans for the mobilization, training, and movement of divisions to overseas areas and with the Navy's elaborate mechanisms for convoy-escort, minesweeping, and antisubmarine activities. Conversely, the unresolved debate as to whether or not nuclear weapons will be used in local wars—and, more importantly, the extent of their use—gives rise to certain anomalies in service planning. The Air Force has consistently held that preparedness for general war implies ability to handle lesser operations, but this gives no answer to the question of how the Air Force would deal with, for example, Viet Minh operations against Laos. Similarly, the Navy position that mobile naval-air forces in the Pacific provide the kind of power needed to deal with problems such as that of Viet Minh aggression does not square with the Army's call for large-scale air and sea lift of major ground units for a similar purpose.

The service failure to reach agreement on a common approach not only means duplication of facilities (or failure to provide these to other services, as with air and sea lift) but also has an impact on allied military planning and on foreign relations. For example, on what basis should our allies develop their military establishment when they have no idea of the role which their forces may be called on to play in combined operations, much less of the level and kind of United States military support which they may expect to receive under certain circumstances?

In large measure the failure to reach decisions concerning the most feasible and desirable strategic concept, and to adjust the level and balance of forces accordingly, occurs because of the injection of the staff views of the respective services into all levels of Joint Chiefs of Staff planning, with the result that every paper becomes a compromise. Not only is the Joint Strategic Plans Committee of the JCS a five-power group (Army, Navy, Air Force, Marine Corps, Joint Staff) but also the Joint Staff itself is made up of a series of tri-service committees (Army, Air Force, and Navy or Marine Corps.) Under these circumstances (and in view of the express desire of the President for unanimous decisions by the JCS) every concept, every plan, every paper either represents a compromise or, worse yet, becomes an amalgam of irreconcilable positions which each of the services accepts because it can do no better.

As long as each of the three services persists in thinking that every threat can be handled best by its own forces, acting in accordance with its own concepts of operation, a truly unified approach to any military problem is impossible. Since the staffing process insures that integrated alternatives are rarely brought forth and never developed in full, the possibility of presenting to the Secretary of Defense or to the President meaningful alternative choices on strategic concepts or force levels does not exist.

Equally noteworthy is the inflexibility of the services in adjusting plans and strategy to new developments in weapons systems. Since strategy is the interrelation of aims and means, it is important, in determining strategic concepts and force levels, to consider the impact of the current revolution in military technology. Our research and development programs have produced major innovations in nuclear weapons, in guided and unguided missiles, and in electronics, to name just three fields. Yet, lacking strategic concepts for their employment, these weapons have largely been added to existing armaments with no coordinated approach for their optimum use.

For example, in attempting to develop a modern air defense, the Army and the Navy have gone from gun to missile while the air force has developed its missiles from interceptor prototypes. It can be foreseen that within a measurable period of time anti-aircraft missiles will have sufficient range to cover large areas and an accuracy equal, if not superior, to that of fighter aircraft; but the interceptor program (as of 1957) was continuing. Fighter-interceptor aircraft require a different system of warning and control from surface-to-air missiles. Consequently, interservice quarrels have arisen over both the use of missiles and the relationship of the Army's electronic warning and control system to that of the Air Force. If a phased comprehensive plan for the integration and development of our air defense exists, it is not readily apparent to the public.

Yet in the opinion of one of the country's most responsible and competent research and development executives a revolution in concept and execution of weapons systems has now become mandatory. According to Major General John B. Medaris, Commander of the Army Ballistic Missile Agency at Redstone Arsenal,

There must be a single direction of a weapons program from conception until delivery to troops. All functions involved in the provision of materiel must be related to a single, coordinated plan. From beginning to end, the management of design, development, procurement, production, storage, issue and maintenance must be treated as a single problem.[5]

Granted that there can be valid differences of opinion over the relative effectiveness of specific weapons, or concerning the best means to implement objectives, the present service positions make each specific operational choice a subject for endless argument. Under the committee system of staff procedures, the result is a compromise in which, although one service may have the edge, each of the others gets something—if only a duplicate of what the other service may have (Nike-Talos, Thor-Jupiter, Strategic Air Command, Aircraft-Carriers).* The results are endless duplication of forces, installations, and projects and the simultaneous development of contradictory programs. As long as each service sees its future tied to espousal of a particular concept or the development of certain weapons, rational objective decisions will be difficult to obtain.

Theoretically, the Joint Chiefs of Staff agency should be able to see problems in the broadest possible perspective; but the Chiefs themselves are also heads of very complex and important military services. Only the Chairman is in a position to look at the problem from a detached point of view. Even the members of the Joint Staff, who are drawn from the various armed services, hardly dare to express fully unbiased viewpoints as most of them realize that they must eventually return to their own services and may find their careers damaged if they advocate a stand contrary to their respective service positions. Many of the original contributions and suggestions that have been made in military planning have arisen in one of the service staffs rather than from the Joint Staff itself. This is no reflection on the high caliber of personnel who have been recruited for the Joint Staff, but rather on some of the limitations of the organizational structure.

Moving down in the Defense Department structure, we see that, when strategic plans promulgated to guide program planning in the services reflect unagreed concepts and compromised policy guidance, planning in the respective services results in inefficient and irreconcilable programs. Since the resolution of compromised issues is achieved only in the process of resource allocation by the individual services, the ultimate decision passes to a lower level which lacks the over-all picture of the strategic military, political, and economic situation upon which the nation's strategic plans should be based. As a result, strategic direction to the overseas unified commands issued from the JCS structure often has been at variance with the logistic support provided by the individual services to their units within such commands for

---

* Nike and Talos are ground-to-air missiles of the Army and the Navy, respectively. Thor and Jupiter are intermediate-range ballistic missiles (IRBM) of the Air Force and Army, respectively.

the implementation of the unified strategic mission. Individual service interpretations of their own tasks in implementing strategic plans prevail because they control resources and logistic support for their respective forces.

Strategic plans may assign one service particular responsibility for a mission or task. However, the lines of authority within the defense structure do not conform to such single assignments. Since existing authority assures to each service cognizance of and participation in a program, the decision-making and planning processes for the accomplishment of the assigned task become fragmented, and the service responsible for the task may have authority and control over only part of the resources essential for its accomplishment. We find this occurring in such basic tasks as continental air defense, where over-all Air Force responsibility through the North American Air Defense Command (NORAD) draws considerable resource support from Army and Navy facilities. Again, the Army is responsible for maintaining flexible forces for quick transportation throughout the globe but is dependent upon Air Force lift capabilities to carry out this charge. Collaboration between the services on such problems is seriously disrupted by unclear and inadequate strategic guidance from the JCS.

When central issues of strategic guidance are not adequately resolved within the JCS, there is a tendency not only for *de facto* and often contradictory decisions to be made at lower echelons in the services but also for the question to be passed upward for ultimate decision to the staffs serving the various Assistant Secretaries of Defense. Here, again, the decisions are often made arbitrarily and under pressure to reach some solution even though the staff may be ill-informed on many of the basic elements of the strategic military situation. Frequently, the Office of the Comptroller, lacking sufficient strategic guidance, will in effect establish this guidance through its budgetary determinations regarding military programs. Similarly, the office of the Assistant Secretary of Defense (Supply and Logistics), in issuing its policy guidance regarding procurement and logistics planning to the services will, in the absence of agreed JCS plans, be forced to make decisions establishing strategic guidance.

A significant result of the difficulties encountered in the Joint Chiefs of Staff organization and procedures for strategic planning has been the impact upon the role of the Chairman of the Joint Chiefs of Staff.

By Reorganization Plan No. 6 of 1953 the Chairman has enhanced authority over the Director and members of the Joint Staff, and by a subsequent Department of Defense Directive this authority was extended to the various joint committees, such as the Joint Strategic Plans

Committee, the Joint Logistic Plans Committee, and the Joint Intelligence Committee on which sit both members of the Joint Staff and representatives of the military services. (See Chart 6.) Nevertheless, the fact that he is divorced from any direct service responsibilities, coupled with his position as the representative of the JCS advising the Secretary of Defense, the National Security Council, and the President, gives him unique opportunities and responsibilities. The role of the Chairman, who is not responsible to any service, permits him to see things in a broad perspective and grants him time to do so. The service members of the JCS have operational responsibilities. Their tie-ins to a particular service and the consequent inability to reach agreement among themselves either on concepts or on the many day-to-day problems of weapons development, such as assignment of responsibilities, force levels, or deployments, place the Chairman of the JCS in a unique position.

Although every effort is made to achieve agreement within the Joint Chiefs when there are split views on issues, the Chairman is the person who takes them up to higher authority for decision, the higher authority generally being the Secretary of Defense, although he may, in certain cases, be the President. As Admiral Radford himself stated:

I think the responsibility and the authority of the Chairman is greater than appears in the law. I have often pointed out to the Chiefs that the more they disagree the more power they hand to the Chairman.[6]

Despite his unique position, the Chairman of the JCS is hampered by a poorly organized and cumbersome apparatus which cannot provide him with the requisite staff assistance to enable him to develop independently valid conclusions. Mention has already been made of the tripartite nature of the Joint Staff and of the interservice committee system through which papers reach the Chairman of the JCS for his consideration. In addition, the diffuse nature of our governmental organization takes some responsibilities out from under the control of the Chairman and of the JCS. For example, national intelligence estimates are approved by the Intelligence Advisory Committee of which the Deputy Director of the Joint Staff for Intelligence is simply a member, along with his counterparts in the Army, Navy, and Air Force. Thus there is no single military judgment either on military intelligence or on the positions taken by the military in the field of national estimates on which the Chairman can base his position. Similarly, the Weapons Systems Evaluation Group reports to the Assistant Secretary of Defense for Research and Engineering and to the JCS as a body, but not to the Chairman; and the Special Assistant for Guided Missiles reports to the

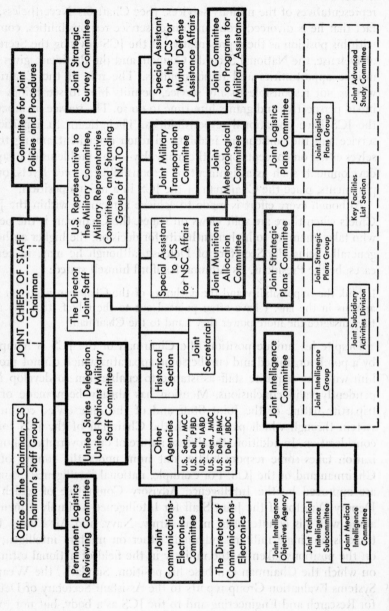

THE ORGANIZATION OF THE JOINT CHIEFS OF STAFF AND THE JOINT STAFF

Secretary of Defense and not to the Chairman of the JCS, although his decisions and recommendations may have a manifest impact both on strategy and on force levels. Conversely, certain important officials, such as the JCS representative on the NSC Planning Board, work *de facto* for the Chairman even though they may nominally report to the Joint Chiefs as a corporate body. Thus the mixed responsibilities of the staff available to the Chairman inhibit preparing for him a unified concept of strategy, of operations, and of roles and missions. The Chairman must, therefore, deal with and form judgments on matters which already reflect very strong service biases and which lean toward the same set of built-in compromises which so often characterize the documents coming up through committee channels for consideration by the JCS.

When we review the present organization and procedures of the Defense Department in the total context of national planning and the vital function of formulating sound strategic plans, it is evident that there are both waste motion and potentially dangerous inefficiency in an area of action fundamental to national security.

Footnotes

1. See, notably, S. Kent, *Strategic Intelligence for American World Policy*, Princeton: Princeton University Press, 1949; and R. H. Hilsman, *Strategic Intelligence and National Decisions*, Glencoe, Illinois: The Free Press, 1956.

2. "An Exclusive Interview with Admiral Radford," *U. S. News and World Report*, February 28, 1955, p. 48.

3. The missions of the services are respectively found in Sections IV, A, 1, V.A.L. and 2, and VI, A, 1 of Department of Defense Directive 5100.1 dated March 16, 1954. This promulgates the revised "Key West Agreement." See Stanley, *op. cit.*, p. 176, for reference.

4. Henry A. Kissinger, "Strategy and Organization," *Foreign Affairs*, Vol. 35, No. 3, April 1957, p. 381.

5. Major General John B. Medaris, "The Revolution in Weapons Development," *Army*, September 1957, p. 35.

6. *Symington Committee Hearings on Airpower*, p. 1457.

Seven

NEW WEAPONS—NEW TASKS

Since a key element in maintaining an adequate defense posture today is our ability to at least match, if not outdo, the enemy in timely development of new weapons and to integrate them into the ready military forces with minimum disruption of efficiency, rapid technological advance has placed heavy requirements upon the Defense Department.

It has increased the magnitude and complexity of decisions to be made while shortening the time within which these decisions must be reached if meaningful and valid programs are to result. It has spurred interservice rivalry by leading each of the services to seek complete control of new weapons systems.* It has complicated the process of strategic planning, which must reflect the impact of new weapons that may never have been tested or may not even be off the drawing boards, and has led to calls for a total reappraisal of the missions of the different services. Moreover, the steadily increasing costs involved in conducting military research and development programs, the small number of truly creative scientists and the increasing cost of producing and operating modern weapons all dictate the need for organization and procedures which maximize economy and make effective utilization of available technological resources.

We can best examine the problems confronting the Defense Department decision-makers in this field by considering them under two broad headings: translating scientific advance into mass-produced new weapons in the hands of troops trained to employ them, which requires fostering innovations in defense programs through full exploitation of creative scientific and professional manpower both within and outside the Defense Department; and the necessary realignment of the tasks and missions of the armed forces.

* A "weapons system" is the entire complex of equipment, support facilities, trained manpower and concept for employment necessary to make a weapon operational.

INNOVATION AND THE INTEGRATION OF NEW WEAPONS

The cycle through which significant technological advances in basic or applied research are introduced to potential weapons applications and are then developed, evaluated, procured, and integrated into forces trained for their use in accordance with strategic plans and tactical concepts is a complex process which cuts across many organizational and procedural lines within the Defense Department.

In the current organization, the Assistant Secretary of Defense (Research and Engineering) has been assigned the principal responsibility for providing advice and assistance to the Secretary of Defense for coordinating this process. His office is responsible for developing policies and establishing procedures for effecting a sound, integrated research and development program, which includes assuring that the nation's best scientific and technical talents are applied to planning and prosecution of military research and development programs. In collaboration with the Assistant Secretary of Defense (Comptroller), his office reviews research and development budgets and construction of laboratories and testing facilities proposed by the military departments. It coordinates weapons development by the military departments with Joint Chiefs of Staff strategic planning. It is in close liaison with the Assistant Secretary of Defense (Supply and Logistics) concerning policies to coordinate the procurement and distribution of newly developed weapons systems, and with the Assistant Secretary of Defense (Manpower, Personnel and Reserve) concerning scientific and technical manpower needs of Defense Department research and development programs. It follows that decisions regarding the integration of new weapons cut across the responsibilities of a great number of staffs at the Office of the Secretary of Defense level alone.

The fragmentation of decision-making, requiring extensive coordination, is in part the inevitable result of the broad range of factors involved in the cycle for integrating new weapons into the armed forces. However, it is compounded by the multiplicity of staff levels in the current defense organization. The staffs serving the secretaries of each of the military departments include offices, usually headed by assistant secretaries, which are concerned with research and development, financial management, procurement and logistics, and manpower. Problems of weapons integration must also flow through this level, which is interposed between the military staffs conducting actual operations and the Office of the Secretary of Defense responsible for over-all coordination and central policy control.

At an historic juncture when time is a crucial element in the technological race with a potential enemy, this fragmentation slows the decision-making process. It also fosters duplication of effort with consequent waste of resources.

It required seven years to bring the B-52 from the planning stage to initial production and four more years will have passed before the Air Force heavy bomber wings are equipped with this aircraft. Meanwhile the Soviet Union has revealed a capacity to introduce comparable new aircraft at a rate which may exceed ours.[1] Mr. Trevor Gardner, formerly in charge of the Air Force Missile Program, has stated that the programs for missiles development have been slowed by "the length of time it takes to get decisions made in the system, the way it is organized."[2]

Duplication of effort by the services may have some justification in the missiles field on the basis of increased insurance of success through alternate approaches, but it is difficult to justify the development of different tanks, vehicles, helicopters, and light weapons by the Army and Marine Corps to meet basically similar requirements. Moreover, duplication of effort in the missiles field, spurred by service rivalries, creates competition between programs for qualified scientists and scarce facilities which both wastes resources and makes the programs more expensive.

The Office of the Assistant Secretary of Defense (Research and Engineering) attempts to achieve coordination in the process of integrating the development of new weapons into the armed forces, but the scope of the problems and the several tiers of Defense Department staffs involved result in many decisions being made either without adequate coordination or even outside the policy altogether. In order to provide coordinated policy direction to military research and development programs, the Assistant Secretary of Defense (Research and Engineering) has established in such functional fields as atomic energy, electronics, ordnance, missiles, piloted aircraft, and psychological warfare about thirteen coordinating committees composed of representatives from military department research and development program offices. Nevertheless, the actual operating decisions are made largely by the military service staffs. Fragmented decision-making at many staff levels inhibiting the timely development of clear policy guidance to the services, interservice rivalry for the control of new weapons, and "vested interests"* within the services and in related civilian industries all

* Note the struggle between the Navy's Bureau of Aeronautics and Bureau of Ordnance for control of missiles development, and the close ties between service research programs and certain industries which exert influence to support weapons which they can develop and produce.

hamper efforts by the Office of the Secretary of Defense.

Moreover, the research and development phase is but one step in the cycle from new concepts to new weapons in the hands of the troops. Beyond questions of which weapons to develop in what priority are complex problems of which weapons to produce in quantity and the timing of their introduction into service use in accordance with the phased replacement of old weapons and training schedules for the appropriate forces. The Office of the Assistant Secretary of Defense (Research and Engineering) collaborates with staffs of other Secretaries of Defense, such as Comptroller, Supply and Logistics, and Properties and Installations, in reviewing and coordinating military service solutions to these issues.

The coordination problem is further complicated by the need to integrate the weapons development cycle with strategic planning conducted by the Joint Chiefs of Staff. Here again the channels of liaison and coordination are highly complex and cut across all levels of the Defense structure. The strategic plans must not only reflect weapons capabilities in terms of strategy and tactics but also their expected time of availability and their impact on the organization, logistics support, and training of the armed forces. We have already discussed some of the shortcomings in strategic planning stemming from the nature of the Joint Chiefs of Staff structure, certain patterns of current Defense Department organization, and the impact of service rivalries. It must be noted here that the absence of strategic plans expressing agreed, detailed guidance to the military services also fosters divergent service programs for integrating new weapons into their forces, programs which not only lead to duplication and waste but also hamper the process of developing integrated weapons systems best suited to the over-all military tasks.

A recent organizational step toward resolving this dual problem of assuring precise implementation of clear policy guidance and effective integration of all phases of the cycle from research and development to operational use of new weapons was the appointment in spring 1956 of the Special Assistant to the Secretary of Defense for Missiles Development.* This is noteworthy in that it is an effort to gain increased effectiveness and speed in missiles programs by concentrating all phases of missiles development under the centralized control of a "missiles czar" directly responsible to the Secretary. His staff is involved in all aspects of the missiles programs—budget, research, development, production, logistic support, maintenance, base facilities, military employment,

---

* Edgar V. Murphree, the first incumbent, was replaced by William M. Holaday in May 1957.

and troop training. The Air Force and Navy have taken similar steps to assign across-the-board responsibilities for new weapons systems to a single organ; the Air Force has established the Western Development Command in the missiles field, and the Navy has its "Lead Bureau" concept.[3]

Closely related to the organizational and procedural problems of integrating new weapons into the armed forces is the question of how best to channel into defense programs the thinking of creative scientific and professional manpower both within and outside the Defense Department structure. The technological advances which lead to new or improved weapons and the concepts for producing and using these weapons ultimately stem from the innovation and imagination of human minds. And since there is a relative scarcity of truly creative scientists, patterns of organization must be found which enable optimum use of available creative talent.

Current Defense Department organization in the research and development field reflects definite attempts to channel the nation's best creative thinking into defense programs. In addition to extensive research facilities and testing grounds, with high quality military and civilian scientific staffs, operated directly by the military departments, the Defense Department makes many contracts with private university and industrial facilities and retains a great number of consultants in a broad range of fields. However, despite these extensive sources of innovation and new concepts, it is debatable whether the present defense organization adequately channels the creative core of the tremendous scientific potential into its programs and operations.

One of the steps taken within the defense organization to bring the views of highly qualified scientific personnel to bear on defense research and development programs was the creation of technical advisory panels under the direction of the Assistant Secretary of Defense (Research and Engineering). These panels, composed of consultants from other government agencies, industry, private research institutions, and colleges, generally parallel the fields covered by the coordinating committees of militiary department representatives established by the Assistant Secretary of Defense (R&E) to review and integrate military research and development programs. However, certain patterns of operation, stemming from the current organization, vitiate the impact of these experts on actual programs.

The fact that the coordinating committees are organized according to functional fields which parallel the respective service organizations tends to restrict the attention of the committees to the same problems with which the service members are concerned in their day-to-day operations and to inhibit innovation and the introduction of novel weapons concepts. The committee system restricts the flexibility of adjusting program priorities, since each service seeks to stress research on its own weapons. Finally, the existence of functionally divided coordinating committees and advisory panels inhibits examination by specialists from diverse fields of the broad implications for the United States strategic position of the latest trends and developments in a wide spectrum of scientific fields.

There should be a two-way interaction between defense planning and operations and scientific innovation if optimum defense policies and programs are to be developed. In strategic planning, for example, advances in weaponry must be reflected in strategic plans, but, if the strategic planners note deficiencies in our weapons arsenal because of enemy developments or changing concepts of warfare, it is their responsibility to guide our scientific effort accordingly.

Because of the lack of clear, agreed strategic guidance from the Joint Chiefs of Staff, and ineffectively coordinated military research and development, our scientific resources today tend to be expended arbitrarily in divergent directions without adequate agreement or concentration on principal strategic military deficiencies. In addition to the consequent waste of resources, there is a danger that the resulting scientific advances may not be channeled effectively by the strategic planners. A novel weapons breakthrough is of little value in terms of stronger forces if it is ineffectively applied to strategic and tactical concepts for its optimum use.

The Weapons Systems Evaluation Group (WSEG), established in February 1949, has developed into a valuable organization for overcoming some of these deficiencies. It offers a means for fostering innovation in defense programs, providing broad over-all analyses of weapons advances, and coordinating technological advances with strategic planning. According to its charter, WSEG is charged with providing "comprehensive, objective, and independent analyses and evaluations under projected conditions of war, which will include . . . present and future weapons systems . . . and . . . the comparative effectiveness and costs of weapons systems." It is also to provide "timely advice and assistance to aid decisions in the allocation of resources for development of the most effective combination of weapons systems."[4]

WSEG functions under the administrative direction of the Assistant Secretary of Defense (Research and Engineering) and is responsive to directives with respect to studies both from him and from the Joint Chiefs of Staff. The director of the Group is appointed by the Secretary of Defense with the advice of the JCS and the Assistant Secretary of Defense (R&E) and is assisted by a research director who supervises the scientific work. WSEG conducts studies for the Department of Defense as a whole, but individual studies must be approved and assigned either through the Assistant Secretary of Defense (R&E) or the JCS. Significantly, the Group also may initiate studies of its own. All findings and conclusions of the Group are strictly advisory and are not binding on any agency of the Defense Department. The group is charged with utilizing the most able professional military and civilian minds and most advanced analytical methods available. The Director may also recommend to the Assistant Secretary of Defense (R&E) contractual arrangements for obtaining necessary professional and analytical services.

A noteworthy recent development under this contract clause was the establishment in April 1956 of the Institute for Defense Analyses (IDA). Until this time WSEG had been operating with a small military- and civilian-scientist staff. The purpose of IDA is to provide the technical management necessary to strengthen and expand the civilian scientific element so as to utilize more extensively the minds and skills of the American scientific community. The initial incorporators of IDA were the presidents of California Institute of Technology, Case Institute of Technology, Massachusetts Institute of Technology, and Stanford University and the vice-president of Tulane University. Additional members are permitted, and each institution is represented on the board of trustees. In this manner an association of universities has been organized to bring the benefits of their intellectual resources to bear upon some of the complex technical and strategic problems raised by scientific and weapons advances.

In practice IDA hires as its direct employees civilian-scientists who are mostly located in the Pentagon and work closely with the military members of WSEG. WSEG-IDA operates as an integrated effort with little differentiation of staffs. Projects undertaken at the request of the JCS, the Assistant Secretary of Defense (R&E), WSEG itself, or another agency of the Defense Department are assigned to project groups composed of the most appropriatae combinations of WSEG-IDA personnel. The close integration of effort is indicated by the fact that the director of research for WSEG is the same individual as the vice-president and research director for IDA, who reports to the IDA board of trustees. IDA thus offers means for drawing additional scientific personnel into the Defense Department organization to support the project groups in particular studies. The close association with universities provides a channel for locating the best available knowledge and expertise on the problems at hand.

It should be pointed out that each of the services also supports weapons systems evaluation groups which have made significant contributions to the problem of anticipating future weapons systems and their associated strategies or tactics: the Army's Operations Research Office of Johns Hopkins University, the Navy's Operations Evaluation Group, and the Air Force's RAND Corporation. These agencies have all been able to tackle problems, such as continental defense or limited war, without inhibiting restrictions arising from service cognizance. A useful relation has been established between all of them and with WSEG.

The trend toward centralization of Defense Department decision-making has become apparent in the operations research field recently, as it has been argued that such research effort should be concentrated in WSEG. However, since all these agencies, WSEG included, perform an essentially advisory function, decision-making resting with those legally entrusted with responsibility, it is debatable whether all the military "think" centers should be controlled by a single rein.

There is still some question whether the products of all these purely *advisory* study groups are adequately channeled into actual programs by the current Defense Department organization. Those responsible for the actual operation of military research and development programs and the development of strategic plans often regard the study groups as too far removed from the realities of the current problems. This attitude is aggravated by the fact that the advisory groups are usually composed predominantly of civilian scientists while the responsible operators and planners are largely military professionals. Thus the channel by which the views of creative civilian scientists might have an impact on defense programs is somewhat obstructed. We have already noted organizational patterns which tend to restrict the impact of scientific consultants through the Office of the Assistant Secretary of Defense (R&E).

The fact that the views of civilian scientists are largely restricted to advisory form throughout the Defense Department inhibits the full consideration of their views concerning decisions relating to technological and scientific innovation. Those who make such decisions must balance existing facts with anticipated developments, and current procedures and policies with novel concepts and proposals, in order to develop optimum programs and strategic plans. However, because the viewpoint of civilian scientists is usually expressed merely as advice, and the scientists do not occupy positions of direct authority in planning and operating defense programs, scientific and technological innovation tends to be given inadequate weight in the decision-making process.

A further factor inhibiting innovation in defense programs is the fact that any large bureaucracy such as the Defense Department tends to suppress innovation within the structure. Staff work continues to be organized largely along highly specialized lines which make it difficult to develop a broad view of alternative solutions to the problems at hand; and the novel insights of specialists are diluted as they pass up through the bureaucratic committee hierarchy. As policy positions are developed, as many as possible of the specialized committees and staff organs participate in order to maintain organizational cohesion; but the result is likely to be compromise solutions which do not fully reflect the advice from lower levels.

Granting the substantial progress made toward the solution of the complex over-all problem of fostering innovation and integrating new weapons into the armed forces, a comprehensive view of the present Defense Department organization compels the judgment that the problem is far from solved. Under present conditions the net effect of our procedures is that we do not realize our national scientific potential. The highly placed executive concerned with technological scientific advance is more a negotiator of successful compromise than a creative leader.

Another factor which has limited the contribution of American scientists in the effort to stay ahead in the race for technological supremacy has been some of the abuses associated with the existing system of maintaining the secrecy of new discoveries. Lloyd V. Berkner has ably stated the dilemmas involved:[5]

Obviously, it would be foolish to advocate complete abandonment of technological secrecy in military matters. Certainly much is to be gained by careful protection of a few very vital secrets that need be known only to a few and that warrant the very special precautions that ensure their protection. Thus, restriction on the specific design of a particular weapon may have real military value, and at the same time have no immediate significance to society. The cover of secrecy is justified in such cases for it yields substantial advantage. But the restrictions placed on scientific and technical information have gone far beyond this sort of thing.

The point is this: For any scientifically advanced nation, and there is every evidence that the Soviet Union is such a nation, there are few if any technological secrets. The only real secret is that you can do something at all, and this you cannot hide. Tell science that someone can do something, and with the industrial and scientific potential at hand, it can, with no further information, equal and even better that accomplishment. This is no boast; it is but the fact of modern technology. Widespread technological secrecy does not deter any enemy so much as it denies our own citizens the opportunity to administer properly their own affairs.

Berkner's views are held by many of America's most competent scientists—the group on whom the country depends to win the technological race.

Closely related to this question is the amount of basic research which should be sponsored directly by the Department of Defense. Many American scientists are concerned that we have concentrated so heavily on applied research that the wells of fundamental discoveries may be in danger of drying up. Scientists thoroughly familiar with the Defense Department's research and development program believe the Department should do much more to support the research out of which new technological advances will flow. On the other hand, the National Science Foundation has proposed to the Bureau of the Budget that basic research should be conducted outside of the defense effort. While most officials within the Pentagon believe that the military have a responsibility for basic research, the steadily increasing costs of weapons production and procurement, as well as development after the research stage, has been making it increasingly difficult to find funds for basic research. If budget ceilings continue to hamper defense programs, basic research will suffer since the demands of actual weapons production must be met first. In any event, government-sponsored and government-financed basic research, on whose results the Defense Departmnt can draw, is essential.

One further item remains to be mentioned. It is a paradoxical fact that the responsibility for the design, development, and production of the weapons which have become the core of American military planning and strategy does not lie within the Defense Department but with the Atomic Energy Commission. There is no need to trace here the history of the legislation which created this paradox. However, it is important to note that the division of responsibilities between the Atomic Energy Commission and the Department of Defense, whatever its advantages in terms of civilian control and operation of a vital national program, does cause additional problems in the design, development and utilization of atomic weapons and in the integration of these weapons into service structures.[6]

Thus despite strenuous efforts to coordinate more effectively research and development programs—and perhaps to some extent because of the methods used to achieve such coordination—we have not been successful either in bringing about a fully rational and unified program or in speeding the processes of innovation and adaptation, either with regard to weapons or with respect to the forces using them.

ARMED FORCES ROLES AND MISSIONS

Inseparably linked to the total problem of innovation in a time of rapid and critical technological advance is the urgent requirement that the strategic assignments of the armed forces reflect the most effective use of new weapons. The organization of the armed forces in terms of their special functions, their roles and missions as defined by national defense strategy, cannot rest on traditional patterns or remain static. It must keep pace with modern science.

The Joint Chiefs of Staff are charged with primary responsibility for making strategic plans which state missions for forces with which to achieve national politico-military objectives. They must establish the nature and tasks of forces assigned such missions, allocate the weapons required to implement such tasks, and outline the general strategy and tactics for the employment of forces and weapons. In order to guide the application of available resources, the strategic plans assign certain priorities to the tasks, forces, and weapons.

We have previously noted the strong tendency for each military service to approach such strategic planning problems from a different point of view—usually one that would result in its being assigned missions and tasks requiring a significant role for its own forces, a situation which makes agreement on common strategic plans extremely difficult. Some service elements continue to harbor jealousies and fears that unification may tend to reduce their significance and prestige, a situation which further aggravates lack of agreement on strategic concepts and even leads to personality conflicts among service personnel. Such influences contribute to making the JCS unable to meet their established schedules for developing certain estimates and strategic plans, to the postponement of decisions, or to leaving them to be made elsewhere. Decisions made elsewhere may not result in optimum over-all defense policies and programs; postponed decisions can seriously jeopardize national security.

The crucial nature of the weapons-roles-missions relationship to effective strategic planning has spurred interservice rivalry by leading each of the services to seek complete control of new weapons systems, both in order to have the self-contained capability of executing its assigned service mission and as a *raison d'être*. Thus the roles-and-missions problem centers today around the many issues arising from the rapid development of new weapons, particularly concepts for their employment and their assignment to the respective military services for the execution of particular tasks.

One of the most notable features of recent defense organization has been a persistent rigidity in the roles and missions of the three services. Despite the tremendous effects of revolutionary weapons, neither the basic legislation on the functions of the armed forces nor the Key West-Newport Agreements of 1948, which amplified and crystallized these functions, has been changed substantially as regards the roles and missions of the armed services. In October 1953 the Key West-Newport Agreements were issued in a form which revised but did not modify the assigned roles and missions. From time to time, the Joint Chiefs of Staff have reached agreement on the assignment of *weapons* to services or have had such decisions made for them by the Secretary of Defense,[7] but this is considerably different from developing a change in roles and missions. Even the JCS "agreements," hammered out with so much difficulty, either have been rendered obsolete by technological advances, as were the Army-Air Force understandings of 1952 on the development and use of light aircraft, or have been honored more in the breach than in the observance.

The current assignments of roles and missions of the armed services, as established by the Key West-Newport Agreements of 1948, list both primary and collateral functions for the respective services.[8] The basic primary functions are set forth as follows:

Army:

1. To organize, train, and equip Army forces for the conduct of prompt and sustained combat operations on land. Specifically:
    (a) To defeat enemy land forces.
    (b) To seize, occupy, and defend land areas.
2. To organize, train, and equip Army antiaircraft artillery units.
3. To organize and equip, in coordination with the other services, and to provide Army forces for joint amphibious and airborne operations. . . .
    . . . .
6. To provide Army forces as required for the defense of the United States against air attack. . . .
    . . . .
8. To develop, in coordination with the Navy, the Air Force, and the Marine Corps, the doctrines, procedures, and equipment employed by Army and Marine forces in airborne operations. . . .

Navy:

1. To organize, train, and equip Navy and Marine Forces for the conduct of prompt and sustained combat operations at sea, including operations

of sea-based aircraft and their land-based naval air components. Specifically:

    (a) To seek out and destroy enemy naval forces and to suppress enemy sea commerce.

    (b) To gain and maintain general sea supremacy.

    (c) To control vital sea areas and to protect vital sea lines of communication.

    (d) To seize and defend advanced naval bases and to conduct such land operations as may be essential to the prosecution of a naval campaign.

2. To conduct air operations as necessary for the accomplishment of objectives in a naval campaign.

3. To organize and equip, in coordination with the other services, and to provide naval forces, including naval close air support forces, for the conduct of joint amphibious operations. . . .

   . . . .

7. To provide air support essential for naval operations. . . .

   . . . .

9. To provide naval (including naval air) forces as required for the defense of the United States against air attack. . . .

Air Force:

1. To organize, train, and equip Air Force forces for the conduct of prompt and sustained combat operations in the air. Specifically:

    (a) To be responsible for defense of the United States against air attack. . . .

    (b) To gain and maintain general air supremacy.

    (c) To defeat enemy air forces.

    (d) To control vital air areas.

    (e) To establish local air superiority except as otherwise assigned herein. . . .

3. To be responsible for strategic air warfare.

4. To organize and equip Air Forces for joint amphibious and airborne operations in coordination with the other services. . . .

5. To furnish close combat and logistical air support to the Army, to include air lift, support, and resupply of airborne operations, aerial photography, tactical reconnaissance, and interdiction of enemy land power and communications. . . .

   . . . .

7. To provide Air Force forces for land-based air defense. . . .

Under collateral functions the following procedures apply to all the services.

The forces developed and trained to perform the primary functions set forth above shall be employed to support and supplement the other services in carrying out their primary functions where and whenever such participation will result in increased effectiveness and will contribute to the accomplishment of the over-all military objectives. . . .

The service member of the Joint Chiefs of Staff having primary responsibility for a function is charged with presenting to the JCS the requirements and plans for the forces of all three services to carry out the function. If there is unresolved interservice disagreement within the field of his primary responsibility, he is supposed to present it to the JCS for resolution. The primary functions involving joint operations of the three services, such as joint amphibious and air defense operations, are to be exercised "in accordance with doctrines and policies of the Joint Chiefs of Staff."

Thus the existing roles and missions generally make each service responsible for conducting operations against its enemy counterpart. However, it becomes clear that, in order to execute its assigned primary missions, each service becomes involved in tasks inseparable from the primary missions of other services. In such overlap of missions and in joint operations the JCS are charged with resolving disagreements and approving joint policies and doctrines. In practice this has proved highly difficult to achieve. Wherever missions overlapped, the fragmentation of functions among the services to conduct operations against their enemy counterparts has led inevitably to the development of different strategic concepts and priorities as to the importance of the roles and missions of the respective services. Moreover, each service has developed weapons to implement its primary missions, a practice which, because of the overlap in such missions, has led to duplication. For example, missiles are regarded variously as extensions of artillery, aircraft, and naval firepower. Each service regards its newly developed weapons as logical extensions of the existing weapons traditionally recognized as essential to the performance of its missions.

The problem of resolving service differences over roles and missions has been aggravated by the changing nature of modern war. Instead of land battles being fought by land forces and sea battles by sea forces, now all conflicts are increasingly taking on the character of combined land-sea-air operations. Land battles involve ground units, combat air support, troop lift, supply aircraft, missiles, and often amphibious assault, strategic sea lift, naval gun and missile support, and sea supply. Air defense involves sea- and land-based fighter interceptors, land- and air-launched missiles, antiaircraft, missile ships, and picket ships. Battles for sea supremacy involve ships, land- and carrier-based aircraft, land- and ship-launched missiles, and ground assault forces to seize and defend advanced bases. Each service, then, in pursuit of its primary mission, whether for land, sea, or air battles, naturally seeks to incorporate land, sea, and air weapons in its preparation to execute its mission.

While the need to resolve differences in strategic concepts and to reduce duplication of effort and resources by the services is recognized, the speed of the development of revolutionary weapons has not been adequately reflected in the form of flexible adjustments in roles and missions assignments. The impact of new weapons has dictated the need for flexible readjustment of missions, but, paradoxically, it has often led to increased rigidity in roles and missions assignments.

Not being sure of the implications for the future, the military services prefer to retain their status and structure as embodied in existing missions assignments. If, for example, the decision were made to rely solely on missiles for air defense, as was done in the United Kingdom,* there would be an automatic cutback in the number of Air Force fighter wings and a corresponding reduction in Air Force personnel strength, funds, position, and prestige. Thus, unless the Air Force could develop or acquire ground-to-air missiles of its own, it would gradually find itself crowded out of the air defense role by the Army and would, in effect, lose both one of its missions and one of its claims to consideration.

Similarly, unless the Air Force can control the development and use of the IRBM (Intermediate Range Ballistic Missile) and its successor, the ICBM (Intercontinental Ballistic Missile), it may find that it no longer has a virtual monopoly on the strategic retaliatory capability of the United States. Ultimately, as manned bombers are replaced by missiles, there may be diminished reason for maintaining the Air Force as a separate entity. Conversely, if the Army is restricted to the development of short-range missiles, it not only loses control of weapons it regards as essential to the performance of its mission but also is debarred from acquiring the strategic retaliatory capability which may give it a larger voice in Pentagon decisions.

We do not mean to suggest that all rivalries over weapons are motivated solely by selfish service considerations. The point is that, since the future of each service is inevitably bound up with the weapons it possesses, each of the armed forces seeks to develop *all* weapons of

---

* One of many decisions announced by the British in their 1957 White Paper on defense was the abandonment of further developments of interceptor aircraft in favor of missiles (*The New York Times*, April 5, 1957, p. 4). Whatever the merits of this particular approach, it represents the end in Great Britain of a battle which in this country is still raging furiously. Sweden also has made the decision to drop any further development of interceptors.

possible use, without much deference to what is being done by other services or to over-all concepts for the use of these weapons. It follows that the problem of assigning responsibilities for weapons, and of adjusting both missions and forces in accordance with these responsibilities, becomes inextricably bound up with the position, prestige, and strength of each service. This is also true, although to a lesser extent, within the services; rivalry expresses itself between submarine and carrier elements of the Navy as well as between the Army and the Air Force over the question of responsibility for air defense.

In the face of such service rivalries, the service "agreements" on roles and missions hammered out in the Key West-Newport documents, which only partially settled the differing points of view at the time, have proven increasingly difficult to implement and interpret as new concepts and weapons continue to be rapidly developed. Most efforts to promote greater unification in the Pentagon have foundered on the rocks and shoals of roles and missions.

The 1948 "agreements" perpetuated air arms for both the Navy and the Marine Corps, but it was not until after the B-36-super-carrier controversy had been investigated by Congress that the dispute between the Navy and Air Force reached a relative draw and each service went ahead in its separate lines of development, aided by the increasing defense appropriations stemming from the outbreak of the Korean War. The Navy continued to design and build larger and more modern carriers, and the Air Force pushed its development of an all-jet, land-based strategic air force. Nevertheless, the disagreement regarding the relative value of land-based versus sea-based strategic air power was only submerged. It reappeared during the airpower hearings before the Symington Committee even though both the Navy and the Air Force were careful to express public agreement. As the Chief of Naval Operations put it, "We have no intention of trying to preëmpt any part of the Air Force's responsibility."[9] However, it did appear that, with appropriate deployment, carrier-based planes and missiles could perform strategic strikes against enemy targets as closely associated with control of the air as with control of the sea.

Another area of continuing disagreement, inadequately resolved in 1948 and intensified by subsequent technological developments, is the degree and nature of Air Force support to Army missions. Army modernization programs have placed increasing emphasis upon battlefield air lift and reconnaissance; and the Army has tried to develop heavier and faster aircraft, principally helicopters, for battlefield reconnaissance and logistic air lift missions. The Air Force has regarded Army aviation as an attempt to develop an organic Army air arm competing with roles and missions assigned to the Air Force by the 1948 accords and supplemented by the Pace-Finletter agreement of 1952. This agreement, embodied in a November 4, 1952 memorandum of understanding between the Secretaries of the Army and Air Force, limited the Army to fixed wing aircraft of not over 5,000 pounds empty weight and rotary wing aircraft (helicopters) without weight limitation. These aircraft were restricted in missions to observation, fire control, and such battlefield chores as liaison and evacuation of wounded. The Air Force retained the missions to supply strategic and tactical air lift between outside points and the combat zone, air lift for airborne operations, and tactical air support of ground operations.

"Exercise Sagebrush" in the fall of 1955 revealed continuing doctrinal controversy between the Army and Air Force despite previous "agreements." The Army had formed a unit called "Sky-Cav," designed to perform airborne cavalry-type missions under conditions of nuclear war. The Air Force contended that this airborne unit violated the 1952 memorandum. The Secretary of the Air Force agreed to permit use of the unit in the maneuver but made clear that his agreement was not to be construed as altering the Air Force position in the doctrinal dispute.

Continued Army-Air Force disagreement was revealed also by the interservice controversy which broke out of the Pentagon into the press in the spring of 1956. A central concern to the Army was the adequacy of Air Force strategic and tactical air lift which alone could give Army Forces the mobility essential to overcoming the lack of manpower and to maintaining a capability to defeat enemy "brush-fire" aggressions in widely scattered points of the globe. Despite continued Army concern, the Secretary of Defense stated in his memorandum of November 26, 1956, which was designed to end service disputes in the roles and missions field:[10] "The current composition of the Air Force structure has been carefully examined and it appears that it provides adequate airborne lift in the light of currently approved strategic concepts."

This same Secretary of Defense memorandum reasserted belief in the basic soundness of the National Security Act of 1947, as amended, and the statement of roles and missions contained in the Key West-Newport agreements. Instead of modifying these agreements, it noted only that operational experience had revealed a need for "clarification and clearer interpretation of the roles and missions of the armed services." The directive substantially upholds the Pace-Finletter agreement of 1952, reduces overlapping service roles in air defense, and makes broad assignments of responsibility for the development and employment of Intermediate Range and Intercontinental Ballistic Missiles (IRBM and ICBM).

In air defense, the Army is given responsibility for point defense (i.e., fixed locations such as cities and bases) with the missiles designed for that purpose, principally the Army-developed Nike and Navy-developed Talos; the Air Force is responsible for area defense. The Army is to continue its development of surface-to-surface missiles, but only up to a 200-mile range, for close support of ground operations. The successful development of close-support missiles will, presumably, make it possible to reduce the number of tactical support aircraft in the Air Force. The Army will continue development of its IRBM, the Jupiter; the Air Force will continue to develop its IRBM, the Thor, and its ICBMs, the Atlas and the Titan. At the same time the Navy continues to develop its own IRBM, the Polaris, for launching from naval vessels and submarines. Significantly, however, despite the continuing Army development of a land-launched IRBM, the memorandum stipulated that operational employment of the IRBM is to be limited to the Navy and Air Force, eliminating the Army completely.

The memorandum of November 1956 reveals the need for making flexible readjustments of assigned roles and missions despite the prevailing rigidity of assignments stemming from the inability of the services to agree upon readjustments through established Joint Chiefs of Staff channels. Differing service missions and strategic concepts, coupled with service prides and prejudices, still make it difficult for the military to arrive at decisions on weapons development and utilization which form the core of roles and missions assignments. Under such circumstances, and intensified by individual service efforts to build public and Congressional support outside the Pentagon, the basic problems are pushed into the political arena for decision by the top civilian officials of the Defense Department.

It is true that, for disinterested evaluations of new weapons, the Secretary of Defense can draw upon the technical capabilities of the Office of the Assistant Secretary of Defense (R&E) and the Weapons Systems Evaluation group.* Nevertheless, to assist him in efficient and realistic resolution of such weapons-roles-missions issues, the Secretary still lacks agreed advice that can come only from those trained and experienced in exercising professional military judgment. The present organization is based on the premise and expectation that such major

---

* The operation and responsibilities of these organs were discussed previously in this chapter.

military issues can and will be resolved through the Joint Chiefs of Staff and existing service structures. The fact that this system has not worked out in practice indicates an urgent need to reexamine and improve a crucial sector of the existing defense organization and procedures.

TWO BASIC MILITARY TASKS

Particular effort has been made to achieve closer correlation between forces and missions for performing two basic military tasks, continental air defense and waging limited war with appropriate flexible striking forces. Although progress has been made, experience has revealed certain shortcomings in achieving adequate correlation of forces, missions, and tasks in these important areas. We consider those shortcomings here since they stem partly from ineffective organization and procedures that are illustrative of the current defense structure.

"Continental air defense" refers to the defense of the continental United States against manned aircraft and their prospective successors, missiles. Whether an effective air defense system is possible is one of the most critical factors in the nuclear equation for the coming era. The implications of a Soviet capability to destroy the United States and at the same time prevent a crippling retaliatory blow are obvious.

Weapons which the Soviets will have available for the next ten to fifteen years, and among which they will presumably have free option to choose, include manned bombers, with or without air-to-surface missiles, sub-launched guided or ballistic missiles, and ICBMs. A major threat to the United States now, and for some years hence, is that of an attack by manned bombers, whether made by them exclusively or in conjunction with an attack by submarine-launched missiles against targets located on both coasts. The objectives of such Soviet attacks might be key industrial and population areas, locks, seaports, and communication centers; atomic energy installations; and strategic bases.

The advent of intercontinental ballistic missiles introduces new complexities into the strategic picture. There is a wide difference of opinion as to when such missiles will be operationally effective (the Soviet Union claimed to have such weapons in its arsenal in the latter part of 1957) and to what extent they will alter the equations of warfare. The advent of long-range missiles would first of all have a great psychological impact, particularly if the Soviet Union acquired them first, as it appears to have done. (Parenthetically, the successful Soviet launching of an earth satellite had even more disastrous consequences to United States prestige throughout the world.) In any event, as of now the Soviet Union possesses enough bombers to seriously harm the United States and will shortly have enough to do any job which missiles could conceivably accomplish.

For the foreseeable future, an effective defense system against air attacks will have the following components:

A warning system extended as far out as possible.

A comprehensive command and information system in depth.

High performance interceptors.

Surface-to-air guided missiles.

Ultimately, as strategic missiles replace manned bombers, and as surface-to-air missiles increase in range, speed, and accuracy, interceptor aircraft may be completely replaced by defensive missiles. Already, technical developments threaten both to outmode the recent division of air defense responsibilities between Army and Air Force and to render obsolete some of the components of our present air defense system. Air defense is admittedly an extremely difficult military task. It involves the broadest concept of many integrated systems in order to provide, in terms of the weapons used and the coordination employed, better-than-reasonable assurance that the enemy's strategic air force will be largely destroyed if it should ever attack the United States.

Present indications of the technological requirements for high-level air defense against known strategic threats do not warrant any arbitrary conclusion that such a defense is possible or impossible for either the United States or the Soviet Union. It is reasonable to expect, however, that a potential enemy will choose that course of action which yields the greatest return for the effort expended, and that he will amend his choice when he has indications that progress in United States defense has rendered his first choice unprofitable. It is difficult to get many sections of American opinion to realize that, given the character of United States governmental processes (such as Congressional debate, hearings, public information policy), the Soviets will always have reasonably good information on the general progress of United States air defense; and that, in turn, this information will usually be sufficient to tell them with reasonable accuracy what options are being closed to them. This fact reinforces the argument that our system of openness of discussion entails a high price for security, for an adequate United States defense system must be planned to cope with all major options.

Consequently, the problem of defending the United States against hostile attack delivered through the air by various types of missiles and air vehicles illustrates better than almost any other the complex and integrated nature of our defense structure. There is no truly natural division of labor in continental air defense between our respective armed services. It is obvious, for example, that our defense against missiles launched against us from enemy submarines might involve our naval forces striking against the submarines themselves or their operating bases and that it might involve the use of our land-based Air Force and Army missile systems against the incoming missiles. Effective defense is certainly going to require an integrated warning line, including seaward extensions, involving Air Force, Army, and Navy personnel.

Our continental air defense, when fully established, will be one of the most complex technologically integrated systems in existence. The planning and the organizational structures within the three services will have to be substantially modified in the process of devising it, since there will be required a continuous strategic long-range planning activity cutting across all United States military forces. In this planning activity, cognizance of the problem cannot be limited, as it often is today, to the special interests of a particular service. None of the services can solve the problem in its entirety with its own resources, and efforts to hold on to information regarding particular parts of the problem because of a service's jurisdictional interests might well prevent an optimum solution.

Continental air defense clearly requires a principle of organization which will permit decision-making at the top level of the military establishment, such decision-making to be based on the completion of comprehensive study of the problem by the subordinate echelons. In this vital instance it may be necessary to separate the responsibility for future strategic plans from daily operation and organization.

Although continental air defense is one of the most complicated offensive-defensive problems which has ever confronted the Defense Department, thus far our approach has not been fully coordinated at the top level. In fact, formal responsibility for some segments of the defense problem has not yet been assigned. Furthermore, a firm general philosophy has not yet been developed for allocating effort among three demanding claimants: strategic striking forces of land, sea, and air; the continental air defense forces; and assistance to our allies in terms of military hardware, equipment, and troops.

The United States has been informed by a man who is one of the Americans most likely to know, General LeMay, that the Soviet Union has a sufficient number of weapons to destroy the key targets in this country unless they are well defended. There is much justification in our policy of trying to convince the enemy, through maintaining a tremendously powerful retaliatory force, that they should not attack us, but if General LeMay is right we must also have the ability to blunt *their* attack should they ever choose to launch one in the face of our deterrent retaliatory capability. In the testimonies before the 1956 Symington Committee the statement was made repeatedly that the facilities and resources that we have allocated to air defense have, in general, not been adequate. Deficiencies in early warning systems and in performance of fighter aircraft, and divergencies in evaluation of missile systems to be employed, were frequent issues of discussion. In short, in the spring of 1956 we were told that we were not ready, and that there was an urgent requirement that the United States undertake many additional and ambitious programs in order to be certain of having an effective air defense in the years ahead.

The public admission of difficulties reflects the views of the many boards and commissions that have advised the government during the last three or four years on the problem of air defense. There is no question that there is a time lag between our defensive preparations and what are soon to be the offensive capabilities of an enemy striking force. This factor becomes all the more critical when it is realized that, for all intents and purposes, the position of almost unchallenged nuclear superiority which the United States enjoyed a few years back has disappeared.

In 1953 Lloyd E. Berkner, a leading American scientist, made an impassioned plea for accelerated air defense. He said:

There is grave danger that through ambiguous assignments of responsibility, that through inadequate and penurious support, and that by continued reliance for decisions on a machine that does not run but moves only when pushed, we shall have the illusion of getting something when it is really nothing and at great cost. There is grave danger that timid and unimaginative leadership will fail to capitalize on the great inventiveness, brilliance and skill of American science and industry properly teamed to produce a result that is cheap, efficient and effective.

In 1957 ambiguous assignments of responsibility because of the Defense Department organization were still complicating and hampering our efforts toward generating a truly effective continental air defense system in time.

It was evident that our continental defense system was not being planned as an integrated entity, and that there was no agency which had both the competence and the authority either to undertake the required over-all planning or to implement its plans if they were adopted. Since there was inadequate coordination between the operating and development agencies, the actual system being developed represented a compilation of weapons and equipment which had been brought into being not by considering the over-all needs of the system but by emphasis on limited service aspects of the problem.*

However, even if the United States possessed a clear net advantage for waging strategic air war, that is, a long-range delivery system superior to the enemy's defenses and an advanced and comprehensive system of defense superior to the enemy's attacking forces, such an advantage by itself would not be sufficient to support our national aims and the world-wide commitments we have assumed in behalf of mutual security. Even when the United States enjoyed a decisive strategic advantage, the Communist bloc was able to expand because the Soviet Union pursued its strategy for the gradual erosion of the free world by attacking or seducing weak countries around the Soviet periphery. An atomic monopoly in American hands did not prevent the Communist guerilla actions against Greece and the pressures against Turkey in 1947, the *coup d'état* in Czechoslovakia in 1948, the Berlin Blockade, or the invasion of Korea.

With the steadily increasing Soviet strategic capabilities for nuclear strikes, the United States and the Soviet Union will approach a condition of nuclear parity during which both sides possess the means for mutual annihilation during an exchange of limited duration. It has been widely observed that under such conditions general war becomes less likely because it becomes increasingly unprofitable to either side. Conditions of mutual deterrence of general war increase the likelihood that conflict will take a more limited form.

The Soviets, reasoning that their encroachment upon nations along the periphery of the Soviet Union in 1947-1950 did not arouse the United States, with an atomic monopoly, to retaliation in the name of the free world, might logically estimate that there is even less likelihood today of strategic retaliation from this country. Given certain conditions, they might judge that they still possess opportunities for peripheral encroachment. Moreover, our retaliating on a thermonuclear scale to limited aggression would be hard to justify if Soviet efforts toward local Communist aggrandizement were conducted with sufficient skill to deny the United States an unequivocal basis for action. We have seen previous instances where our attempts to justify the projected use of United States forces against Communist forces were unsuccessful—for example, in Vietnam during the so-called "civil war" in which the Communists were successful in wresting half that nation away from the free world.

Since joining the North Atlantic Treaty Organization in 1949, the United States has actively supported mutual free world security efforts as the best way of assuring peace in a very troubled world. At the present

---

* New directives were issued to the joint command for North American air defense (NORAD) in the fall of 1956, but it is still too early to assess their full effectiveness.

time we are members of NATO, the Association of American States, and the Southeast Asia Treaty Organization; we participate in the Military Committee of the Baghdad Pact and have taken other measures in the Middle East consistent with the Eisenhower Doctrine; and we have, in one form or another, military agreements with forty-four countries situated outside the Soviet periphery.

In the context of such international commitments, and beginning with the Presidential "State of the Union" message in 1954, United States military policy has relied heavily on nuclear weapons to provide mutual security; and current American military policy is based on the contention that the United States' tremendous nuclear striking power should deter the Soviets from undertaking overt aggression, either against ourselves or our allies.

The "new look" taken at this policy in 1953-1954 gave some recognition to the fact that local limited wars of the kind that took place in Korea or Indochina might also occur in the future. It was decided that the primary means for containing limited types of aggression was the build-up in countries located around the Soviet periphery of indigenous forces assisted in certain ways by the United States—principally with arms, money, training, advice, and in some instances air and sea forces. In terms of that concept, our own ground forces were to be considerably reduced and, in general, concentrated in a strategic reserve to be held in the United States.

There has been no quarrel in the United States, even in the Pentagon, with such a general strategic concept. However, there has been some serious questioning of the means employed to implement it. First, there is the question as to whether or not the actual strategic reserve that we have maintained is large enough to fulfill our manifold commitments. Secondly, there is a question whether there actually exists sufficient air or sea lift in a high state of readiness to carry the troops and supplies needed to reinforce threatened countries in time to prevent their takeover.

Again, as in the case of air defense, solution to this critical problem has been prevented by the inadequate correlation of forces and missions to carry out the closely integrated operations, involving all the armed services, required to wage limited local wars effectively.

The Army has perhaps greater interest in the implementation of this strategic policy than the other two services. Most of the military assistance rendered to countries around the Soviet periphery involves Army equipment and Army training and supervisory personnel. Moreover, Army units would comprise the bulk of the strategic reserve used to backstop any country threatened by limited Communist aggression. Yet the Army is powerless to act without having the type of transportation for its troops and supplies which, under current missions assignments, only the Air Force and the Navy can give it; and the whole problem of meeting limited aggression has been of secondary interest to the Air Force and, perhaps, to the Navy. As a result, Air Force and Navy preparation for such a mission has not been anywhere nearly as advanced as has the support which has been given the fleet air arm in the Navy and the Strategic Air Command of the Air Force—both designed to participate principally in the strategic air war of nuclear destruction. By 1957 there were indications that both the Air Force and the Navy were giving increased attention to the problems of limited war, yet both seemed to believe they could cope with such conflicts "with the forces that are maintained for general war."

We come down to the fact that, regardless of shifts in emphasis, the question of roles and missions is at the core of arguments over the provision of means to implement United States military policy, and that as long as service disagreements continue and the organization for strategic planning and for determining roles and missions fails to operate effectively United States capabilities of dealing with peripheral Communist encroachments are seriously weakened.

Another factor inhibiting United States capability to counter peripheral aggression effectively is failure to grapple with the problem of allocating scarce resources. The present lack of agreed, precise strategic plans and the duplications of service missions and forces to accomplish overlapping primary functions aggravate this problem. Strategic planners face the difficulty of assuring preparedness for general war, including the unquestioned need to maintain effective offensive air power and an effective defense against Soviet air attacks, while simultaneously finding resources to combat more limited local aggressions. This is an admittedly difficult dilemma during a time of rising dollar costs, increasingly expensive modern weapons, and strict ceilings on the defense budget. Strategic planners and those charged with the direction of military operations have become reluctant to continue to deploy the shrinking United States armed forces around the world for fear that to do so might cause our dwindling forces to be committed in the wrong places and thus weaken our over-all strategic deterrent versus the Soviet Union and perhaps our ability to fight general war should it occur.

A further issue complicating the development of means to meet peripheral aggression, compounded by inadequacies in the existing strategic planning organization and procedures, is the problem of reaching agreement upon the proper balance of conventional and nuclear weapons for the conduct of the broad range of military tasks facing the United States armed forces. The introduction of nuclear weapons for use in a tactical as well as strategic manner increases the tendency to reduce conventional capabilities in favor of increased mobility and striking power. This trend could lead us to over-reliance upon nuclear forces, thus reducing the range and flexibility of actions available to meet the various forms of local Communist aggression such as civil war, guerilla action, or covert infiltration. On the other hand, both the United States and its allies have found the maintenance of large conventional armed forces increasingly difficult in light of economic limitations and in view of the ever-present possibility that nuclear weapons might be employed against allied forces armed only with conventional weapons.

The debate over whether or not to use tactical nuclear weapons in localized situations has a direct impact on the problem of command organization and procedures which results from the increased likelihood of future military actions occurring in peripheral situations. In the event of "brush-fire" outbursts we shall need to react swiftly and powerfully in order to impress immediately on the enemy our willingness to employ whatever of our capabilities are necessary to force him to desist from further aggression. In turn, the ability to react swiftly depends upon speed and precision in streamlined decision-making, from the immediate theater area all the way up to the highest levels of government. This important problem will be further discussed in the next chapter.

Footnotes

1. *Symington Committee Hearings on Airpower,* p. 1114.
2. *Ibid.,* pp. 1859-1862.
3. "Coordinating the Military Effort," address by Thomas S. Gates, Secretary of the Navy, at the National War College, Washington, D.C., April 24, 1957.
4. Department of Defense Instruction 5128.8, April 13, 1956.
5. Lloyd V. Berkner, "Is Secrecy Effective?" *Bulletin of the Atomic Scientists,* February 1955, p. 62.
6. For a discussion of both the causes of this situation and some of its implications see the unpublished manuscript *Policy and Organizational Problems in the Military Applications of Atomic Energy,* specially prepared for the American Project Series by Lt. Col. Niel M. Wreidt, USA.
7. The latest such decision, relating to responsibilities for the development and use of various types of missiles, was contained in a memorandum of November 26, 1956, to the Armed Forces Policy Council, subject: "Clarification of Roles and Missions to Improve the Effectiveness of Operation of the Department of Defense." The memorandum is reported as Appendix C in the Association of the United States Army publication, *The Security of the Nation. A Study of Current Problems of National Defense,* Washington, 1957.
8. Department of Defense Directive 5100.1, March 16, 1954; subject: "Functions of the Armed Forces and the Joint Chiefs of Staff." For ready reference, see Stanley, *op. cit.,* p. 176.
9. *Symington Committee Hearings on Airpower,* p. 1379.
10. Memorandum to the Armed Forces Policy Council, entitled "Clarification of Roles and Missions to Improve the Effectiveness of Operation of the Department of Defense," cited above.

Eight

READINESS FOR ACTION

EMERGENCY DECISIONS

It is obvious that forces in being cannot alone constitute adequate preparedness for instant action. There must be a controlling administration and command system capable of rapid decision-making, a structure in being and embracing effective decision-making procedures before any emergency occurs. In short, the decision-making process of the Defense Department while operating effectively within the government framework for developing and implementing a national "cold war" strategy, must be capable of instantaneous transition to waging a "hot war," whether in limited or general form.

The Defense Department has made considerable progress since the Korean conflict toward maintaining a level of logistic and mobilization preparedness capable of rapid reaction with adequate military force. Progress has also been made in the integration of military and politico-economic cold war planning. But there are continuing serious problems.

A basic flaw in the present system is the relationship between the Joint Chiefs of Staff and the Office of the Secretary of Defense to which we have given some previous attention. Hoover Commission studies, the Rockefeller Committee, and the President's message accompanying Reorganization Plan No. 6 have all called attention to the need for closer cooperation and coordination between them. The Secretary of Defense in 1954 issued a directive that the JCS ". . . shall effectively, fully, and completely collaborate with all parts of the Office of the Secretary of Defense to insure broadened participation in strategic and logistic planning at the early stages of staff work on any major problem being considered."[1] Nevertheless, one year later the Hoover Commission stated that a major obstacle to effective administration of the Defense Department was the fact that "decisions and information do not flow freely from the Joint Chiefs of Staff to the Assistant Secretaries of Defense."[2]

The intrinsic nature of the present Joint Chiefs of Staff structure and the restrictions on its use obstruct the procedure of providing sound military advice to civilian superiors. Since close collaboration with the staffs in the Office of the Secretary of Defense is inhibited by the fact that no JCS views are firm until the individual chiefs personally have expressed their corporate views in writing, it is exceedingly difficult to develop agreed staff-level views. Consequently, strategic considerations developed by the JCS and political-economic-logistic factors concerning the Assistant Secretaries of Defense can be formally blended only at the top after the Chiefs themselves have taken a position.

Under the pressure of an emergency, such an absence of effective staff collaboration on all aspects of the problems at hand results in piecemeal and unrealistic decisions reflecting poor balancing of factors and of civilian and military views. During the peacetime development of plans for wartime mobilization and operations, the absence of appropriate balance of civilian and military views and of close collaboration between staffs concerned can result in unrealistic plans which fail to meet the emergencies when they occur.

The Joint Chiefs of Staff as a corporate body were restricted by the 1947 National Security Act to advising the Secretary of Defense, the President, and the National Security Council on strategic plans and implications. They were given no corporate command authority. Those limitations, intended to assure civilian control over the exercise of military power, almost completely inhibit top-level professional military direction of military operations in time of emergency. Moreover, although the pressure of emergency operations demands a speed and precision of communication in the Defense Department decision-making process which is normally found only in military command channels, these channels have become devious and confused as a result of the multiplication of staff levels and the tendency of civilian policy staffs to intervene in operations.

To some degree, the multiplicity of channels through which the flow of Defense Department business passes is a result of the attempt to maintain civilian-military balance by dividing decisions between military and nonmilitary and the laudable effort to decentralize operations. However, present practice, under which the various services carry out most of the contacts with the working military units in the conduct of day-to-day administration, often on behalf of the Secretary of Defense, is far from satisfactory. Problems arise both because of frequent difficulty in differentiating between policy guidance issued by the Office of the Secretary of Defense and lower-level administrative instructions initiated by the services. They likewise arise because at the service level the same agency receives different types of instructions from different sources. Some are issued by the Secretary of Defense, some on behalf of the Joint Chiefs of Staff (JCS), and some under a service masthead.

A directive to a unified commander—say, the Commander-in-Chief, European Command—may be issued by the Secretary of Defense directly, by the Secretary through the Department of the Army as his executive agency, by the JCS directly, by the JCS through the Department of the Army, by the Chief of Staff of the Army, under the authority given him to act in the name of the Secretary of Defense,[3] or, in administrative or purely Army matters, by the Department of the Army on its own authority. Similarly, communications from the theater commander may take any one of the major routes described, or, in the situation above, may follow NATO* channels through the Standing Group, through the United States representative on the NATO Council, or through the Defense Representative, Northern Atlantic and Mediterranean Area, to the Assistant Secretary of Defense (International Security Affairs). The existence of so many channels hampers efficiency and enables interested parties to make whichever approach they think will best facilitate a decision in their favor or may be useful in initiating a reclama† after getting an adverse decision.

To some extent this complexity in communications channels is caused by the dichotomy between civilian control of policy and supposed military freedom of action in the field of strategic planning and guidance. Actually, the cause of the confusion lies deeper than this. Theoretically, the theater commanders are responsible directly to the Secretary of Defense; in practice, however, the various theaters have been regarded as fiefs by the particular service which inherited responsibility for them by the accident of World War II. Thus, the Army has long regarded Europe and the Far East‡ as its particular prerogatives; the Navy has continued responsibility for the Pacific, for the Atlantic, and, in a very complex fashion, for the Mediterranean; and the Air Force has had the functional commands of the Strategic Air Command and Continental Air Defense, as well as a few detached "provinces" such as Spain and North Africa. Where no previous command arrangement existed, as in the Middle East or in the southern part of Latin America, it has been very difficult to establish one because no service will willingly relinquish

---

* North Atlantic Treaty Organization.

† Request for a new policy.

‡ On July 1, 1957 the Navy became executive agent for the entire Pacific area, including the Army's Far East Command.

to another the privileges and prerogatives of dealing with such an important personage as the theater commander.

Behind this situation there also lies the fact that the military chief of a service which acts as executive agency for the Secretary of Defense transmits strategic guidance and, in an emergency, can direct strategic operations through the theater commander in a given area. Thus the development of strategic concepts for an area, the determination of command arrangements, to some extent the establishment of levels and types of forces, and the exercise of a whole host of related powers depend on close relationships between a given service and the nominally independent theater command for which the service is supposed to act as executive agency on behalf of the Secretary of Defense.

Given these circumstances, and the fact that the administrative and logistic organizations are not completely unified within a theater, multiplicity of communications channels and resultant policy and operational confusion are likely to continue. Policy guidance sent from the Office of the Secretary of Defense may frequently be modified or negated by instructions from the Joint Chiefs of Staff. What is sent out from a service department will frequently have more weight with the "unified" commander—and be more partisan—than what may come from either the Joint Chiefs or the Secretary of Defense. Although the Secretary of Defense has assumed the responsibility for the conduct of strategic operations (through his designated executive agency), he has not in practice assumed the corresponding responsibility for approving strategic plans and strategic guidance. Thus he has, to some extent, reduced his own authority—although it must be noted that this is an area of such sensitivity that failure to take more positive action is understandable at this stage in the development of the Defense Department.

In terms of the decision-making process, the current organization and procedures of the Defense Department structure not only raise grave doubts as to its capability for instantaneous reaction with effective military force; they also bring into question its capability to conduct effective combat operations. In fact, some critics of the Defense Department contend that it is not really designed to run a war.

We have noted that, as the principal military advisers to the President and the Secretary of Defense, the JCS are restricted to a strategic planning responsibility. The fact that the members of the JCS are at the same time the military chiefs of the services is supposed to provide the necessary link between advice and operational responsibility. Significantly, however, while the members of the JCS have command responsibility in their individual services, the corporate body of the JCS has no command responsibility. Under present procedures, therefore, while the JCS would provide direct military advice to the President and the Secretary of Defense, commands under wartime conditions would follow the President-Secretary of Defense-secretary of a military department-military chief of staff line.

Under the strain of wartime and the need for rapid decision-making, it might well be desired to utilize the JCS as a corporate command body directly under the Secretary of Defense, or even directly under the President, as the JCS operated in World War II and the Korean War. If such modifications should prove necessary, who would be responsible for determining what emergencies required a change in procedures, and what would be the risks of making such changes in the initial phase of a global conflict? It would seem preferable to establish and develop procedures in peacetime that will remain constant in time of war.

Some observers have raised questions as to whether our present system would be effective in controlling the scope of military operations should war, either local or general, occur suddenly.

One such operation would be the pre-planned strategic nuclear strike at an enemy homeland. According to various spokesmen, there would be no hesitation, if NATO were attacked, to carry out counter-air strikes deep in enemy territory, in which at least some elements of the United States Strategic Air Command would be immediately and directly involved. If the sweeping predictions in regard to a "three-day war" are to be believed, the tempo of the air attacks involved, once begun, would preclude any further interference by civilian officials until great damage had been done to airfields, road and rail junctions, industries, and people —not to mention the crippling of military units, material, and installations. In other words, once the retaliation "button" is pressed, the machine may grind through its operation with only such hindrances as the enemy may interpose, despite the political desirability of calling a halt.

Limited war presents an even more challenging problem. If full play is to be given to political efforts to limit both the scope and the consequences of the war, then obviously some system of restraints must be imposed on our military commanders. Yet the imposition of restraints would run counter, at least to some extent, both to our established concept of giving the theater commander broad freedom of action and, more important, to the military necessities of modern war. Will any one in uniform willingly risk another "Clark Field," wherein his striking forces may be irretrievably crippled while he awaits more information or decisions from higher headquarters? And yet the tremendous political and military implications attendant to the employment of nuclear weapons dictate the retention of control over their use by the top civilian authority, namely, the President.

It is not clear to what extent a theater commander can exercise the rapid and independent judgment necessary to react quickly. Moreover, it is questionable whether the channel from him to the chief of staff and secretary of the proper military department, to the Secretary of Defense, to the President works rapidly enough to permit effective initial reaction if the decision is to be made in Washington. Finally, the very complexities of the defense structure may not permit rapid execution of agreed strategic and operational plans to implement the decisions once they have been made.

Even more important than the question of *how* the dilemma confronting the theater commander might be resolved in an emergency is the question of by whom it is to be resolved. Ultimately and logically, decisions on the employment or disengagement of United States forces must be made by the President. Equally logically, he should weigh the views of both his military and political advisers. Yet no mechanism exists to bring together rapidly in practiced harness the President, the Secretary of State, the Secretary of Defense, and the Joint Chiefs of Staff. In time of emergency these individuals may be scattered in separate places a hundred miles apart around Washington.

Even if they all stay in Washington, who will be charged with winnowing out, either in advance or at the time, the relative political and military situations for streamlined presentation to the President? There is no command post where such data may be assembled and orders disseminated either at the White House, the National Security Council, or within the Office of the Secretary of Defense.

If existing procedures are followed, reports from the theater commander would go to the JCS, possibly through one of the military departments. Thence JCS estimates and recommendations would go to the Secretary of Defense, presumably through the Assistant Secretary of Defense (International Security Affairs), who is charged with politico-military planning and policy. Either here or at the JCS level the views of the Department of State would have to be sought and considered. Finally, unless the responsibilities of the civilian Secretary of Defense for the conduct of strategic operations are to be completely ignored, he, his advisers, and the members (or possibly only the chairman) of the JCS would meet with the President and the Secretary of State, or with the full National Security Council.

If the past is any guide, it appears that, confronted in a time of military emergency with the present time-consuming process of decision-making, there would be a reversion to the previous practice in times of crisis. Decisions would be made by a very few top officials without benefit of complete or considered political-military advice.

It is indeed ironical to reflect that, although the United States has facilities for integrated political-military decision-making, including Allied participation, in an isolated outpost like Berlin, it has no comparably efficient mechanism in the headquarters of the United States Government in Washington.

Footnotes

1. Department of Defense Directive 5158.1, July 26, 1954, *Method of Operation of the Joint Chiefs of Staff and Their Relationships with Other Staff Agencies of the Office of the Secretary of Defense.*
2. *Business Organization of the Department of Defense*, p. 14.
3. Department of Defense Directive 5001.1, March 16, 1954, *Functions of The Armed Forces and of The Joint Chiefs of Staff.*

Nine

MONEY AND MANAGEMENT

THE BUDGET

It goes without saying that the maintenance of national security requires a careful balance between military preparedness adequate to deter enemy aggression and the preservation of a strong and growing national economy. Thus planning for and meeting the ever-increasing costs of defense requirements are subject not only to considerations of over-all national security policies and programs but also to domestic economic and political conditions. It follows that basic decisions affecting the magnitude and composition of the defense budget may be made outside the Defense Department through the channels of the Treasury Department, the Bureau of the Budget, and the White House, not to mention the Congress, which provides the actual defense appropriations.

This has been true in the case of both political parties. In the Spring of 1946 President Truman indicated that the military budget would be decided for the subsequent two years on the basis that the armed services would be apportioned one third of the national budget remaining after fixed debt and government administration costs had been met.[1] In 1957 President Eisenhower both imposed a limit of $38 billion on defense spending for FY 1958 and established a similar ceiling on new obligational authority which could be requested for FY 1959. In both cases concern for the strength and growth of the economy appeared to be a motivating factor. In his exchange of correspondence with Secretary of Defense Wilson in January 1955, President Eisenhower stressed the need for a carefully evaluated balance of defense requirements and domestic economic and political conditions. The President wrote that, in building the defense structure, "to do less than the minimum would expose the nation to the predatory purposes of potential enemies. On the other hand, to build excessively under the impulse of fear could, in the long run, defeat our purposes by damaging the growth of our economy and eventually forcing it into regimented controls."[2]

We have noted that inadequate coordination on the government-wide level between the budget cycle and formulation of over-all national security policies and programs has tended to separate budget from other planning within the Defense Department, restricting the ability of the defense planners either to establish realistic goals in terms of available financial means or to justify additional appropriations to meet absolutely necessary requirements.[3]

The cyclical differences between schedules for budget presentation and those for the development of national policy and derived military strategic and logistical plans have been recognized by many authorities as one of the major causes of delay, confusion, and duplication of effort which has characterized some of the Defense Department's operations. Generally the fiscal cycle precedes and overshadows the considerations of policy questions, an inversion which is not always advantageous to our security position.

There are also other external factors that bear upon Defense Department budgeting and spending. The fact that three to five years may elapse between preparation of a budget and the expenditure of appropriations has resulted in monies being spent for programs which were no longer valid. On the other hand, imposing budgetary ceilings or making very sharp cuts in military department requests for funds has frequently required a complete reworking of the budget, with consequent delays in developing and implementing programs. Moreover, the procedural requirement that appropriations must be rejustified to the Assistant Secretary of Defense (Comptroller) and the Bureau of the Budget before allocations of funds to specific programs can be obtained has further hampered operations.

Granting these surrounding conditions, we would judge that greater obstacles to achieving optimum defense programs with maximum cost-efficiency result from current trends in organization and procedures for conducting strategic planning and for exercising the comptroller functions within the Department of Defense itself. The necessity for close integration of strategic planning and the budget cycle was recognized in the Key West Agreement, which in its present form[4] states that it is one of the duties of the Joint Chiefs of Staff

to prepare and submit to the Secretary of Defense, for his information and consideration in furnishing guidance to the Departments for preparation of their annual budgetary estimates and in coordinating these budgets, a statement of military requirements which is based upon agreed strategic considerations, joint outline war plans, and current national security commitments. This statement of requirements shall include: tasks, priority of tasks, force requirements, and general strategic guidance concerning development of military installations and bases, equipping and maintaining the military forces, and research and development and industrial programs.

In practice, the fact that the Joint Chiefs of Staff structure has experienced distinct difficulties in developing agreed strategic concepts, and especially a joint logistics plan to support such concepts, in time to meet annual budget cycles has vitiated the JCS guidance required by this directive.

In the absence of clear, agreed military strategic concepts and plans, the guidance issued to the military departments for preparing their annual budgets is determined largely by civilian staffs in the Office of the Secretary of Defense who must make assumptions and decisions which ideally should be made by experienced military professionals. Moreover, the absence of clear, agreed military guidance means that each of the military departments develops its budget requirements on the basis of its own unilateral strategic concepts and plans. Since the Joint Chiefs of Staff, although they review major material and personnel requirements of the armed forces, do not review the budget as a whole,[5] the independently developed military department budgets are not considered by the JCS in relation to JCS *joint* strategic concepts and plans —regardless of whether those *joint* concepts and plans are in the form of clear agreements or vague compromises. It is plain that such circumstances foster both costly duplications and potentially dangerous gaps in essential defense programs as embodied in the military department budgets submitted to the Secretary of Defense.

An even more significant result of present procedures is that the civilian staffs at the Office of the Secretary of Defense level, who review the military department budgets under the general supervision of the Assistant Secretary of Defense (Comptroller), in effect make the ultimate determinations regarding differing service strategic concepts and plans. It is true that final hearings on proposed budgets bring together the top military and civilian officials of the Defense Department, and that final decisions are made by the Secretary of Defense prior to forwarding the composite budget to the Bureau of the Budget. Nevertheless, the recommendations forwarded to the secretary inevitably reflect the judgment of the staff producing them; and under the present organization and procedures, it appears that advice on strategic military concepts and plans, which ideally should come from trained and experienced military professionals, is not always developed in a timely or agreed manner. The military advice available is not channeled effectively into the budget preparation process, where the ultimate decisions on strategic concepts and plans are made in lieu of agreed military views. Domination of the defense budget process by the civilian staffs at the Office of the Secretary of Defense level again reflects the general tendency toward increased centralized civilian control—in this case through the comptroller operations.

To return to the political-economic content of the present discussion, if optimum defense programs are to be attained, organizational and procedural means for exercising effective fiscal controls must balance two basic groups of factors: first, the military facts of the strategic situation and the military requirements derived therefrom, and, second, the availability of resources in terms of the economic and political capabilities of the society. When, as occurs under present procedures, service rivalries and difficulties in determining agreed strategic concepts, roles, and missions vitiate military guidance as to the strategic situation and the derivative military requirements, and the voice of the predominantly civilian fiscal control staffs becomes a determining factor in policy decisions, there is the grave risk that the end result will be unrealistic and unbalanced defense programs incapable of supporting military tasks basic to national survival.

It must be admitted that the whole issue of achieving appropriate balance in fiscal and budget policy is highly complex. Every fiscal official, from the Secretary of the Treasury down, is confronted with claims for "defense" money which would reach astronomical totals unless rigorously screened and checked; and yet there does not exist within the Treasury Department, the Bureau of the Budget, or in the Defense Department itself a completely systematic basis or institutional machinery for distinguishing those claims which deserve priority when measured against some rational and comprehensive security concept. This is particularly important since there is some skepticism among civilian officials as to the real validity of budgetary requirements submitted by the military. Moreover, although justification for a particular claim on the national defense budget is often documented in great detail and with impressive arguments, the whole budget is generally developed on a piece-by-piece basis. Since there is no agency which attempts with any success to show the interrelationship of the various items which make up the defense budget, decisions as to which force or item (for example, the Strategic Air Command or the fleet air arm; tanks or transport aircraft) should get what amount of money are often determined by subjective influences and political pressures.

In 1956 the Defense Department, at the direction of the National Security Council, attempted to handle the problem through the device of making a functional budgetary breakout for such items as air defense, the strategic striking force, etc. The idea was to bring together in one place the costs of joint operations, now scattered through separate service budgets, in order to compare them with other joint defense operations and individual service programs and establish priorities more realistically geared to the actual military tasks at hand. However, the complexities of the operation, the fact that some types of forces have two or more missions, and the opposition of the services to both the process itself and the establishment of any meaningful system of priorities made the resultant breakout both incomplete and relatively useless. The idea was good, and even the poor results obtained represent a step forward. However, the basic situation is still that, unless we are able to devise a far more rational system than the present one for arriving at strategic requirements and demonstrating their budgetary implications, the Treasury, the Bureau of the Budget, and the Congress must decide fundamental questions of national security, *via* the budget process, on a somewhat haphazard basis.

OPERATING ECONOMY

Maximum economy in operation consistent with the attainment of established defense objectives has been a basic objective of the defense establishment ever since unification. In his exchange of correspondence with Secretary of Defense Wilson in January 1955, President Eisenhower tersely reemphasized this objective:

> If we are to support active and effective forces of the order indicated over a period which may last for decades, we must practice a strict austerity in day-to-day operations.[6]

The influential role of the civilian budget and fiscal management staffs in the budget process, resulting in increased centralized civilian control exercised through the defense comptroller operation, is paralleled by the increasing reliance upon these staffs to achieve economy in defense operations. Their role is emphasized by the fact that the 1949 amendments to the National Security Act spelled out in considerable detail the organization for fiscal management within the Department of Defense.

Title IV of the National Security Act establishes one of the Assistant Secretaries of Defense as comptroller of the Department and a comptroller and deputy comptroller in each of the military departments. It provides that the secretary of each military department, subject to the authority, direction, and control of the Secretary of Defense, shall assure that budgeting, accounting, progress and statistical reporting, internal auditing, and related administrative and managerial procedures be organized and conducted in a manner consistent with the operations of the Office of the Comptroller of the Department of Defense. The comptroller for the Department, the Assistant Secretary of Defense (Comptroller), has received from the Secretary of Defense the authority to exercise "functional control" over all the comptroller functions and organizations throughout the Department. "Functional control" is defined as "the power and duty to prescribe policies and procedures, to require compliance therewith, and to review or audit activities within the area of responsibility."[7] Assistant secretaries for financial management have been established in each military department; they either serve as the comptroller for that department or delegate the responsibility to an official directly responsible to them. They exercise general supervision and "functional control" over the comptroller activities of their respective departments, subject to direction and control of their own superiors.

The hierarchy of comptroller structures has grown steadily in influence to the point where it not only acts as a channel for coordinating the defense budget and for furthering operating economy but also is increasingly relied upon as the principal means for exercising control and discipline throughout the Defense Department. The staffs of the Assistant Secretaries of Defense and the military department secretariats have relied increasingly upon the budget process, financial allocations, and fiscal policies to assure that implementing actions in the military departments follow the basic policies which have been issued by the Office of the Secretary of Defense in accordance with its responsibility for central policy control.

The evolution of the comptroller channel as the most effective means for exercising control has resulted partly from the ineffective operation of other organs and procedures within the Defense Department. The comptroller function includes gathering a great deal of diverse information on defense operations through the process of accounting, auditing, and statistical and progress reporting.

The difficulties the politically appointed officials have experienced in obtaining adequate information from other sources on which to base their decisions has led them to rely increasingly on the comptroller. For example, the absence of agreed strategic guidance from the Joint Chiefs of Staff has led the Assistant Secretaries of Defense to look increasingly to the Assistant Secretary of Defense (Comptroller) for information to assist them in developing policies to guide military department operations. Moreover, the multiplicity of staff levels and confused channels of communication within the present defense structure make it difficult for the staffs responsible for policy development to obtain necessary information from operating levels and to assure precise implementation of policies throughout these operations. The clearly defined comptroller hierarchy thus offers a readily available alternate source of information and means of exercising control.

It is debatable whether this increasing reliance on the comptroller channel is desirable in view of the limitations of fiscal controls as management tools. Even though the comptroller operation has proved an invaluable means for coordinating the budget and to some extent for increasing economy in operations, there are always dangers in substituting decisions by civilian comptroller staffs for agreed professional military views on strategic concepts and plans.

In addition, the information gathered by the comptroller does not necessarily provide the data in meaningful form required by officials in other functional fields. For one thing, procedures established by the comptroller at the present time are rarely set up to gather data on the basis of missions or key tasks, particularly when these cut across service lines. Consequently, the information is obtained in rather artificial or arbitrary categories to serve comptroller needs—categories which may not reflect, or may misrepresent, factors required for valid decisions by officials working on other problems. Still further, the increasingly extensive reporting and accounting requirements laid on the military departments by comptroller operations has created demands for additional trained clerical personnel, frequently unavailable, and necessitates major changes in techniques at lower levels, with the result that, particularly at field installations, many offices have not yet been able to supply the desired information.

Over and beyond the above considerations, we would question the extent to which fiscal controls which have been used successfully in private industry can effectively be utilized within the Defense Department. It can be said that whereas a large manufacturing corporation has as its mission the delivery of a known product at known places at known times and in known quantities, the Department of Defense has the mission of delivering an uncertain product to unknown places at unknown times and in unknown quantities. In a business organization the establishment of comparatively few basic elements, such as a break-even point and how many items to produce in a year, constitutes a program. In the Defense Department repeated program reviews and rapid changes, such as introducing a new weapon into mass production before an earlier model has been integrated into operational use, make demands on the fiscal data and fiscal control machinery which are unknown to private industry.

It should be noted that the present defense structure also places great emphasis upon effective "business" organization and administration outside of the comptroller area. Indeed, six of the Assistant Secretaries of Defense* are basically "management vice presidents," most of their management areas being also the responsibility of parallel assistant secretaries in the military departments, for example, financial management, manpower, and logistics.

The current defense organization has admittedly achieved some real economies in defense operations.

A significant contribution to economy and efficiency in supply management was achieved by the development of a single supply catalogue with uniform military standards and specifications for all supply items. By establishing a system for identifying and classifying all items in the military supply systems, standardization has been advanced; and the catalogue is today a valuable tool for mobilization planning, procurement, and distribution. Established by the Munitions Board in 1948, the cataloguing and standardization program was intensified† after Congressional inquiry into the Korean experience revealed serious deficiencies in the supply system.

By 1957 the identification and classification of the estimated 2,400,000 items in the military supply systems had almost been brought up to date. Standardization is continuing to progress under a program set up in October 1954 which instructed the military departments to accelerate their programs to simplify procurement, expand cross-servicing, improve logistic support, conserve critical items and materials, and reduce maintenance and distribution costs. In fiscal year 1955 alone, 157,000 items were eliminated from the military supply system, and savings from standardization were estimated at $29 million annually.[8]

In order to enhance effective management procedures leading to greater economy in operations, an Advisory Committee on Fiscal Organization and Procedures was established within the Department of De-

---

* The Assistant Secretaries of Defense (Comptroller), (Manpower, Personnel and Reserve), (Research and Engineering), (Supply and Logistics), (Properties and Installations), and (Health and Medical).

† The Defense Cataloguing and Standardization Act of 1952 set up the Defense Supply Management Agency within the Department of Defense. The functions of this agency were transferred to the Assistant Secretary of Defense (Supply and Logistics) by Reorganization Plan No. 6 of 1953.

fense to investigate and make recommendations regarding budgeting, accounting, and financial activities. More than twenty reports were completed before the conclusion of its work in 1954, and many of the recommendations that resulted were implemented immediately. The over-all recommendations were turned over to the Hoover Commission for integration into its reports. Altogether, the Hoover Commission, established in 1953 to make studies and recommendations that would "promote economy, efficiency, and improved service of the public business," had published by the end of 1955 a total of eighteen Commission and twenty task force reports which related to or were primarily concerned with the business organization and management of the Defense Department. Topics included military procurement, depot utilization, real property management, commercial and industrial activities, disposal of surplus property, budgeting and accounting, civilian personnel, and research and development.

While recognizing the progress made in promoting operating economy, the 1955 Hoover Commission *Report on the Business Organization of the Department of Defense* found that there were still areas which required improved organizational techniques. It noted the importance of existing management staffs at the predominantly civilian levels of the military department secretariats and in the Office of the Secretary of Defense, but it also made recommendations* as to how these could be better organized to achieve economy in defense operations. We would note here simply that those recommendations indicated a trend

---

* It recommended that a civilian position be created in the Office of the Secretary of Defense to improve planning and review of military requirements through such procedures as maintaining contact with the National Security Council and the Joint Chiefs of Staff, coordinating the Office of the Secretary of Defense guidance for the preparation of requirements by the military departments, and providing a system for reviewing defense plans and requirements computations. It recommended that the functions of the Assistant Secretary of Defense (Supply and Logistics) and the Assistant Secretary of Defense (Properties and Installations) be combined as well as those of the Assistant Secretary of Defense (Research and Development) and the Assistant Secretary of Defense (Applications Engineering) to better coordinate the broad areas of logistics, research and development, personnel, and finance. It further recommended that the duties of the military department assistant secretaries be regrouped to conform to this same pattern recommended for the Office of the Secretary of Defense. It proposed common procedures to assure that each Assistant Secretary of Defense and the assistant secretaries of the military departments in the management fields would be responsible for screening requirements and budget review in their program areas, although these offices were already accomplishing these functions under individual techniques of program monitorship. The report also recommended establishing the often discussed "fourth service" concepts in the form of a "Defense Supply Administration," which would be a civilian-run agency reporting to the Secretary of Defense and would be responsible for administering supply and service activities common to all the military services.

toward even further centralization of control in the hands of predominantly civilian officials with increased staffs, and that, since the "management vice presidents" already exercise considerable control over the business side of the defense establishment, there may be some question as to the extent of increased efficiency which would result from increasing this authority.

A new technique to improve economy and efficiency in defense management which does not disrupt basic lines of authority and responsibility has been devised in the form of the Single Manager Plan. Under this plan, as established in January 1956,[9] the secretary of one of the military departments is designated by the Secretary of Defense to be responsible for the organization and operation of a particular assignment of common-use items or common-service activities for all of the armed services. It is designed to apply the "best supplier" principle in order to reduce duplication of effort by the military departments and to improve effectiveness and economy of supply and service operations throughout the Defense Department. The secretary of the military department designated as single manager for some particular operation, such as the purchase of all food or oil for all services, appoints to operate the program an executive director who is subject to approval by the Secretary of Defense but responsible to the secretary appointing him. The organization that is then established to operate the assigned single-manager function is expected to make maximum use of existing facilities and personnel in all three military departments, and the services are expected to eliminate whatever becomes surplus as the result.

The influence of the Office of the Secretary of Defense upon the single-manager operation goes beyond merely approving the appointed executive director. This director is assisted by an administrative committee of which he is chairman and which includes representatives from each of the three armed services, from the office of the Assistant Secretary of Defense (Comptroller), and from offices of other appropriate Assistant Secretaries of Defense concerned with the particular supply operation. With such influence assured, the single-manager concept offers an effective tool for increased centralized control over the military services by the Office of the Secretary of Defense. For example, if the single-manager concept were applied to any great extent in the field of procurement and supply, the services' existing leverage for influencing the development and implementation of over-all defense programs through their own procurement and supply programs would be curtailed.

SINGLE MANAGER ORGANIZATION

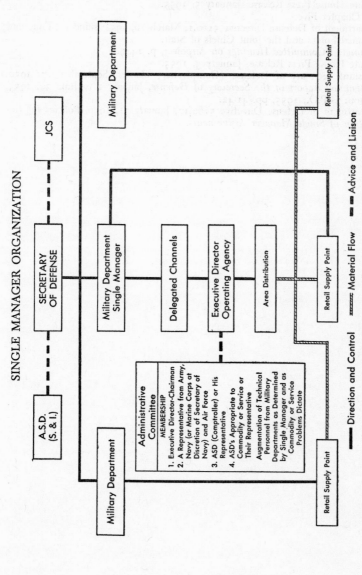

Source: Department of Defense comments on the Hoover Commission *Report on Business Organization of the Department of Defense,* March 1956.

Footnotes

1. Millis, Ed., *The Forrestal Diaries, op. cit.,* p. 162.

2. White House Press Release, January 5, 1955.

3. See Chapter Five.

4. Department of Defense Directive 5100.1, March 16, 1954; subject: "Functions of the Armed Forces and the Joint Chiefs of Staff."

5. *Symington Committee Hearings on Airpower,* p. 1449.

6. White House Press Release, January 5, 1955.

7. Assistant Secretary of Defense (Comptroller) charter, September 27, 1950.

8. *Semiannual Report of the Secretary of Defense,* January 1 to June 30, 1955, Washington: G.P.O., 1955, pp. 41-42.

9. Department of Defense Directive 5160.12, January 31, 1956, *Policies for Implementation of Single Manager Assignments.*

Ten

MOTIVATION AND MORALE

No matter what may be the organization design of the Defense Department, today or in the future, the structure will always depend ultimately upon the vitality of human manpower. Plans, programs, equipment and weapons are worthless without human beings to develop and utilize them. In short, the number and quality of personnel manning the defense machine will be a vital determinant of the adequacy with which the Defense Department fulfills its tasks for maintaining the national security.

In one sense the manpower problems of the Defense Department are unique in that the structure combines civilian and military personnel whose conditions of employment are controlled by separate personnel systems. However, the fundamental personnel requirements for effective operation of the Defense Department are common to both the civilian and military categories; namely, to attract and retain sufficient qualified and competent manpower, and to maintain their motivation and morale.

In order to satisfy these basic personnel requirements the defense organization must be so constituted as to offer the following incentives: adequate salaries geared to the jobs performed and comparable to remuneration for similar work outside the department; opportunity for career development and promotion; opportunity to perform meaningful work; and recognition of conscientious effort. Although Defense Department personnel policies and programs have recognized these requirements, recent inquiries have indicated major continuing problems in attracting and retaining both the civilian and military manpower necessary for effective defense operations.

CIVILIAN MANPOWER

The problem of obtaining sufficient qualified civilian manpower for the Defense Department is to a great extent part of the over-all problem of attracting and retaining civilian personnel for government service as a whole. We shall not attempt to deal with the familiar elements of this general problem here. Rather, we shall examine some of the critical problems which require continuing attention in order to meet the needs of the defense organization. These problems can be broken down into two categories: career civil service personnel; and politically appointed personnel.

Both the cause of many civilian personnel problems in the defense structure and the urgency for their resolution stem from the magnitude and complexity of the tasks befalling the Department of Defense today. The demands of national security have developed the Defense Department into the world's largest organization by any standard of measurement. Its personnel must make decisions and take actions which involve more people, more money, and more material than any of their counterparts in private industry. The activities of almost every private, commercial, and industrial enterprise in the nation's economy, from the simplest tasks to the most complex arts and sciences, have counterparts in Defense Department projects and operations. And it is upon the politically appointed civilian leaders of the defense structure that there falls the responsibility to assure effective management and civilian control over these gigantic operations, with the indispensable support of professional civilian and military staffs. Failure to resolve some of the personnel problems hampering the performance of defense tasks "will have a profound effect on our National Defense," as the Cordiner Committee stated in its report.[1]

The recent survey by the Cordiner Committee discovered that in the category of career civil service personnel the Defense Department is "suffering alarming losses of established career civilians, engineers, scientists, and managers."[2] In the field of top level career civilians it noted that turnover is increasing, quality is decreasing, and many positions are remaining unfilled. Moreover, it pointed out that the current losses of older, experienced personnel are being aggravated by the fact that the input of new college graduates at the professional starting level is inadequate, both in quality and quantity. The report concluded that, "The situation is fast becoming critical. Increasing losses of top talent and the lack of input at the bottom cannot long continue without serious effect upon the military establishment."[3]

Causes of these difficulties were traced by the Cordiner Committee to the inadequacy of three of the four basic incentives. Although the Defense Department mission offers real meaning to the work of the top-level career civilians, there are inadequacies in compensation, prestige, and chances for personal improvement.

The system of compensation for civil servants was highlighted as the basic cause of the problems at hand. Fixed by statute, it lacks the flexibility and response to competitive pressures which characterizes industrial systems. Yet the Defense Department is in direct competition with industry for scarce skills in top civilian scientific, engineering, and managerial positions. This competition is heightened by the technological revolution which has intensified the need for both scientific and managerial skills in new fields. An extensive survey of comparable positions in government and industry cited by the Cordiner Committee report showed that the pay of scientific, professional, and managerial personnel is 15 to 20 percent higher in industry than in government. Moreover, retirement and other so-called "fringe benefits," which formerly added to the attractiveness of government employment, were found to be matched or exceeded by those common in private industry today.[4]

In the area of personal improvement and opportunity for advancement the Cordiner Committee reported that, while high quality programs for the improvement and training of civilian technicians and supervisors had been developed in the Defense Department, comparable attention had not been given to the needs of senior civilian executives and scientists at the level of GS-12 and above.[5] The need for greater recognition in personnel programs of the necessity to maintain the prestige of senior civil service officials *vis-a-vis* their counterparts in non-government occupations was also noted. This was found to be especially true in the case of scientists and engineers.[6]

It is worthy of note that these career civilian personnel problems had previously been pointed out by the Hoover Commission in its *Report on Special Personnel Problems in the Department of Defense*[7] as deserving particular attention. Among other points, the Hoover Commission report recommended continued study and adjustment of the compensation system in terms of the civilian economy and comparable positions outside government. It pointed out the need for more adequate career opportunities which would challenge civilians to earn advancement to higher positions. It suggested increasing training of promising civilian executives by the Defense Department, both within the department and at outside institutions, in order to develop competent managers and technicians in sufficient numbers. The report also concluded that more careful differentiation could be made between military and civilian positions in management, support, and technical functions. It was argued that this would result in more efficient use of available civilian and military personnel, more effective operations, and clearer lines of opportunity for advancement for both military and civilians.

In addition to making such recommendations to improve the career civilian personnel system and make a civilian career in the defense establishment more attractive, the *Report on Special Personnel Problems* supported the recommendation of the 1955 Hoover Commission Task Force on Personnel and Civil Service that there be established a Senior Civil Service. The Senior Civil Service was conceived as being composed of the highest quality career civil servants in terms of experience, training, and capabilities. Individuals would be selected for this category at the pinnacle of the career ladder on a limited and highly selective basis. In short, it would represent an "elite corps" of top-level civil servants who had outstanding competence and broad experience. They would not be directly associated with any one agency but would be assigned from time to time to various agencies to perform specific tasks of particular difficulty or importance. The defense organization would be one of the agencies benefiting from their periodic assignments and from the element of prestige such a "corps" would add to government service.

We would emphasize in this connection that the problem of obtaining qualified civilian personnel to fill political positions and of retaining such personnel for a sufficient period of time continues to be a particularly acute one in the defense organization.

The political positions embrace some of the most important functions within the defense structure since their holders are the principal authorities for exercising civilian control over the armed forces. Under contemporary conditions of international affairs, the decisions encountered in exercising such civilian control are becoming increasingly complex and have tremendous impact on both our defense preparedness and our over-all national security posture. Ultimate Defense Department decisions regarding defense aspects of national security policies, relating political and economic conditions of the nation to military requirements, and equating political-military factors in the strategic direction of the armed forces are made by top civilian appointees. Yet recent experience has revealed considerable difficulty in obtaining personnel qualified for these positions and retaining them long enough for efficient and effective decision-making.

Some of the basic causes of this difficulty can again be traced to inadequate compensation, frustration of career development, and lack of prestige or recognition. For example, political appointees receive relatively low compensation in terms of salary offered similar executives in private industry. Moreover, "conflict of interest" restrictions (which often require appointees to sell valuable stock holdings), lack of previous experience in government, and various personal frustrations also affect attitudes toward government service.

Under prevailing conditions individuals accepting political appointment have a broad range of motivations. At the highest levels, duty, patriotism, and a desire for government experience are necessarily more predominant than the relatively low financial compensation. Prestige and financial reward are more influential at lower levels. In any event, highly personal motivations constitute significant factors in determining how effectively the defense organization will be able to fill its important political positions, and it is difficult to develop an effective procedure or system for supplying such highly qualified manpower under these conditions. It becomes even more difficult when the element of prestige has been decreased by the proliferation of political positions in the Defense Department bearing the rank of assistant secretary (currently there are about 40 such positions) and when financial compensation is hardly comparable to similar top civilian executive positions.

The 1955 Hoover Commission *Report on Special Personnel Problems in the Department of Defense* made recommendations toward alleviating some of these problems. It called for increasing the compensation of the Secretaries and Assistant Secretaries of the Defense Department and for increased recognition by individuals called to these positions, and their employers, of the importance of such service and the necessity to commit themselves for longer periods of time. It urged clarification and simplification of conflict of interest laws. Furthermore, it suggested that means be found to give potential political appointees experience in political positions at lower levels, and opportunities for advancement in political positions, before they are placed in top positions of political responsibility.

Thus far little has been done, save for increases in compensation, to carry out such proposals. Obtaining and retaining adequate civilian manpower, both career and political, continues to present the Defense Department with basic problems. Successful resolution of this issue is as important as achieving a well-balanced supply of military manpower in the fighting forces.

MILITARY MANPOWER

The quantity and quality of military personnel required in our armed forces must be directly related to the nature of the principal military tasks confronting the defense establishment, especially to the requirement for a capability for instantaneous reaction. Since there would be neither time nor favorable conditions to permit the conduct of mobilization after an exchange of nuclear blows, and since a deterrent to limited local wars depends heavily upon a capability for flexible but rapid counteraction, the United States must maintain sufficient armed and trained manpower at peak readiness. The current world situation places an incalculable premium on highly trained forces ready to utilize instantaneously the concepts and weapons stemming from the rapid advances in military technology.

It is a paradoxical fact that, at a time when the United States is spending more for peacetime defense in both absolute and relative terms than it ever has in its history, it is experiencing great difficulty in attracting to and retaining in the armed services the high quality personnel which the advanced weapons systems inceasingly require. In their testimony before the Symington Committee in the spring of 1956 all the services testified that their manpower problem was one of the most acute with which they had to contend.

Recognition of this crucial problem gave rise to the appointment in May 1956 of the Advisory Committee on Professional and Technical Compensation, with Ralph J. Cordiner, President of the General Electric Company, as chairman, to advise the Defense Department regarding administrative and legislative measures which would enhance the ability of the military services to attract and retain the scientific, professional, and technical skills required today and in the future. Particular attention was given to the effect of present compensation practices on the problem of personnel procurement and retention. In its report of March 1957 on compensation for the armed services[8] the Committee spelled out some of the elements of the problem:

Since the end of fighting in Korea, the number one problem of the military forces has been excessive personnel turnover. . . .

. . . we have been unable to retain the people we train long enough for them to gain the experience required to meet the qualitative needs of the Services. This applies to both officer and enlisted personnel and is of critical importance in the higher skills requiring the longest and most expensive training. Individuals possessing the more easily produced skills are remaining in service in greater numbers than the higher skilled.

Strategy and tactics are undergoing radical change in anticipation of future developments. The machinery of modern defense is becoming even more fantastically complex and technical, and the weapons system of today is regarded as but a passing stage in the headlong rush of technological discovery. Yet, strangely enough, the principles and practices which guide the recruitment, motivation, compensation, and development of men have not changed substantially in the history of our country. The times call for a sharply increased investment of time, thought and money in the development of men.

Although the Army, the Navy, and the Marine Corps—and to a much lesser degree the Air Force—all maintain and depend on inactive components, the major burden of responsibility for the military preparedness of the nation has been and is now being borne by the active duty forces, which include both regulars and sizeable increments of draftees, National Guardsmen, and reserve officers. Whatever the present value and future roles of the reserve elements, it is to the career personnel that the nation must look for military leadership and for the bulk of the forces needed for immediate response to enemy action. Moreover, many of the same factors which impel individuals to a career in the regular forces act upon and influence those in the reserve components. Accordingly, when studying motivation and morale we may ask ourselves: How, then, have the professional forces fared?

Despite growing national dependence upon professional military personnel, the regular armed services have experienced increasing difficulty in obtaining, training, and retaining the skilled professionals they need to perform their tasks. As noted in the January 1957 report of the Symington Committee:

Air Force witnesses labeled as their No. 1 deficiency the inability to obtain, train, and retain skilled personnel. Army and Navy witnesses also pointed out the seriousness of this growing problem.

Principal problems encountered by the services include high rates of turn-over with low re-enlistment levels, shortage of experienced officers, rising training costs stemming from increasingly complex technical equipment and the high turnover rate, and difficulties in attracting and retaining technically and professionally qualified personnel.

The testimony before the Symington Committee of Brigadier General Horace Wade, Director of Personnel, Strategic Air Command, is particularly illustrative of some of the problems:

In January 1953 we were 80 per cent effectively manned. This has now regressed to 78 per cent. This does not tell the complete story. We are talking about the over-all manning for all career fields. In some career fields and skills our effective manning is below 50 per cent.[10]

... In other words, 71 per cent of our strength will have less than 2 years in the Strategic Air Command. The majority of these first- and second-year people will be inexperienced and will lack SAC know-how. The people whom we have to rely on to do the training and get the job done come to approximately 29 per cent. . . .[11]

The testimony of Captain David Martineau, Navy Bureau of Personnel, before the same committee included the following statements:

. . . There are two principal problems in the officers Corps: (1) the shortage of pilots and (2) the shortage of experienced officers with 4 to 10 years' commissioned service.

Now as to enlisted levels. . . . At the present time some 210,000, or 36 per cent of the total, have 4 or more years of naval service. The remaining 64 per cent are in their first enlistment, with less than 4 years' service.

The re-enlistment rate of those completing their first 4-year enlistment is presently averaging only 10 per cent.[12]

Major General Booth, Assistant Deputy Chief of Staff for Personnel, pointed out to the same committee that 71 per cent of the Army's enlisted strength is composed of personnel with less than 3 years' duty, and that law requires the Army to accept 2-year enlistments to coincide with the 2-year obligation of the draftee. As a result, he stated:

This situation causes an endless parade of people through units which are required to be combat-ready, making it nearly impossible for commanders to achieve a sufficiently high standard of operational efficiency.[13]

The causes underlying these difficulties in maintaining the professional armed forces at adequate levels of preparedness have been receiving increasing attention. During his testimony in the course of the Symington Committee hearings, Lt. General Emmett O'Donnel, Jr., Air Force Deputy Chief of Staff for Personnel, noted some of the reasons for the inability to retain professional military personnel in the Air Force. His reasons, which in effect apply to all the services, were summarized in the report of the Symington Committee, in the following manner:

The basic reasons for both officers and airmen leaving the service after considerable investment in their training are: substantially higher salaries paid in private industry, poor housing conditions, inadequate dependent medical care, need for survivor benefit legislation, insufficient severance pay for reserve officers, better working conditions and working hours in private industry, shifting geographical locations interfering with family life, need for restoration of commissary and base exchange rights, lack of education benefits, inadequate pay structure with lack of provision for adjustments of cost of living increases.[14]

Many of these factors are related to the broad problem of adequate compensation, but they also imply inadequate advancement opportunities and failure on the part of Congress, if not the public, to recognize and improve the conditions under which the personnel of the armed forces perform their vital task.

The most recent study of problems related to attracting and retaining qualified professional military personnel in the armed services, conducted by the Cordiner Committee, also concentrated on the issue of adequate pay. However, it noted that "compensation practices are not alone to blame, nor can they alone provide a final or easy solution" to the problems at hand.[15] The Cordiner Committee gave particular attention to the impact of rapid technological advance upon the military services in terms of the resulting increased demands for scientific, professional, and technical manpower today and in the future. It emphasized the need to attract and retain highly qualified personnel to cope with the complex weapons and the problems of modern warfare. Pointing out that the development of men qualified to perform the professional and technical tasks of the modern armed forces required considerable "lead time" in experience and considerable investment in training, the Committee found that this development process was being frustrated by a compensation system which "discourages re-enlistments and frustrates even the devoted career man."[16]

In comparing compensation received by military personnel and civilians in comparable positions, the Cordiner Committee analyzed enlisted and officer personnel separately. Particularly in regard to technician positions in civilian life and of enlisted personnel, the Committee found that:

1. The Service man concluding his first tour of duty can normally expect higher pay in starting a civilian job than he received in Service.

2. Promotional opportunities in civilian life are greater than those afforded the career enlisted man.

3. Fringe benefits no longer favor the enlisted man over his civilian counterpart, except for the 20-year retirement option.[17]

In addition, it was found that, particularly in the field of new and expanding technologies, such as electronics, servicemen upon leaving the service take civilian jobs similar to their military positions more often than jobs in other occupational fields.

Cordiner Committee recommendations for improvement of the compensation system for enlisted personnel were pointed principally at correcting the imbalance in military personnel resulting from imbalanced re-enlistments. Career incentive legislation passed during 1954, 1955, and 1956 had contributed to a general increase in the re-enlistment rates during those years from 24 per cent in 1954 to 43 per cent in 1956. However, men in the occupational specialties requiring long and expensive training and experience, technically complex positions in which the services require the highest re-enlistment rate, were re-enlisting after their first tour of duty at only *one-half* the rate of those in the less complex and more easily trained categories.[18]

The Cordiner Committee concluded that the existing compensation practices of the armed services were such an inhibiting factor in obtaining qualified personnel that, "A fundamental modernization of the personnel compensation system of the Armed Forces constitutes the basic first step in the process of the development of the highly skilled force needed today and in the future."[19] Accordingly, the committee set forth certain "modern compensation principles" to guide the improvement of the system. Among other features, these included relating the compensation to the state of the national economy in order that the military career personnel would enjoy rises in the living standard, making compensation reasonably comparable to that paid in the civilian economy to persons with similar positions and occupations, designing the compensation system to encourage meritorious performance and advancement rather than survival for a lengthy period of time, and recognition in terms of compensation for special skills and performance.

The principal problems revealed by the Cordiner Committee in fulfilling current requirements for officer personnel were serious deficits in both experience and quality. Apparent inability to retain younger officers entering since World War II has resulted in a shortage of 28 per cent below service requirements in the 4- to 14-year service group, a group which is particularly important because it represents more than half the total officer requirement and because its members, such as pilots, deck officers, and company commanders, constitute the backbone of operational units. A special study of Army lieutenants revealed that the average efficiency of those electing to continue in the service after completion of their obligatory tour is lower than the average for career officers, indicating that the more qualified junior officers with higher potential return to civilian life at the first opportunity. It was felt that the less qualified officers at the junior level, which is in most direct contact with the troops, contributed to low levels of re-enlistments among enlisted personnel. As with enlisted personnel, the Cordiner Committee concluded that retention of officers can be directly related to the compensation system.

Up to the present the lack of sufficient numbers of qualified and experienced junior officers has been compensated for by the substantial resources of trained and experienced officers carried over from World War II. However, within six years many of these World War II officers will have completed 20 years service and will leave active duty. Unless the trend among junior officers changes, the lack of sufficient experienced and qualified officers will be intensified and the armed forces will face a severe depreciation of top quality leaders.[20]

In this connection it should be noted that obtaining an adequate supply of professional officers in the future is likely to remain a continuing problem, as indicated by the rate of officer resignations by graduates of the military academies, which has been increasing rapidly since 1951. For example, it is estimated that about one fourth of the 1953 and 1954 classes of West Point will have resigned within five years after graduation. The class of 1950 had only 11.5 per cent resignation after five years, but the 1951 class had 20.9 per cent. Similarly, the Annapolis class of 1952 lost 21 per cent through resignation by June 30, 1956, and Air Force appointees from the West Point Class of 1952 registered a 20 per cent resignation rate by June 30, 1957.[21]

Although shortcomings in the compensation system for the personnel of our regular armed forces, with related impairment of advancement opportunities, have been demonstrated by the findings of the inquiries mentioned above, it would be shortsighted to overlook other factors which undermine the motivation and morale of the fighting men forming our first line of defense.

Disunity in a supposedly unified Defense Department directly affects the spirit and morale of its military manpower. An organization which fosters service rivalries and suspicions tends to make the professional military man more concerned with the survival of his own service than with a joint effort in the over-all defense and national interest. When time is consumed in competing with rival services, his loyalties become even more closely wedded to the service of his origin through which he must seek his advancement. Such conditions are not only detrimental to the effectiveness of defense planning, programs, and operations but also frustrate the able military professional attempting to serve the over-all security interests of his country; and they undermine his feeling of performing a worthwhile and meaningful job.

The career military man also becomes discouraged when he feels that appropriate military advice is not receiving adequate consideration in the councils of the Defense Department, and consequently the national government, responsible for deciding the basic issues of our national survival. We have noted earlier how the multiplicity of staff levels, the tendency for policy staffs at the Office of the Secretary of Defense level and in military department secretariats to exercise direct operational control, the trend toward increasing centralized civilian control, and the inability of the Joint Chiefs of Staff structure to produce agreed military advice have obstructed the channels for expressing professional military advice and have often resulted in basic military decisions being made by civilian staffs. Under such conditions, a military career seems to some less desirable than operating in a civilian capacity within the Defense Department.

The effects of lack of recognition within the Defense Department are heightened by continuing public attitudes within our society which further undermine the attractiveness of the military career. There is still a strong undercurrent in American social thought which regards the career military man with suspicion. The traditional distrust of large standing forces expressed throughout United States history, and clichés regarding the rigid, militaristic "military mind," have left their imprint both on the public and on Congress. On the other hand, it is an ironic fact that at the same time that the military profession is confronting these obstacles which reduce its attractiveness as a career, men with a professional military background are being increasingly sought by private industry, which has apparently found them highly capable executives.

The facts and figures we have cited hardly need elaboration. The hard-core spirit and integrity of the nation's professional armed forces are beyond question. Their awareness of the imperative need for total readiness is unimpaired. But, for reasons largely beyond their control, they face, in a very real sense, the threat of a kind of starvation at a time when they must bear a maximum responsibility.

To date there has been little recognition, either in the government or outside it, of the vital need for changes both in the factors adversely affecting service morale and motivation and in the system of compensation. With the exception of proficiency pay for enlisted men, the Cordiner proposals remained buried within the Executive Branch until the post-sputnik furore focused attention upon them. Moreover, while Congress has revealed an increasing respect for military advice on problems of national security, this has not been matched by a willingness to pass the legislation necessary to provide the salary and "fringe benefits," such as health, education, housing, and other family support, which are basic to maintaining the military profession as an attractive career. At the present time there seems to be a need to enhance respect for the military as a profession and otherwise to increase its attractiveness. If this is not done, the nation is in danger of diluting its reservoir of qualified professional military manpower to such an extent that we shall be no longer capable of performing the military tasks essential to our national survival.

Footnotes

1. *Report of the Defense Advisory Committee on Professional and Technical Compensation*, Vol. II, *Civilian Personnel*, Washington: G.P.O., 1957, p. 4. Hereafter referred to as *Cordiner Committee Report: Civilian Personnel*.
2. *Ibid.*, p. 4.
3. *Ibid.*, p. 5.
4. *Ibid.*, pp. 5-6.
5. *Ibid.*, p. 10.
6. *Ibid.*, p. 9.
7. Commission on Organization of the Executive Branch of the Government (Second Hoover Commission), *Special Personnel Problems in the Department of Defense*, Washington: G.P.O., 1955.
8. *Highlights of a Modern Concept of Compensation for Personnel of the Uniformed Services*, Defense Advisory Committee on Professional and Technical Compensation, Washington: G.P.O., March 1957, pp. 1 and 5.
9. *Symington Committee Hearings on Airpower*, p. 28.
10. *Ibid.*, p. 69.
11. *Ibid.*, p. 73.
12. *Ibid.*, pp. 1042-1043.
13. *Ibid.*, p. 867.
14. *Ibid.*, p. 31.
15. Report of the Defense Advisory Committee on Professional and Technical Compensation, *Highlights of a Modern Concept of Compensation for Personnel of the Uniformed Services*, *op. cit.*, p. 4.
16. *Ibid.*
17. *Ibid.* p. 107.
18. *Ibid.*, pp. 28-29.
19. *Ibid.*, p. 6.
20. *Ibid.*, pp. 60-65.
21. *The Army Times*, Vol. XVII, No. 51 (July 27, 1957), p. 188.

Eleven

A SUMMARY EVALUATION

The preceding six chapters have dealt with specific problems and shortcomings in the operation of the Department of Defense. It has been argued, for instance, that the cost of our military program is increased by the fact that we have no agreed strategy for dealing with the wide range of military problems confronting us and, hence, no integrated concept for the development and utilization of our armed forces. Evidence has been cited to the effect that we are slow both in introducing new weapons into our military arsenal and in resolving differences over who shall use them and where and against what targets they shall be used. Attention has been directed to the overlapping of perhaps obsolete service roles and missions, and to the problems of effective and efficient civilian control of the military. Here we shall attempt, in terms of our critical yardstick, a summary evaluation of the total performance of the Department of Defense as presently organized and operated.

Before so doing, it is essential to make one point clear: the intent of our judgments is not to criticize responsible agencies or individuals past or present. There is no question as to the fact that strenuous efforts have been and are being made to improve the effectiveness of the Department of Defense and the governmental machinery of which it is a part. It is even possible to recall the earlier statement that "more has been accomplished toward achieving truly effective teamwork for national defense in the past ten years than in the previous one hundred and fifty"[1] without negating the conclusion that much still needs to be done if our existing organization is to be fully effective in discharging the manifold responsibilities laid upon it.

We would emphasize, then, that the sole purpose of the following evaluation is to establish a framework for future decisions.

CIVILIAN CONTROL

In general, the major efforts to assure effective civilian control have been made in the field of administration. Personnel policy, methods of procurement, systems of supply and maintenance, and similar "business activities" of the Department of Defense and of the military services have been placed under close control and supervision by civilian officials and staffs. While the military, by reason of their operational requirements, still have major responsibilities in the logistical field, they are increasingly subject to detailed policy direction by a civilian secretariat and a largely civilian staff. In fact, some authorities have gone so far as to recommend establishing throughout the Department of Defense the system used by the Navy (where producer logistics are directly under the management of a civilian under-secretary) and granting to civilian officials power to manage and control all supply and service activities.[2]

It is questionable whether increased civilian supervision of Defense Department activities has really led to effective civilian control.

The difficulties in obtaining well-qualified people with the requisite leadership capabilities for government posts, the relatively short tenure of those who enter the higher ranks of government service, and the size and complexities of the defense apparatus all combine to make civilian direction of "business activities" less effective than it might be. More important, the areas in which policy control is of paramount importance are not administration or logistics but strategic concepts, war plans, and force requirements, fields which the military regard as peculiarly their own domain; and there is still ineffective civilian control over these areas.

It is clear that, since power over the military services is divided between the executive branch and the Congress, which has no real means of assessing and judging between alternate strategic concepts or other implementing programs, civilian control in the sense of relating basic military policy to national purpose poses a long-range problem. In the whole area of planning and implementing military policies and programs the diversity of civilian authorities to which the military are constitutionally and legally responsible obscures the appropriate role for the military both in their advisory and command responsibilities.

Part of the reason for the relative ineffectiveness of civilian policy control within the executive branch lies in the staff apparatus at Department of Defense level. The Secretary of Defense has no organized secretariat, no office to coordinate civil and military policy across the board, and no agency to evaluate military requirements for men, money, and material. In brief, there exists no civilian counterpart (or counterpoise) to the Joint Chiefs of Staff. As a result of the fragmentation of authority among the civilian assitants of the Secretary, many decisions are necessarily made with little knowledge of their broader ramifications or consequences. Whatever the competence of the Secretary of Defense, better staff organization would increase both his official capabilities and his range of control.

The efforts made thus far to increase civilian control over the military have had certain undesirable side effects. First of all, attempts to increase civilian control through the extension of civilian supervision have resulted in an over-layering and over-centralization of the defense establishment, with consequent delays and inefficiencies in operation. Second, they have led to the establishment of divers channels of communication and control, to a fragmentation of the decision-making authority, and to diffuse and divided loyalties among both military and civilian personnel. Thirdly, they have caused adverse reactions among those military personnel who consider the scope of their authority unduly diminished and their competence questioned. Lastly, efforts to extend civilian control, coupled with the growing scope and complexities of militiary affairs, have led to the simultaneous operation of civilian and military authority in the same fields of activity and the consequent blurring of lines between them. Whether good or bad in itself, this practice is the cause of considerable personal competition and some dissatisfaction on both sides.

It must be concluded, then, that despite extensive or intensive civilian supervision of military operations, the proper kind and extent of civilian control over the Department of Defense is a problem still to be resolved. Neither Congress nor the Executive Branch possesses the means to judge fully the implications of policy decisions, to relate force levels and programs to particular strategic concepts, and to control wisely the rate of growth (or decline) of expenditures in support of various programs. The crucial question is what can and should be done to make civilian control possible without vitiating the over-all effectiveness of our defense establishment or unduly restricting the military in the execution of their heavy responsibilities.

PARTICIPATION IN NATIONAL POLICY FORMULATION

By its very nature the Department of Defense is so constituted as to make difficult its effective and coordinated participation in the formulation and implementation of national policy. Not only is it composed of three separate military services; it also contains an extremely powerful and influential office with quasi-legal status as an independent entity—

the Joint Chiefs of Staff.[3] Indeed, the Joint Chiefs have access to the National Security Council which is separate from that of their nominal superior, the Secretary of Defense, the only instance in government of such a situation. Moreover, by its method of handling defense legislation and appropriations and by writing into the National Security Act the right of the service chiefs and departmental secretaries to appeal over the head of the Secretary of Defense[4] Congress has insured that independent voices shall be heard on various policy issues. Thus, neither organizationally nor politically can the Department of Defense operate on the same basis as an integrated agency such as the Department of State.

The problems created by a diffuse organization as they affect Defense Department determination and implementation of national policy are complicated by the ambiguity of the language in which policy decisions are phrased. Despite the most strenuous of efforts, it has been almost impossible to obtain from the National Security Council and its related agencies more than statements of general policy guidance in which the vagueness of language may be acceptable to the various participants but is inadequate to direct the integration of various programs into a cohesive and effective effort. In fact, there is serious question as to whether military program formulation and implementation are adequately related to policy either timewise or in substance. Moreover, it is nearly impossible to determine from the budget of the Defense Department those items which are authorized by any specific major National Security Council program or policy.[5] The result, in the words of one study group, is that

In the absence of means to consider, at the NSC level, the relative balance among programs, the real decisions appear to be made within the Service staffs of the Defense Department. Programs are often continued as a result of past momentums and because there exist powerful convictions within the Services to support on-going activities. New programs, by contrast, often suffer from a lack of such support.[6]

In other words, even the President, with the help of the National Security Council, has been unable to bring about programs for the implementation of strategic concepts compatible with national policy. This has been aggravated by the fact that, since the processes of national security policy formulation are not coordinated with the budget cycle, objectives and means are inadequately correlated.

In addition to the problems in national security planning caused by the vagueness of policy directives, the lack of correlation between policy and programs, the heavy impact on strategic decisions of Congressional legislation and appropriations, and the organizational dichotomy in the Defense Department, there is another factor to be considered. Unlike the heads of other agencies, the Secretary of Defense cannot be simply the spokesman for the policies and programs recommended by his subordinates; except in times of recognized crisis the gap between requirements and available resources is too large. Normally he is virtually compelled not only to present compromise proposals on national security requirements but also to serve as the instrument for the further reduction of military expenditures while at the same time formulating programs which ostensibly support national policy. The result is largely to deny him the support of his peers and the confidence of his subordinates, since neither can be satisfied by the position he takes. Although the elements of personal competence, persuasiveness, and forcefulness undoubtedly enter into the balance, the Secretary of Defense is almost bound to be weighted down by the difference between increasing requirements and constant, or diminishing, resources. Under these circumstances, fully effective Defense Department participation in national security planning is difficult whatever the organizational changes made.

These observations suggest one of the Secretary of Defense's principal functions and responsibilities—the absolute necessity for his continued appearances before the Congress and certain executive agencies in the varied roles of suppliant, expositor, advocate, and defender of the policies underlying national security, defense needs, methods, and goals. This is one of the most exacting obligations of the Secretary, and a great deal of the success of the defense effort depends on his competence in this field and his ability to gain the trust of both parties by operating the Department in a strictly nonpolitical fashion.

MAXIMUM READINESS

There is not much question that our armed forces today are more powerful and better prepared than at any period in our peacetime history. Although there are admitted difficulties in maintenance and in the flow of trained personnel, our Strategic Air Command is in a high state of operational readiness, with some elements constantly on the alert. Our naval combat elements, our tactical air and ground forces overseas, and, to a lesser extent, those in the United States are constantly being trained, exercised, and maneuvered to keep up a keen edge of effectiveness. Despite equipment which is not in all instances of the most modern types and a personnel system which, especially in the Army, actually inhibits combat efficiency, the tactical elements of the armed forces are undoubtedly able to react to enemy attack with great speed and effectiveness. Whether these forces are mentioned at a level adequate to meet our many world-wide commitments is open to debate.

It is also questionable whether we have developed an adequate system for the command and control of these ready forces. The existing mechanism for the correlation of information, for the preparation and presentation of coordinated staff advice, and for speedy decision by civilian authority on politico-military questions of national importance is cumbersome. Moreover, our diffuse and complicated channels of communication, both within the services and between the Commander-in-Chief, the Department of Defense, and the field commands, delay the receipt of information, hamper the execution of policy decisions, and tend to separate strategic direction of operations from policy control—a tendency which is reinforced by our growing reliance upon preplanned and relatively inflexible retaliatory attacks. Grave doubts have been expressed as to whether our system is adequate for the control of military operations in either general or local war.[7]

The problem of speeding up the machinery of command and assuring in its operation the precision necessitated by today's far-flung and complex military security requirements is a formidable one. Nevertheless, it must be faced.

SOUND STRATEGIC DOCTRINE

As the Department of Defense now functions, the difficulties inherent in drawing up strategic plans which embrace the entire spectrum of possible hostilities and which simultaneously provide both for immediate readiness and for future preparedness are compounded by organizational and procedural patterns which tend to vitiate sound strategic planning, to perpetuate service rivalries, and to cause something less than full consideration of both national policy objectives and the forward movement of technology.

The fact that the future of each service is intimately tied up with the strategic concept adopted makes even specific operational details the subject of endless argument. Under the committee system of staff procedures the result is a compromise in which, although one service may have the edge, each of the others gets something—if only a duplicate of what another service may have. In joint planning, emphasis upon giving each service control of all the means essential to the prosecution of its mission results both in endless duplication of forces, installations, and projects and the simultaneous development of mutually contradictory programs. As long as each service sees its future tied to the espousal of a particular concept or the development of certain weapons, rational decisions concerning strategic doctrine and roles and missions will be difficult.

Although planning under the existing structure has led to an increasingly influential role for the Chairman of the Joint Chiefs of Staff in advising the Secretary of Defense upon the resolution of differing views on strategic concepts and plans, the chairman lacks the comprehensive, coordinated staff support necessary for him to perform this role effectively.

Among the illustrations of consequent inadequacies in strategic planning which come readily to mind, at least in hindsight, are those which deal with concepts for the employment of nuclear weapons. When, in 1950, the United States and its NATO allies hammered out both a strategic concept for the defense of Western Europe and plans to raise and equip the forces needed for that defense, little consideration was apparently given to the tactical use of atomic weapons by either side. Whatever the cause, and whatever the difficulties of prejudgment, the fact remains that the forces raised under the initial and modified NATO concepts have in some respects become obsolescent even while they are being equipped. As Admiral Radford testified, our Mutual Defense Assistance Programs "were embarked on under conditions a good deal different from those today."[8]

Were this all, it could be excused by the difficulties of forejudging developments in a period of rapid technological change. However, the plans for the defense of the NATO area still reflect a dichotomy between conflicting strategic concepts. Both the Army's plan for the mobilization, training, and movement of divisions to overseas areas and the Navy's elaborate mechanisms for convoy-escort, mine-sweeping, and anti-submarine activities seem incompatible with a concept which envisions the large-scale, mutual use of nuclear weapons against ports, communications centers, depots, arsenals, and other similar facilities. Conversely, the Air Force position that preparedness for general war implies the ability to handle conflicts of lesser magnitude would appear to be opposed to both Army and Navy measures to prepare for the possibility of limited war in such areas as Southeast Asia and the Middle East.

Other instances could be cited to show both the time lag in our decisions and the lack of foresight in our declarations of policy. The policy decision to retaliate against Communist aggression in a manner and at times of our own choosing, first announced by Secretary of State

Dulles in March of 1953, implicitily rested upon the superiority of the United States in nuclear weapons and delivery systems. But in that same year the Soviets exploded the first thermonuclear bomb; and scarcely two years later, at Geneva, we tacitly recognized the fact that growing Soviet capabilities to attack the United States made impossible a liberal application of the policy of "massive retaliation." Similarly, the various proposals for the "thinning out" of United States forces abroad, which had such severe repercussions in the summer of 1956, apparently represented something less than a timely and balanced appraisal of either the political situation abroad or the relative trends in the United States-Soviet military capabilities. This was particularly the case in our 1957 announcements of plans to reduce our armed forces in the midst of disarmament negotiations.

In part the difficulties mentioned spring from service rivalry, in part from failure to make adequate and timely evaluation of technological developments, and in part from the time required to carry out even the best-laid and most foresighted programs. Whatever the cause, the judgment must be made that our mechanism to formulate strategic doctrine responsive to national policy has shown grave defects of operation.

ORDERLY INNOVATION

There is considerable evidence that in the development, procurement, and integration of new weapons, surely one of the most important military functions of our time, the Soviet Union is now, on balance, very nearly equal to us and in some fields such as guided missiles possibly ahead of us.[9] This is in direct contrast to the situation at hand immediately after World War II, when the Soviet Union was far behind the United States, especially in the development of nuclear weapons, jet aircraft, heavy bombers, and all the complex equipment of modern airpower. Significantly, the Soviets appear to have been progressing at almost twice our pace, as indicated by the speed with which they followed up our initial development of atomic and thermonuclear weapons with similar devices of their own.

In part, the relative speed of the Soviet advance is due to the slowness of our pace. It took us seven years to bring the B-52 bomber from planning stage to initial production,[10] and it will require another four years to completely equip with this airplane the heavy bomber wings in our Strategic Air Command. It took almost as long to produce the Army's anti-aircraft missile, Nike Ajax; and other advanced weapons such as Snark and Bomarc have gone through similar periods of gestation. The result of such time lags in a period of rapid technological change is that the usuable life of weapons is shortened almost to the vanishing point. In some instances, equipment is obsolescent before it is even produced, much less in the hands of troops.[11]

Examination of our present procedures reveals avoidable causes for the delays in this process which so closely concerns our national security.

In the opinion of qualified observers, one such cause is the failure to effect a closer relation between research and development and military planning, that is, to make full use of available scientific advisors[12] and of advisory elements such as the Weapons Systems Evaluation Group. Another cause is the relative scarcity of research and development funds and shifting emphasis in their use; for example, research on a nuclear-powered aircraft has twice been dropped and twice been reinstated. A third cause is the complex process required to obtain approval of, funding for, and evaluation of research and development projects—a process which is complicated by interservice rivalry over the development and use of various weapons systems.

The process of innovation is currently delayed by the duplicatory research and development programs carried out by the various services and by the existence of "vested interests" both in the services and in related civilian businesses.[13] The appointment of a "missiles czar" to effect coordination in one field gives evidence of official concern with the problem; but the fact that the Army and the Marine Corps are developing different tanks, motor vehicles, helicopters, and light weapons to meet basically similar requirements indicates that much still remains to be done.[14]

It must be concluded that, at a time when we must foster innovation in all defense programs, not merely the technological and weapons fields, the current structure of the Defense Department is characterized by bureaucratic procedures which tend to suppress creative thought and action, and that the views of our most qualified scientists, largely restricted to an advisory capacity, are ineffectively channeled into actual defense programs and policy decisions.

FLEXIBLE ADJUSTMENTS IN MISSIONS

At the present time each of the three services is basically responsible for conducting operations against its enemy counterpart. Under these circumstances it is not only natural but inevitable that each service, confronted with essentially different and fragmented tasks, has developed both a distinct strategic concept and a differing order of priorities from that of the other two services.

That this is no isolated criticism is borne out by the testimony of the military chiefs themselves. As General Twining stated in a discussion of the contribution made by naval airpower to our strategic striking force, "I don't know where those [Navy] carriers are going to be . . . so the Strategic Air Command has to be just as big, just as strong, and just as ready, regardless of this Navy contribution."[15] And General Taylor, defending the Army's development of a 1500-mile missile, argued that,

The primary function of the Air Force is to destroy enemy air power and for the Navy to destroy enemy naval power. . . . If you accept the fact that the Army exists to destroy hostile armies, then any missiles which would destroy hostile ground forces should be available to the Army.[16]

It is true, as Admiral Radford stated, that the

roles and missions paper is a guide for the development of peacetime forces. . . . It does not mean that a unified commander in time of war, or a commander in the field in time of war, cannot use an Army man or an Army unit to do something that the roles and missions paper says that the Air Force has the primary mission to do or vice versa.[17]

Nevertheless, there have been no basic changes in the roles and missions of the several services since they were first written in 1948, and only minor changes in operational responsibilities.[18]

Some progress has been made in the establishment of functional military missions, largely through the medium of the unified and specified commands. Perhaps the most successful effort has been in the field of air defense, where long study of this topic by the National Security Council and pressure by civilian scientific advisors resulted in the establishment of an air defense command. Ultimately this evolved into a triservice organization, the North American Air Defense Command, whose Commander-in-Chief has the responsibility for "stating his operational need for new and improved weapons systems and for recommending to the Joint Chiefs of Staff all new installations of any type."[19] Thus, in this one instance, the problem of determining roles and missions in a given field and planning for their implementation has been taken from the two services most vitally concerned, as well as from the Joint Chiefs of Staff, and has been given to an ostensibly neutral unified command.

However, not even this move has served to end interservice wrangling over their respective air defense missions. And when we look beyond this single example we find that not even this elementary step has been taken with respect to other unified and specified commands. This is particularly true with respect to military preparations for waging limited wars with flexible United States striking forces. Despite the attention which has been devoted to this problem, our present inability to develop agreed strategic concepts, the overlapping assignments of service roles and missions, and the present devious command channels continue to inhibit our ability to plan or conduct joint operations with flexible forces to meet this task.

MAXIMUM COST-EFFICIENCY

Virtually every study, report, or budgetary hearing on the Department of Defense tends to cite examples of waste, over-procurement, or poor handling of material, with consequent cost to the taxpayer. Without challenging the truth of these statements it is suggested that they tend to overlook the fact that the excess cost of national defense derives from quite different causes—causes relating to fiscal procedures and to duplications of forces and installations resulting from overlapping and frequently contradictory service roles and missions.

With respect to fiscal procedures, we would note that efforts to obtain increased economy have had side effects which are not conducive to efficient operation. First of all, the three to five years which normally elapse between preparation of a budget and the expenditure of the sums obtained has meant that monies were frequently requested—and appropriated—for programs which were no longer valid. Conversely, the imposition of budgetary ceilings, or very sharp cuts in service requests, have frequently necessitated a complete reworking of the budget, with consequent delays in the development and implementation of programs. Thirdly, the practice whereby appropriations must be rejustified to the defense comptroller and the Bureau of the Budget before allocations of funds can be obtained has further hampered operations.

In terms of cost, however, perhaps the greatest single factor has been the inability of the Joint Chiefs of Staff and of the military departments to agree upon a joint logistics plan which will support an agreed strategic concept. Although the Joint Chiefs of Staff are charged by the National Security Act with the "preparation of joint logistic plans and assignment to the military services of logistic responsibilities in accordance with such plans"[20] they have not always been able to reach agreement in time on the annual plans needed for program guidance. Accordingly, each of the three services has used its own "unilateral" plan, based on its own concepts of strategy and its own estimates of requirements. To the extent that there have been duplications or inconsistencies among the three sets of plans, these have been projected into all subsequent estimates,[21] including those for mobilization planning. Although both the appropriate Department of Defense offices and the

Joint Chiefs of Staff do review major material and personnel requirements of the military forces, the Joint Chiefs of Staff do not review the budget as a whole;[22] nor do they relate the various service budgets to the strategic concepts and military programs which the budgets are designed to support. In the absence of agreed military advice, civilian budget staffs in effect resolve differing military concepts and plans through their budget determinations. Under these circumstances it is relatively easy for both major duplications and large gaps to appear in the service budgets presented to the Secretary of Defense.

All that has been said should not minimize the fact that considerable economies have been obtained through "squeezing the water" out of service programs. However, there is some question whether the methods used for this process have not cost more than they have saved and have failed to touch the basic causes of waste and duplication. In all probability, major economies are realizable only through realignments of functions which might preclude costly competitive efforts among the three services.

MOTIVATION AND MORALE

It is obvious that the Defense Department must make effective use of that most valuable of all resources, skilled and competent manpower; for military manpower forms the heart of the fighting machine and civilian manpower is the key to effective management. The effective military utilization of weapons and equipment developed by our scientists and engineers requires skilled and competent personnel, as evidenced by the recent report of the Cordiner Committee. As also evidenced by that report, the armed forces are not retaining the personnel they need either for research or for operations.[23]

In part this may be due to the traditional United States distaste for military service; in part to the strains put upon family life by the requirements of the military profession. In large measure it is undoubtedly caused by the 50 per cent decline over the last forty years in the real income of field grade and general officers.[24] The individual in the services who is told he cannot expect pay increases because efforts to make military service financially as appealing as civilian life could put an intolerable burden upon the treasury naturally reacts with some bitterness to this attitude.[25]

While the problem of retaining high-caliber personnel is to some extent beyond resolution by organizational changes, these do have a bearing on such intangibles as morale, service pride, and job satisfaction. There is some evidence to the effect that over-centralization, over-layering, and the disheartening complexities of staff operations tend to reduce the sense of accomplishment of many of our officers, and hence contribute both to inefficiency and to lowered morale and motivation.[26] The net result has been to make military service less attractive, particularly among officers assigned to higher level service staffs or to joint staffs. To the undeniable frustration of finding oneself many times removed from the decision-making level is added the belief that service of this nature does not materially advance one's career.[27]

In the field of civilian personnel the problem takes two dimensions; we need both career officials and political appointees. The position of the former resembles in many respects that of the officer in the armed services—relatively low pay, slow advancement, and debarment from key positions, with something of the same results. Political appointees of skill, competence, and devotion are becoming increasingly difficult to find, and their average tenure of eighteen months is much too short.[28] Here again, relatively low pay is a factor, but more important are the loss of position (and possibly of pension rights) in civilian life, the problems occasioned by "conflict of interest" laws, and distaste for exposure to politically-motivated criticism and censure. While the Defense Department may not have achieved the record of twenty-one refusals reported for one high position in government, it is not far behind. New responsibilities, as well as new emoluments, will be required to change the present pattern.

Footnotes

1. Stanley, *op. cit.*, p. 138.
2. *Business Organization of the Department of Defense*, pp. 29-30.
3. For a discussion of the theoretical and actual positions of the Joint Chiefs of Staff, see Samuel P. Huntingdon, *The Soldier and the State*, Cambridge: Harvard University Press, 1957, pp. 432-437 and 374-399.
4. Section 202(c)(6), National Security Act of 1947, as amended. Reprinted as Appendix II in Stanley, *op. cit.*, p. 154.
5. For specific reference to the need for program budgeting and for a shortening and rearrangement of the budgetary cycle, see Arthur Smithies *The Budgetary Process in the United States*, *op. cit.*, Chapter XI. The general discussion of the gap between policy formulation and program implementation is supported by studies of the Second Hoover Commission.
   Commission of Organization of the Executive Branch of the Government (Second Hoover Commission), *Five Staff Papers Prepared for the Task Force on Procurement*, Washington: G.P.O., 1955. (Hereafter cited as Second Hoover Commission, *Five Staff Papers*), Vol. One, pp. A-6 to A-16.
6. *Ibid.*, Vol. One, p. A-16.
7. See, for example, Henry A. Kissinger, "Strategy and Organization," *Foreign Affairs*, Vol. 35, No. 3, April 1957, pp. 387-389.
8. *Symington Committee Hearings on Airpower*, p. 1463.

9. Unpublished report of the Subpanel on International Security Affairs, Special Studies Project, Rockefeller Brothers Fund, Section I. See also the testimony of former Deputy Secretary of Defense Reuben Robertson before the House Committee on the Armed Services, as reported in the *Washington Post and Times-Herald,* May 10, 1957.

10. Second Hoover Commission, *Five Staff Papers,* Vol. One, p. B-3.

11. With respect to this see the testimony of Mr. Reuben Robertson, *loc. cit.,* and that of Admiral Arthur Radford, Chairman of the Joint Chiefs of Staff, before the Symington Committee (*Symington Committee Hearings on Airpower,* p. 1471).

12. For illustration, see the testimony of Dr. Vannevar Bush, President of the Carnegie Institute of Washington, and Dr. James R. Killian, Jr., President of MIT, before the Riehlman Subcommittee of the House Armed Services Committee, quoted in Second Hoover Commission, *Five Staff Papers,* Vol. One, pp. A-51-52.

13. For information on how interservice rivalry results in the duplication of research and development, see the comments of Senator Saltonstall during the Symington Committee Hearings (*Symington Committee Hearings on Airpower,* p. 1469). The recent case of Colonel John Nickerson, whatever view one takes of it, is an example of "vested interest," actual and theoretical.

14. *The Washington Post and Times-Herald,* April 3, 1957.

15. *Symington Committee Hearings on Airpower,* p. 1840.

16. *Ibid.,* p. 1285.

17. *Ibid.,* p. 1468.

18. The latest and most important of these changes were contained in Secretary of Defense Wilson's Memorandum of November 26, 1956, "Clarification of Roles and Missions to Improve the Effectiveness of Operation of the Department of Defense," reprinted as Appendix C in the Association of the United States Army, *The Security of the Nation. A Study of Current Problems of National Defense,* Washington, 1957.

19. *Ibid.,* paragraph 3, p. 28.

20. Section 211 (b)(2), National Security Act of 1947, as amended; reprinted as Appendix II in Stanley, *op. cit.,* p. 154.

21. Cf. Second Hoover Commission, *Five Staff Papers,* Vol. One, pp. B-5 to B-8.

22. *Symington Committee Hearings on Airpower,* p. 1449.

23. Defense Advisory Committee on Professional and Technical Compensation, *Highlights of a Modern Concept of Compensation for Personnel of the Uniformed Services,* Washington: G.P.O., 1957, esp. charts on pages 27, 29, 61, and 63.

24. *Ibid.,* p. 14. The bulk of the recent West Point and Annapolis graduates resigning from service cited either low comparative income or disruption of family life as causes for their separation.

25. Editorial, *The Wall Street Journal,* April 12, 1956.

26. See Eli Ginzberg, "Human Resources and National Policy," an unpublished paper prepared for the Special Studies Project, Rockefeller Brothers Fund, pp. 20-21.

27. For an interesting analysis of the opinions of Joint Staff personnel concerning their chances of advancement, see Second Hoover Commission, *Five Staff Papers,* Vol. One, p. A-63.

28. *Ibid.,* p. A-64.

Part III

THE APPROACH
TO THE PROBLEM

INTRODUCTION

So far our discussion of Defense Department organization and procedures has been built around the "yardsticks" by which we have attempted to evaluate the effectiveness of the Department. This is a valid and valuable method for the critique, since it enables us to discuss past difficulties, the effects of organizational changes, and residual problems in a common setting. When it comes to outlining possible changes, however, this method of approach loses some of its value.

The first reason for this is the interrelation of various organizational systems and procedures, which makes almost impossible any discussion of measures applicable to a single category of problems. For example, decisions on the number, powers, and tasks of the various assistant secretaries, while directly pertinent to the question of civilian control, will also affect the manner and method in which the business operations of the Department are conducted. Similarly, as will be shown, our budgetary and fiscal procedures can be used not only to bring about greater economy but also to promote effective civilian control—and to enable a more direct relationship between national security policy and military programs. Thus to discuss in full one "yardstick" is virtually to cover every change which might be recommended.

The second reason why our former approach is not suited to a discussion of organizational changes is found in the very machinery the renovation of which we are considering. The functions, the powers, and, in some instances, the procedures of the various offices and agencies within the Pentagon are set forth in a number of key directives, some of them based on law and others deriving from the authority vested in the President and the Secretary of Defense. To evaluate clearly the impact on these offices of various proposals it would be necessary to consider as a whole those recommendations pertaining to a given agency or agencies. Thus, regardless of what has been said elsewhere, changes affecting the Assistant Secretary of Defense for Research and Engineering would have to be grouped in order to determine what should be done to alter existing systems and procedures. To prevent duplication, this is better done outside the framework of the "yardstick." For these reasons, it is proposed in the following chapters to discuss changes which might be made in various organizations and offices, such as the Joint Chiefs of Staff, the Joint Staff, the Office of the Secretary of Defense, and the unified and specified commands. In so doing, every effort will be made to consider together those proposals which are particularly relevant to a given set of yardsticks: thus Chapter Thirteen deals with changes largely affecting civilian control, the readiness for action of our defense machinery, and national policy formulation; Chapter Fourteen will similarly cover matters most pertinent to the development of sound strategic doctrine, service roles and missions, etc.

Before considering various organizational changes which will, in our judgment, improve the effectiveness of the Department of Defense, it is necessary to consider some of the reasons why these and other changes have not already been made. Accordingly, the next chapter will consider some of the factors which affect the range of possible changes within the Defense Department.

Twelve

THE LIMITS
AND PROBLEMS OF REFORM

Within the Department of Defense there are continuing organizational problems, such as those concerning the position and functions of the Joint Chiefs of Staff, which seem to have remained virtually unaltered throughout the successive reorganizations of the Defense Department from 1947 down to the present time. Divers solutions to these problems have been offered, partly derived from service views and positions, and partly in accordance with the primary interest of the proponent in civilian control, readiness for war, economy of operations, or some other objective. Thus it has been proposed at various times that we eliminate the Defense Department entirely, place all service-supported functions in a separate organization under the Secretary of Defense, reorganize the three services either on a completely functional basis (land, sea, and air) or on a completely integrated basis (like the Navy), reallocate all units (regardless of service) into task forces or commands, or merge the three services into one.

That these and other changes have not been made may result, in part, from the fact that they were not responsive to the problem. However, entirely aside from the merits of proposed change, there are four major factors which both shape the nature and the structure of the Defense Department and inhibit major changes in the organization of that department. These factors are service rivalry, Congressional interest and influence, the particular American interpretation of civilian control, and the trend toward centralization within the Department.

SERVICE RIVALRY

The first and perhaps the most profound influence on the structure of the Defense Department is the rivalry among the three services. Contrary to popular belief this is neither something which is nurtured on the playing fields of Philadelphia, where Army meets Navy in the annual football classic, nor is it donned simultaneously with a service uniform. Rather, it is the result of a combination of factors—the proudly-held traditions of the three services, the relative newness of Defense Department loyalties as opposed to those of the military departments, and, above all, the growing sense of professionalization of the military.

As already mentioned, the tremendous and ever-accelerating changes in military technology have both lent an air of haste to decision-making and outmoded the traditional division of roles and missions among the three services. However, because of the newness of these weapons and the lack of practice in their integrated use, because each service has concentrated on the development of certain systems, and because there has been honest disagreement as to the effectiveness of some weapons and the circumstances under which they could and should be used, there has been no real agreement on strategic concepts. Each service supports a concept which enables it to claim a decisive role, and seeks to control weapons and elements which will enable it to carry out that role virtually independently of operations of other services. Thus the Air Force, Army, and Navy all cite a need for weapons systems capable of striking at targets deep in enemy territory—and these may be the same or adjacent targets.[1]

Behind these differences lies in most instances an honest feeling that other members of the armed forces cannot and do not understand the capabilities of their sister services or the role which each of them can play in deterring and defeating aggression. Each service is afraid to entrust to another, or to any independent authority, the power to determine national strategy and military policy lest an "unbalanced" approach be taken which would imperil national security. It was certainly a belief of this nature which motivated the long struggle of the Navy against unification in 1944-1947, and which has prompted continuously expressed fears from some military circles concerning the establishment of an Armed Forces General Staff or a single Chief of Staff.

However, it would be denying human nature to argue that all interservice rivalry represents only honest concern over the security of the nation. Loyalties to the service as an institution affect many of the positions taken, as they do in any bureaucracy, in any system of human organization. Thus the struggle for control of ground-to-ground and surface-to-air missiles has a vital meaning to the Air Force entirely aside from any differences over military policy. If operational responsibility for these missiles were given, for example, to the Army, then the Air Force could anticipate a gradual phase-out of manned fighter-bomber and fighter-interceptor aircraft, and eventually manned strategic bombers, without replacement. This would leave the United States Air Force with virtually no reason for independent existence, and certainly no claim to predominance within the Department of Defense. Similarly, control of all these missiles by the Air Force would mean the loss by the Army of tactical support and antiaircraft capabilities, as well as the virtual elimination of the Navy's strategic striking force; in both cases the force concerned would lose in strength, in position, and in prestige. Thus interservice rivalry is a powerful factor operating against too much unification or coordinated direction of the Defense Department.

Closely allied with rivalry among the services as a factor inhibiting organizational change is the existence within the services of various "power centers." Establishments such as the Army's Corps of Engineers, the Navy's Bureau of Ships, and the Air Materiel Command have all the interests of any vested bureaucracy in maintaining the *status quo*. More importantly, they have developed by virtue of their functions considerable outside support which gives them tremendous political power both within their services and in Congress. Reorganization plans which run counter to the interests of these and similar "power centers" are likely to receive short shrift, as did the proposal in 1948 to divorce the Army Engineers of their responsibility for civil works.

Related to interservice rivalry, and indeed both a part and a derivative of it, is the factor of personal and professional relationships. The armed forces, particularly at the higher levels, are still bound tightly together by group loyalties and professional ties, which extend in many instances to corps, bureaus, and commands. Moreover, the service itself (if an organization may be personified) expects loyalty from its members and has its own methods of dealing with those individuals who do not conform to the desired standard.[2] This personal attachment to a particular service, although it has many good results, can also lead to rationalization of views, to a tendency to identify national interests with service positions, and to handicapping the individual who might try to rise above the level of branch or service rivalries.

In this connection, it is no discredit to the caliber of the individuals concerned to point out that the Chiefs of Staff of the Army and the Air Force, the Chief of Naval Operations, and the Commandant of the Marine Corps are compelled, by the very nature of their assignments as military heads of their respective organizations, to think in terms of service concepts and positions; indeed, they would be derelict in their service responsibilities if they did not do so. Moreover, both the bulk of their experience and their display of the qualities which led to their

selection have been largely within the confines of a single service.*
Under these circumstances, and whatever the intent and the sincerity
of the individual, it will be difficult for him to free his thinking from
the channels of his own experience and the interest of his own service.

The increasing bitterness of interservice rivalries has led powerful
service members to seek outside support for their positions and programs. Through quasi-official organizations, such as the Association of
the United States Army, the Navy League, and the Air Force Association, through members of Congress sympathetic to a given point of
view, as well as through business interests either personally or financially
connected with the service, efforts to promote pressure groups are
carried out. Within the government, moves are common to obtain the
support of a powerful official who will support a particular program,
such as the maintenance in Korea of United States forces, or the provision to NATO allies of new weapons. Moreover, there are literally
dozens of biservice or triservice alliances on different questions within
the Pentagon and the Joint Chiefs of Staff. Thus the Army, Navy, and
Marine Corps may join in opposition to the Air Force concept of large-
scale delivery of thermonuclear weapons by the Strategic Air Command;
conversely, the Air Force and the Army may oppose extensive development of heavy aircraft carriers, or the Air Force and the Navy may
coalesce against the Army's demand for increased air and sea lift. In
these maneuvers, personal relations, individual persuasiveness, and the
trading of votes are sometimes more important determinants than the
rationality of the decision itself in terms of the national interest.

The rivalry at the top, which is closely connected with the futures
of the respective services, is reflected in the positions and attitudes
of more junior officers—and, indeed, of their civilian co-workers. While
on most issues working relationships are extremely good, the younger
officers cannot help coalescing around the strategic concepts and positions of their services like filings around a magnet. Even if they desired
to do so, they could not take positions contrary to those stated by their
superiors. Thus the rivalries of the services are personalized and transmitted throughout all levels of the Department of Defense.

* For example, of the nine members of the Joint Chiefs of Staff since August
1953, only General Matthew B. Ridgeway had any extensive experience with high-
level multiservice and multinational commands. General Maxwell D. Taylor served
only briefly as Commander-in-Chief, Far East; General Nathan F. Twining was
Commander-in-Chief of the relatively small Alaskan Command, and Admiral Arthur
Radford, although he formerly held the position of Commander-in-Chief, Pacific,
had under his command no Air Force elements and only a very small Army headquarters, to which no combat forces were assigned.

This factor, and the air of animosity which it lends to the defense of service positions, is one whose importance must not be ignored. It lends credence to the arguments of those who maintain that only persuasion and cooperation will end service rivalries, that differences cannot be resolved by "putting everyone into a single unit." In a sense this is true, but only so long as no system is adopted for resolving and re-resolving the inevitable controversies among those who wear the uniform, of whatever color. Thus the Army has settled in the past, by command decision, problems of the relationship of the Armor branch to Infantry tank companies, of the Artillery to Infantry mortars, and of the Transportation Corps to Army aviation. Although it is unlikely that any of these differences have been settled in perpetuity, both these and new problems of organizational relations can be resolved by the same mechanism. The recent decision by the Secretary of Defense on operational responsibilities for guided missiles is evidence that a similar system can be applied to broader areas of conflict.

CONGRESSIONAL INTEREST AND INFLUENCE

Congress quite properly has a major interest in the armed forces, since it is charged by the Constitution with responsibility for raising and supporting them. Congress has exercised its Constitutional prerogative through an extensive amount of detailed legislation, resolutions, investigations, and informal relations with the military departments, as well as through its control of appropriations. Before World War II Congressional consideration of major issues of military policy was infrequent and sporadic; however, during the postwar period Congress has been deeply and continuously involved in substantive issues. Prominent among these issues have been the initial unification act and subsequent plans for the reorganization of the Defense Department. It is not necessary to trace all the ramifications of the hearings and debates, but, since Congressional influence has caused a degree of rigidity in the organization and conduct of military affairs which both guides and limits executive branch action in these fields, it may be useful to outline certain Congressional concepts of organization.

First of all, Congress apparently has been motivated by a strong desire to maintain civilian control over the military and a fear that the establishment of a single service, or of a triservice chief of staff with plenary powers, would seriously hamper effective civilian control. This has been no less true recently than it was in 1944-1947 during the debate over unification, or in 1949 when the office of Chairman of the Joint Chiefs of Staff was created. In 1953, when the Congress was considering the recommendations of the Rockefeller Committee that the Chairman of the Joint Chiefs of Staff be given additional powers over members of the Joint Staff, violent opposition to this move arose. One representative argued that these provisions of Reorganization Plan No. 6 violated the spirit of the Constitution and might "open doors to military tyranny"; another charged that the proposed measure was "destroying all that Congress has tried to do to hold the control of the military within the civilian. . . ."[3] President Eisenhower, in a letter supporting the plan, acknowledged the "misgivings some members of Congress have with respect to service 'merger' and its alleged concomitants, a single military chief over all the Armed Forces and an over-all General Staff system with command powers."[4] In the subsequent debate one proponent of the bill even admitted that "we have a heritage of distrust and suspicion of the military."[5] And as late as July of 1956 a number of Senators of both parties, liberals and conservatives alike, joined in denouncing the idea of a single armed service and voiced their fears of a "Prussian General Staff."[6]

This antipathy among some members of Congress to a high degree of unification of the armed forces probably springs also from another source—fear that such an organization would deprive Congress itself of any possibility of effective control. So long as there are a number of military elements with whom Congress can deal it has a better chance of determining the areas of difference among the military, or between them and their civilian superiors, and of obtaining that information which is the essential basis of policy action. To this end Congress wrote into the National Security Act of 1949 a proviso permitting the secretary of a military department or a member of the Joint Chiefs of Staff to present to Congress "on his own initiative, after first so informing the Secretary of Defense, any recommendation relating to the Department of Defense that he may deem proper."[7] Although some such measure is perhaps essential if Congress is to be given the advice and information which it needs to properly discharge its Constitutional functions, the precedent set has had obvious implications for those officers who wish to air service rivalries. The period since 1949 has been marked by at least three major investigations into conflicting strategic concepts and their supporting military programs.[8]

Finally, it should be noted that the attitude of Congress toward the armed forces is marked by a basic dichotomy: Congress both seeks to promote the national interest and represents local interests at the national level. In executing the first function, Congress is concerned with broad questions of strategy, military policy, and economy; in carrying out the second it is subject to all sorts of pressures from clothing manufacturers, farmers, professional societies, and various patriotic organizations. The task of correlating these dual—and frequently conflicting—interests is made more difficult by the size and complexity of national security programs. Faced with the almost insuperable task of determining what is needed for what purposes and in what amounts, the tendency is either to make token across-the-board reductions in requested funds or to fall back upon particularistic examination of details irrelevant to the broad questions of national policy. It is here that local interests have full sway (as shown by recent attempts to require by legislation the continued operation of certain military hospitals), and it is here that opposition arises to methods of budgetary presentation which would relate military programs to national policy. More specifically, virtually every Congressman is interested in the number of people in his state or district who are employed at military installations or under military contract, and demands detailed data on these points; he is less interested in, because less able to cope with, lump presentations of sums needed to pay military and civilian personnel. Unless the Congress can be convinced that the national interest is better served—and Congressional control over military policy better exercised—by measures such as the mission-type organization and the program budget, it is likely to continue its opposition to them. The triumph of the general over the particular interest is one of the major requirements for valid and supportable changes in Defense Department organization and procedures.

THE PRINCIPLE OF CIVILIAN CONTROL

There can be no question as to the ultimate primacy of civil control over the military and civilian responsibility for—as well as authority for—the direction of military affairs. This statement is particularly true today when the reciprocal impact of military and political affairs in both domestic and foreign fields necessitates the closest civilian coordination and control of military policy and strategy. As President Eisenhower stated in forwarding to Congress the Rockefeller Plan for reorganization of the Defense Department, our aim must be to establish

clear and unchallenged civilian responsibility in the Defense Establishment. . . . Basic decisions relating to the military forces must be made by politically accountable civilian officials.[9]

However, the way in which this principle is conceived and implemented is of transcendent importance to the organization and effective functioning of the Department of Defense. To date there have been four major ways in which civilian control has been effectuated within the Department.

First, as recommended by the Rockefeller Committee, the Secretary of Defense has assumed responsibility for directing the operations of the armed forces and has established a channel of responsibility which runs from the Secretary of Defense to the designated civilian secretary of a military department to the commander of a unified or specified command.[10] The Joint Chiefs of Staff have officially been deprived of the command authority which they acquired during World War II and have been placed in the role of advisors to the Secretary of Defense.[11]

Second, there have been established at both Department of Defense and service levels numerous civilian assistants with broad supervisory powers over military activities and with delegated authority for making policy decisions. In large measure the offices of these civilian assistant secretaries are also staffed by civilians.[12]

Third, there has been a tendency to separate out and establish direct civilian control over nonstrategic military matters, such as personnel, research and development, procurement, supply, and medical services. In the Department of the Navy this functional division of responsibilities is of long standing and is sanctified both by tradition and by law; in the other services and in the Department of Defense the principle of direct civilian control of business administration and producer logistics is neither so clearly established nor so universally accepted.

Finally, civilian control has been implemented to a large degree through the establishment of fiscal and budgetary mechanisms which, in the absence of other means, have been used to effectuate policy control.[13]

Thus there are in the United States both powerful sentiments for civilian control of the military and, in the hands of Congress and the executive branch, many instruments for the exercise of this control. Nowhere is there a theoretical challenge to the principle of civilian control; however, behind this ostensible agreement lie deep and lasting differences as to the methods of its application. Usually these take the form of arguments over "decentralization," i.e., the extent of detailed civilian direction of service operations, civilian versus military staffing of offices concerned with administration and logistics, or the adequacy and the impact of fiscal and other controls. But the real question remains: Are the military to run the Department with civilian support or are the civilians to run the Department with military advice? As one observer remarked, the situation is not unlike that "which would exist in the Department of Justice if the Attorney General and his top aides were West Point graduates who had never had any legal training."[14]

Legally—and perhaps logically—the argument is all in favor of the civilian position; in any event, civilian occupation of key positions, civilian staffing, and detailed supervision of military activities by civilians have become equated with civilian control. This is to some extent a perversion of principle in that the valid objective of maintaining policy control by politically appointed civilians has been extended to the increased use of civilians in other than policy positions. The responsible military officers have both memories of greater freedom during and immediately after World War II and professional reasons for considering their civilian chiefs largely unqualified to pass judgment on questions of weapons, the tactics of their employment, the strategy which best utilizes them, and the force levels needed to support that strategy. This difference of view concerning civilian competence and the nature of civilian control in large measure explains the fact that the Joint Chiefs of Staff, for example, have tended to be isolated from the rest of the Office of the Secretary of Defense and to maintain, to a considerable degree, channels of control and communication independent of those used by the civilian authorities.[15] Whatever the cause of these differences, it will be necessary to provide in any future organization for both the principle and actuality of civilian control, the proper utilization of military men and of their professional advice, and smoother relationships among the two groups. That this will be difficult goes without saying.

Another factor which markedly affects both organizational concepts and civil-military relations is a basic difference in approach between these two groups.[16] In modern military education the professional officer is trained to determine and analyze alternative courses of action, together with their advantages and disadvantages. If a staff officer, he submits the results to his commander for decision; if a commander, he chooses the course of action which seems best and executes it. In either case the theoretical emphasis is upon both a full presentation of alternatives and a speedy decision based on logical choice. In practice, of course, the development of courses of action and the selection of a particular one may be affected by ignorance, subjective weighing of argumentation and personal or professional bias. However, the system is stamped indelibly upon the minds of the military and is a requisite part of the decision-making process in military organizations.

The same is not true of the civilian counterparts with whom the officer in the Pentagon must deal, nor of the system under which he and they must operate. The process of decision by compromise is both philosophically and organizationally built-in to Pentagon operations and, indeed, to the relations between the Department of Defense and the other departments of government.* The separate administration of the service departments required by law, the committee system of procedures embodied in the Joint Chiefs of Staff, the existence of many functional assistant secretaryships—all combine to create a situation in which neither the process of decision-making nor the type of decision made conforms to those with which the military man is familiar. It is no wonder that many come to regard service in the Pentagon as a completely frustrating experience!

And yet the officers of the three services are not only thrust into these circumstances but also compelled to master them. At the higher levels of operations civilian and military officials are inextricably intermingled; no true differentiation of their functions is really possible. Although some areas, such as procurement or law, properly afford greater scope for civilian skills and specialties, the officer still can make an irreplaceable contribution in the form of knowledge of military requirements and lower-level military operations. Work in such fields as intelligence and logistics planning, while primarily military, also involves large numbers of civilians with specialized knowledge of technical competence. The question to be considered is how, and on what terms, the contributions of both civilian and soldier can best be used and the differences in their approaches to common problems reduced.

THE TREND TOWARD CENTRALIZATION

Another factor which must be considered in reshaping organization and procedures in the Department of Defense is the trend toward centralization. With the advent of World War II the rather diffuse operational structure of the Army and Navy tended to become more tightly controlled. Measures such as combining the posts of Chief of Naval Operations and Commander-in-Chief, United States Fleet, consolidating the administrative and technical services of the Army under one head, and exercising closer direction of training and readiness programs were but forerunners of a step of transcendent importance—the formation of the Joint Chiefs of Staff.† By the end of World War II this body had become, in effect, a single command for the direction of all our military efforts in the various theaters of war and the locus

---

* Note in this connection the speech of former Secretary of Defense Wilson, cited in Chapter One.

† Strangely enough, the Joint Chiefs of Staff did not become a statutory body until 1947. They owed their early existence and powers solely to letters exchanged by General Marshall and Admiral King.

of military advice on politico-strategic questions. Similarly, the economic side of the war effort headed up to the two Under Secretaries of the Army and the Navy and through them to the War Production Board and other government agencies concerned with the economics of war.

This centralization within the services tended to continue after the war, partly because of habit but more largely because the magnitude and complexity of the problems confronting the military departments apparently necessitated top-level decisions. On top of this departmental structure was superimposed the National Military Establishment, which grew, with increased centralization of authority, into the Department of Defense. Although in theory operations are reserved largely to the three services, and the various assistant secretaries are not to engage in operations or interject themselves into the chain of command, this is not true in practice. Nor, indeed, can it be true. It is humanly impossible to issue directives so detailed and so correct as to cover every possible nuance of policy and to insure without constant checking that these directives are correctly understood and applied. The official who contents himself with writing "policy" will soon merit the criticism of one Congressman that the "Assistants [Assistant Secretaries] grind out meaningless directives while the military departments go their own separate ways."[17]

This problem of increased centralization is not unique with the Department of Defense; during the last generation the size, complexity, and cost of operations, governmental and private, have spurred efforts to make more information available to decision-makers and to place additional instruments of control in their hands. Thus inventory control methods, cost-accounting systems, management surveys, and similar devices have multiplied; and both the means of obtaining and the necessity for having centralized control have increased. In the Pentagon the problem is magnified by the size of the machine involved, by the range and complexity of the matters which must be handled, and by the newness of the system. Unless and until the heads of the military departments and their subordinates can be so placed that loyalty to the Secretary of Defense does not conflict with loyalty to a service, centralization of decision-making authority is likely to remain necessary. Here the problem is to acknowledge both the existence of the trend and the possibilities inherent in the new methods for obtaining and presenting information without becoming bogged down in an administrative morass of our own creation.

PRINCIPLES OF ORGANIZATION

From the consideration of the preceding factors it may be possible to arrive at a statement of principles which could govern the organization of the armed forces and the Department of Defense. It is important to remember that, since the framework of our military establishment already exists; we are faced with the task of modifying an existing structure rather than with the job of building on newly-cleared ground. Moreover, as the previous discussion has attempted to show, there are factors which will manifestly affect the extent and direction of our remodeling. For example, the military perfectionist might be tempted to create immediately a single armed service with a single military chief—a step which certainly would solve many of the organizational and procedural problems discussed earlier. However, such a revolutionary move could be expected both to encounter immediate and vehement opposition within and outside the services and to create problems of centralization of policy and of civilian control as it has been understood and applied in the past. Moreover, such a system would not necessarily bring about closer collaboration between the military and the scientist in the development and introduction of new weapons. The military might, in fact, be able to control research and development more easily than is possible now. Thus factors other than the strictly military must be given consideration in formulating and implementing principles of organization.

At the present time the organization of the Defense Department is based on a set of principles expressed in the Declaration of Policy preceding the National Security Act of 1947.[18] This preamble states that it is the intent of the Congress to

Provide three military departments, separately administered, for the operation and administration of the Army, the Navy (including naval aviation and the United States Marine Corps), and the Air Force, with their assigned combat and service components; to provide for their authoritative coordination and unified direction under civilian control of the Secretary of Defense but not to merge them; to provide for the effective strategic direction of the armed forces and for their operation under unified control and for their integration into an efficient team of land, naval and air forces but not to establish a single Chief of Staff over the armed forces nor an armed forces general staff (but this is not to be interpreted as applying to the Joint Chiefs of Staff or Joint Staff).

Whether or not such principles form a valid basis for defense organization may be debatable; in fact, it can be argued that some of them tend to cause trouble rather than to cure it. Nevertheless, they do reflect some of the strongly held views of the Congress of the United States, to which cognizance must be given.

Entirely aside from the legal principles governing defense organization, there are certain more pragmatic guidelines which should govern any proposed reorganizations. Although it may seem premature to reach this conclusion in advance, it is obvious that any changes must be:

a. Designed so as to facilitate, rather than to make more difficult, solutions to the problems previously discussed.

b. In accordance with the basic principles of the United States Government and our long-held theory of civil-military relationships.

c. Responsive to the past traditions of the armed forces and the attitudes and beliefs of the men therein, both civilian and military.

d. Reflective of the present situation in the Defense Department, and the causes therefor.

e. Consistent with trends in weapons and sufficiently flexible to permit easy change as technological advances indicate.

f. Where possible, evolutionary rather than revolutionary in order to ease the shock of change and prevent a possible dislocation during the present period of protracted crisis.

g. Interim, both because of the above and because future trends may ultimately require extremely radical and far-reaching changes. For example, within the foreseeable future we may have to cope with the problem of whether or not to create a "Space Navy."

Footnotes

1. For a similar comment see Kissinger, "Strategy and Organization," *loc. cit.*, p. 381.

2. For evidence of at least the belief in this form of retribution, refer to the study by Dartmouth University already cited (Second Hoover Commission, *Five Staff Papers*, Vol. I, p. A-63), and the more recent book, *Soldiers and Scholars*, by J. W. Masland, and L. I. Redway, Princeton: Princeton University Press, 1957.

3. Congress of the United States, House of Representatives, *Hearings on House Joint Resolution 264 (Rockefeller Plan)*, Washington: G.P.O., 1953, pp. 136 and 149.

4. *Ibid.*, p. 202.

5. Congress of the United States, House of Representatives, *Congressional Record*, June 26, 1953, p. 7602.

6. B. W. Leach, *American Problems of Forces and Organization*, Serial 87, Harvard University Defense Seminar, 1956-1957, pp. 8-14. The incident referred to took place on July 23, 1956.

7. Section 202 (c) (6), National Security Act of 1947, as amended.

8. As Admiral Radford testified, our democratic system does not lend itself to rapid decisions in peacetime because the military services affected turn to Congress (*Symington Committee Hearings on Airpower*, p. 1466). Huntingdon, *The Soldier*

and the State, op. cit., p. 420, also noted the tendency for those services or groups which were weak in the executive branch to appeal to Congress for support.

9. Congress of the United States, House of Representatives, *Message from the President of the United States Transmitting Reorganization Plan No. 6 on Department of Defense Organization,* Washington: G.P.O., 1953, p. 2.

10. Section II A 14, DOD directive 5100.1, *loc. cit.*

11. *Ibid.,* Section II A. For the statement of Mr. Eisenhower to this effect, see the *Message from the President of the United States Transmitting Reorganization Plan No. 6,* p. 7. For the testimony of Admiral Arthur Radford, Chairman of the Joint Chiefs of Staff, to the effect that the Joint Chiefs of Staff have only advisory power, see *Symington Committee Hearings on Air Power,* p. 1455.

12. In 1954 the proportion of civilians in staff positions within the four Secretariats was as follows: Defense, 83 per cent; Army 57 per cent; Navy, 84 per cent; and Air Force, 69 per cent. Second Hoover Commission, *Five Staff Papers,* Vol. I, p. A-66.

13. For a description of the use of fiscal policy to shape force levels, see "Mystery Man of the Pentagon," *Colliers,* January 22, 1954, pp. 30-36.

14. Stanley, *op. cit.,* footnote, p. 138.

15. For a summary of criticisms levied by various individuals and groups, see *ibid.,* p. 131. The Second Hoover Commission stated that "decisions and information do not now flow freely from the Joint Chiefs of Staff to the Assistant Secretaries of Defense" (*Business Organization of the Department of Defense,* p. 14), and attributed weaknesses in planning to the "inevitable partisanship of the Joint Chiefs of Staff, their lack of time for planning, their reluctance to share the planning task with the Assistant Secretaries of Defense and others, and the reluctance of the civilian secretaries to assume responsibilities in military planning" (*ibid.,* p. 16). See also Second Hoover Commission, *Five Staff Papers,* Vol. I, pp. A-48 and A-68-69.

16. The importance of this point was suggested by a presentation made by Samuel P. Huntingdon to the Harvard Defense Studies Program (Harvard Memorandum Serial No. 51, 10 December 1955).

17. House of Representatives, *Hearings on House Joint Resolution 264,* p. 114.

18. PL 253, 80th Congress, July 27, 1947, as amended to June 1953. *Committee Print No. 3,* House Committee on Armed Services, 83rd Congress, 1st Session, Washington: G.P.O., 1947. For speedy reference, see Stanley, *op. cit.,* p. 154.

Thirteen

COMMAND AND STAFF

The causes and results of present organizational defects in the Department of Defense point the way to substantive and procedural improvements. Although the factors we have discussed set limits beyond which changes would be difficult, they also indicate the direction of movement for any initial effort; and, fortunately, since the boundaries are wide, initial steps of considerable importance can be taken without running into major obstacles.

The moves which will be suggested here do not involve substantial adjustments in the present mechanism. They require few if any changes in law. Moreover, since they are necessary in themselves, any progress in the directions they indicate is ground gained toward more remote objectives. We shall examine, then, in some detail a few of the organizational and procedural steps which can and should be taken to improve civilian control within the Department of Defense, to strengthen the effective participation of the Department in national security planning and implementation, and to enable both a speedier and a more controllable response to possible enemy action.

THE POSITION OF THE JOINT CHIEFS OF STAFF

A *sine quo non* to the effective operation of the defense system is a clarification of the role and position of the Joint Chiefs of Staff. At present, this body is by law "principal military advisors to the President, the National Security Council, and the Secretary of Defense,"[1] and is charged, among other things, with responsibility for the preparation of strategic and logistic plans, review of major material and personnel requirements of the services, and provision for the strategic direction of the military forces, all "subject to the authority and direction of the President and the Secretary of Defense."[2]

The Secretary himself, as "the principal assistant to the President in all matters affecting the Department of Defense . . ." is responsible for "directing the conduct of operations by the armed forces."[3] The crux of the matter is the manner in which the Secretary exercises his authority, especially with regard to strategic planning and the resultant determination of service roles and missions, force levels, and requirements. If he leaves too many of the basic decisions to the military he risks losing direction of the defense effort; if he does not to a large extent rely on them he has neither the knowledge to make, nor the means to implement, decisions concerning the conduct of military operations. The settlement of this issue requires that the Secretary establish an organizational system which will give full weight to military advice while retaining substantive control over broad policy objectives.

The first step in the proper exercise of policy control by the Secretary is to put into practice the oft-avowed statement that the Joint Chiefs of Staff are purely an advisory body, and, like other staff agencies of Department of Defense, have only such directive authority as the Secretary may delegate to them. In practice, the Joint Chiefs of Staff have continued to exercise independent authority, without reference either to the Secretary of Defense or to the civilian secretaries of the military departments. There are, of course, motives for this in terms both of a desire for maximum security of military plans and in the feeling that strategic planning and related operations are properly the concern of the military in general and of the Joint Chiefs of Staff in particular. Yet many of the decisions taken by the Joint Chiefs of Staff—decisions which are never referred to the Secretary of Defense for his approval—inevitably affect the policies and the operations of the military departments in a wide variety of ways. A precise statement by the Secretary of Defense as to the areas in which the Joint Chiefs of Staff are delegated directive authority, as is done in the charters of the assistant secretaries, would go far to clarify the situation; an equally precise reservation as to the areas in which only the Secretary or his Deputy could grant approval of plans and policies would largely end the present difficulties.

In connection with this statement of areas wherein the Joint Chiefs of Staff may only advise on policy and not determine it, other steps should be taken. A system should be established whereby the Joint Chiefs of Staff positions on such matters as National Security Council policy papers, NATO, SEATO, and other Allied proposals, and similar matters of national import are discussed with the Secretary of Defense before referral to any other government agencies, thus avoiding the appearance of divided counsels within the Defense Department and preventing the Joint Chiefs from confronting the Secretary with a *fait accompli*. When, from the agenda of the Joint Chiefs of Staff, the Secretary of Defense determines that matters of outstanding importance and broad scope are to be considered, he might chair the meeting himself or transfer the discussion to the wider forum of the Armed Forces Policy Council, on which also sit the secretaries of the three departments. Since the Chairman of the Joint Chiefs of Staff is already required to keep the Secretary informed, by monthly status report, of all items on the Joint Chiefs of Staff agenda and of Joint Chiefs of Staff deliberations on such items, this would require only a slight change in existing procedures.

However, the full implementation of the proposals made above might well involve altering the positions of the Joint Chiefs of Staff as advisers to the National Security Council, with independent membership on the National Security Council Planning Board,[4] and terminating such direct relationship with other agencies as State-Joint Chiefs of Staff "briefings." The Secretary might go so far as to arrange, if necessary by a change in existing law, that the Joint Chiefs of Staff are primarily military advisers to the Secretary of Defense, and that their advice will be given directly to the National Security Council or to the President only when the latter so directs or when the Joint Chiefs of Staff wishes formally to protest a decision of the Secretary of Defense. The aim of such measures would not be to downgrade the position and prestige of the Joint Chiefs of Staff but to insure that the Department of Defense speaks with a more united voice on politico-military matters.

As part of moves to promote better coordination and mutual understanding of problems, the Secretary might further encourage more personal and less formal contact between the Joint Chief of Staff and his principal staff assistants, and between members of his staff and members of the Joint Staff. The participation of appropriate assistant secretaries in the deliberations of the Joint Chiefs of Staff and of the Armed Forces Policy Council might be one means to this end. More importantly, the Secretary might promote the interchange between the Joint Staff and other offices of liaison officers, who could serve as the nucleus for the staffing in an emergency of a Department of Defense command post. These measures would go far to end the isolation of the Joint Chiefs of Staff and could help the Joint Chiefs of Staff to make their advice more fully responsive to the questions at issue.

One more procedural step would involve the establishment of a joint message center, through which would pass all communications to and from the Joint Chiefs of Staff and the Office of the Secretary of Defense, and the opening of Joint Chiefs of Staff files, documents, and material to properly-accredited staff members of the Office of the Secretary of Defense on the same basis of security clearance and "need-to-know" which holds for service representatives. (It is rather anomalous that a staff officer within a military department can have access to Joint Chiefs of Staff documents but a staff officer of the Secretary of Defense officially cannot.)

The measures outlined above would help to insure the ready availability of all pertinent material on a given matter, would make easier the coordination of policy directives, and would facilitate the establishment in an emergency of a Department of Defense command post with adequate records and means of communication. Moreover, the use by the Secretary of Defense of the Joint Chiefs of Staff as a staff agency with specified powers would facilitate the direction of operations in an emergency and accustom both military and civilian officials to cooperative effort in dealing with strategic problems.

At first glance the measures proposed may seem to intrude into the military sphere too many elements of civilian authority and direction; indeed, many among the military who are both accustomed to and desirous of having a "free hand" may characterize them as harsh or restrictive. However, there is nothing in the proposals made which is not responsive to the *de jure* authority of the Secretary of Defense and the *de facto* responsibilities of his office; their sole purpose is to insure that these responsibilities, if they are to be continued, are adequately discharged. In fact, many of the suggestions for closer liaison, greater exchange of information, briefing of the Secretary on policy matters, and attendance of civilian officials at Joint Chiefs of Staff meetings are— surprisingly enough—already included in a directive by the Secretary of Defense.[5] What is needed is a spirit of mutual trust and confidence which will make their implementation truly effective.

CHANNELS OF COMMUNICATION AND COMMAND

Parallel with the suggested clarification of the status and functioning of the Joint Chiefs of Staff should go a similar delineation of command channels. As has previously been noted, the channels of communication within and outside the Pentagon are so confused and confusing as to hamper both the speed and precision of decision-making and the exercise of control by the Secretary of Defense and the service secretaries. Although the Rockefeller Committee recommendations, many of which were subsequently embodied in the 1953 revision of the Key West Agreement, helped somewhat to improve matters, the situation in some areas is still obscure.[6] The regrouping of elements of the Office of the Secretary of Defense and service offices into similar functional staffs would help to untangle channels of communication and control within the Pentagon, as would the measures previously recommended for clarifying the position and authority of the Joint Chiefs of Staff. However, even changes of this nature would leave largely untouched the complex command and control arrangements outside the Pentagon, where a single officer in the field may at one and the same time be responsible to two or more headquarters with entirely different authorities and channels of communication.*

As much of the confusion results from the Executive Agency concept, the essential step is to stop using the services as intermediaries between the Secretary of Defense and the unified and specified commands. The latter are relatively few in number and can be directly controlled. Thus all directives and policy decisions emanating from the Secretary of Defense, or from any of his staff agencies, including the Joint Chiefs of Staff, should go straight to the various field commands and should clearly indicate the authority under which they are issued. Similarly, all messages from unified and specified commands concerning over-all policy, requests for guidance, changes in force levels, matters affecting the execution of the prescribed mission, etc., should go directly to the Secretary of Defense, who can then take, or cause to be taken, the necessary action.

Because of the obvious danger of end-runs and departmental action to handle messages in ways most propitious for the service, the only feasible solution appears to be the establishment of a Department of Defense message center, as previously suggested. This would replace the separate Joint Chiefs of Staff, Department of Defense, and service centers through which messages to and from the various commands are presently channeled. To this center should come all messages and papers from the Joint Chiefs of Staff and from unified and specified commands save for those clearly pertaining to routine administrative details such as the transfer of personnel or the shipment of materiel, which should go to the appropriate service. Through this center should pass all cor-

---

* Thus the Commander-in-Chief, United States Air Force Europe, as the commander of a major air element, must carry out policies and directives prescribed by the Chief of Staff, USAF; as the commander of a specified command (a single-service command established to carry out a given function) he receives orders from his nominal superior, the Secretary of Defense, through the Department of the Air Force as executive agency; while as the commander of a component command (a service element in a unified command), he is responsible to and receives missions from the Commander-in-Chief, Europe. (*Symington Committee Hearings*, p. 1228.) To make matters worse, the Department of the Army is executive agency for the European Command as a whole, and thus can transmit instructions affecting the Air Force component. In addition to United States command channels, elements of our forces in Europe also receive orders through NATO channels, but this is beyond our consideration.

respondence from the Secretary of Defense, or from the Joint Chiefs of Staff acting in the name of and under the authority of the Secretary of Defense, so that all decisions and directives could be logged, monitored, and checked for coordination and consistency. Since the same message center would handle internal correspondence among and from the various elements of the Office of the Secretary of Defense, this procedure would be relatively easy.

If the measures recommended were implemented, the line of command would run directly from the Office of the Secretary of Defense to the unified commands, and much of the confusion concerning channels of communication and sources of authority should be ended. With the Secretary of Defense himself, or the Joint Chiefs of Staff on his behalf, providing strategic direction for the conduct of combat operations, control over the theater commander would be tighter and his access to the decision-making authority more direct—a matter which will be further discussed later on. Moreover, although the measures described may appear to foster centralization they should in actuality have the opposite effect through freeing the various commanders from detailed direction by interested services. To the maximum degree, the services should deal directly with their own elements in the component commands, following closely the directives from the Office of the Secretary of Defense, and keeping a clear line between policy matters and those pertaining to routine administration. Given time, the adjustment to the new procedures should be both easy and painless.

ORGANIZATION FOR CIVILIAN CONTROL

However, there is still a third line of effort which must be pursued: that of clearly establishing both the means and the system for civilian control within the Pentagon. It is perhaps tiresome to introduce every discussion of civilian control with the prefatory reminder that it is not the principle but its implementation which is under examination. In the present instance, since the principle of control has been interpreted by some as requiring the multiplication and civilian staffing of policy offices and the supervision of operations in such detail as to be virtually indistinguishable from their direction, such a reiteration is perhaps doubly necessary. While true civilian policy control could be made relatively easy, and even the merger between military strategy and national strategy handled without too much difficulty, direction of military administration—the "business side" of the Defense Department—poses vexatious problems.

The first of these arises from the fact that it is virtually impossible to carve up service activities into "military" and "nonmilitary" areas or to divide all problems and policy decisions into unique and easily-definable increments. Even assuming that such boundaries could be drawn, there is no reason to suppose that they would be valid; indeed, the Rockefeller Committee recorded its belief that it is not possible

to make a sufficiently clear distinction between military affairs, on the one hand, and on the other hand civilian affairs (such as political, economic, and industrial affairs) to serve as a practicable basis for dividing responsibility between military and civilian officers, or for establishing two parallel lines of command.[7]

Nor is such a system necessarily desirable. After a hundred years of experience the Army abandoned a similar method of separating producer and consumer logistics, the Air Force has never adopted it, and there are at least some indications that the Navy system works because it existed rather than the other way around.*

The second difficulty is that the system of civilian control over business activities almost inevitably results in two distinct channels of command, especially at the higher levels. Since no one has yet figured out how to rotate civilian clerks or mechanics into Korea, the military necessarily retain both their logistical units and installations and the staff structures needed to direct them, the heads of which are theoretically responsible to their military chiefs. In practice, however, they are equally responsible to the functional assistant secretaries at service or Defense Department level, who exercise supervision over their activities and issue policy guidance affecting them. This, coupled with the tendency of the various secretaries to acquire staffs of their own, leads to greater centralization of authority, increased control over operations, and the imposition in the decision-making process of many time-consuming barriers. Moreover, it must be recognized that the coordinating and directing power of the Office of the Secretary of Defense renders the various service assistant secretaries increasingly impotent to pass on matters of great importance.

As has been mentioned, problems of coordination and control arise from the multiplicity and diversity of assistant secretaryships and similar high-level civilian positions within both the Department of Defense and the military departments. Moreover, there is an element of validity to the charge that much of the work done by these offices results from "taking in each other's washing." Coordination is usually more difficult

---

* In the same way, the handling by civilians of supply functions in the German Army originated in a 17th Century accident, and was only terminated as a result of experience in World War II.

among separate staff agencies than within them. Accordingly, in order both to simplify channels of communication and to streamline the organization, it is proposed to regroup those staff agencies concerned with the "business" side of the Department of Defense into four offices: personnel, funds, research and development, and logistics (to include both the present functions of supply and logistics and those pertaining to properties and installations and health and medical services).* Thus the civilian elements of coordination and control would be exercised largely in those areas having the greatest importance with respect to demands on the economy and to the impact on the public. In addition, since the Defense Department should speak with a single voice in politico-military affairs, the Office of the Assistant Secretary of Defense for International Security Affairs should be continued. While it is questionable whether other officials, such as the General Counsel and the head of the Office of Public Information, warrant the prerogatives of assistant secretaries, that is of small moment here since their impact on internal Pentagon policies and procedures is relatively unimportant.

Correspondingly, the assistant secretaries and high-level civilian officials of the military department could be regrouped into similar functional offices, as recommended by the Second Hoover Commission.[8] This step would be easy to take, would simplify and clarify channels of communication, would establish common representational membership on various committees, and could, if desired, enable straight-line functional supervision of business-type operations from the Office of the Secretary of Defense down through the various bureaus and technical services.

However, in carrying out the measures proposed, laudable though they may be, care must be exercised lest we perpetuate one undesirable feature. A common organizational structure within the top-level staffs of the three departments and within the Office of the Secretary of Defense could encourage functional direction of activities as well as functional supervision, with the result that each senior staff officer or official within the services would in effect report to two superiors: his own chief plus the corresponding functional assistant secretary at the next higher level. Unless both tact and care are exercised, the service secretaries and military chiefs could increasingly find themselves bypassed through the use of technical channels to and from the Office of the Secretary of Defense.

* It should be noted that this much of this proposal is not original with the authors but was advocated by the Second Hoover Commission, *Business Organization of the Department of Defense*, p. 21.

The solution proposed for this complex problem is simple in execution if radical in nature: make the military chief of each service directly responsible to the secretary of that department for the execution of all tasks, administrative as well as military. Under this concept, the line of authority would pass directly from the secretary to the service chief, whose staff would be responsible to him alone, not to a functional assistant secretary. The various assistant secretaries could relinquish their supervisory authority over various military activities and concentrate on determining and controlling policy in both the political-military and the business fields. As a corollary to this move, the authority of the military chiefs and their deputies to act for and on behalf of the service secretary should be strengthened so that fewer matters need be routed through secretarial channels.

Behind this apparently simple proposition lies the philosophical belief that the military can and should be trusted to run their own affairs subject only to policy control. This control must be retained by the Secretary of Defense and his assistants, and, more directly, by the service secretaries and their various assistants, and exercised through the provision of policy guidance, through the monitoring and where necessary the approval of policy directives, and through the primary power to replace ineffective or unresponsive officers—a power which has been too recently and too thoroughly exercised to leave any doubt as to its efficacy. With the military chief of each service directly and singly responsible to the secretary for all operations of the department, the need for civilian supervisory offices could be minimized, and the various secretarial staffs reduced.[9] The end product should be clarification of the channels of command and communication, increased decentralization of operations and delegation of authority, and the virtual elimination of one "layer" of offices. If both civilian officials and responsible military officers live up to this new division of functions, the results can only be good.

A STAFF FOR THE SECRETARY OF DEFENSE

Despite the improvements which have been suggested, it is both natural and inevitable that many matters be referred for decision to the Secretary of Defense. It is foolish to presume that two or three people, in addition to functioning as secretaries of major committees, can in fact monitor and coordinate the flow of actions through the immediate Office of the Secretary. Nor is the situation helped by the fact that the Secretary and his Deputy each have small personal staffs rather than a combined functional staff.

Although the Secretary of Defense is legally prohibited from establishing a military staff other than the Joint Staff,[10] he is specifically authorized a personal staff and "military assistants." There is no reason why these assistants should not be formed into a highly qualified secretariat which could:

a. Check the coordination and interrelation of papers presented for approval.

b. Brief the Secretary (and his Deputy) on the meaning and import of decisions recommended by his staff assistants, the Joint Chiefs of Staff, or the services.

c. Keep the Secretary informed concerning the status and results of actions and decisions taken on his behalf by his subordinates.

d. Follow through on the implementation of decisions and on actions requested by the Secretary or the Deputy Secretary.

In other words, the Secretary of Defense would be given at least the same assistance as is the Chief of Staff of the Army through the institution of the Secretary, General Staff. Such a system, in small scale and on a modified basis, has worked well within the Office of the Assistant Secretary of Defense for International Security Affairs, where the Executive Assistant, the Military Assistant, and the Executive Officer among them perform functions similar to those outlined above.

However, the secretariat could and should be given tasks even more difficult than those outlined previously. First, it should provide staff assistance to the Secretary or Deputy Secretary of Defense and to the Armed Forces Policy Council in reviewing military requirements and relating them to strategic planning and to national policy—a function which at present is partially carried out by the Defense Comptroller and partially left undone. Secondly, it should have the specific responsibility for the coordination to assure long-range planning in the various fields of national security from political-military affairs to weapons technology. Here also is an assignment which "cuts across the board" and on which efforts to date can best be described as spasmodic.

In time of peace it would appear preferable to keep this secretariat separate from the Joint Chiefs of Staff secretariat and from the offices of the other staff assistants. In this way the Secretary of Defense can be assured both of the separate preparation of recommendations and of their impartial review. However, in time of war the members of the secretariat, augmented by additional people from other staff offices, could merge with certain elements of the Joint Staff and the liaison group previously mentioned to form a functioning command post for the Secretary of Defense. As a prerequisite to this, as well as an essential part of their normal assignment, the members of the secretariat should maintain close liaison with both the Joint Staff and other offices within the Office of the Secretary of Defense and with the offices of the service secretaries.

Footnotes

1. Section 211(a), National Security Act of 1947, as amended.
2. *Ibid.*, Section 211(b).
3. Section 202(b), National Security Act of 1947, as amended, and Section IIA, Department of Defense Directive 5100.1, March 16, 1954 (the revised Key West Agreement).
4. George Fielding Eliot, in an article entitled "The Splintering Wedge," *Army*, Vol. 7, No. 9, April 1957, p. 54, recommended that the Chairman of the Joint Chiefs of Staff serve only as adviser to the Secretary of Defense at National Security meetings, and that the Joint Chiefs of Staff function as advisers to the President only on request. Implicit in this recommendation is the conviction that the Secretary of Defense must be the civilian spokesman for National Security interests.
5. Department of Defense Directive 5158.1, July 26, 1954, *Method of Operation of the Joint Chiefs of Staff and Their Relationships with Other Staff Agencies of the Department of Defense.*
6. *The Report of the Advisory Committee on Army Organization*, December 18, 1953, points out on p. 31 that phrasing in the Rockefeller Committee report and the Presidential Message on Reorganization Plan No. 6 "raises doubts as to the Secretary's authority" when the Army is executive agency, especially with regard to direct communication in an emergency between the Chief of Staff of the Army and the Secretary of Defense.
7. *Rockefeller Committee Report*, p. 3. This view is supported in part by *Report of the Advisory Committee on Army Organization*, pp. 18-19 and 45.
8. *Business Organization of the Department of Defense*, p. 24.
9. It should be noted that the departmental structure of the Army and the Air Force lends itself to these suggestions, and that of the Navy does not. However, there seems no reason why the Chief of Naval Operations cannot exercise the responsibilities indicated, which have been sought by many incumbents of that office. (Huntington, *The Soldier and the State, op. cit.*, p. 301.)
10. Section 203(c), National Security Act of 1947, as amended.

Fourteen

OPERATIONS

It should not be imagined that even the full implementation of the measures previously advanced would automatically solve all problems of defense organization. None of the actions discussed will end service rivalries (although they may help to lessen them), nor do they delve very deeply into the problems of roles, missions, strategic concepts, force levels, and weapons which are at once both the cause and the result of our present difficulties. However, even among those who recognize that conditions are not wholly satisfactory there are some (including former Secretary of Defense Wilson)* who judge that the Secretary has all the power and authority he needs, and who maintain that "revolutionary" steps toward further unification are both unnecessary and unproductive. Although dissatisfaction may be expressed with some specific operations of the Department, the measures suggested to alleviate difficulties usually are not far-reaching.

There is no doubt considerable validity in these views, especially as they relate to the legal powers of the Secretary of Defense. Although he is specifically denied authority to transfer, reassign, abolish, or consolidate the combatant functions assigned to the military services by the National Security Act,[1] and must report to the Congress on actions taken with regard to other functions, he undeniably has far-reaching powers. Not since the time of James Forrestal has any Secretary complained of lack of authority, nor has any assertion of such authority been openly and successfully challenged. But to state that the Secretary's power is ample is not to agree that it alone is equal to the task: there are definite limits to the time and the capabilities of any one man. Despite the strenuous and usually far-sighted efforts of various Secretaries of Defense, the powers of vested interests continue. As long as weapons are intimately bound up with services, and as long as technological changes continue at the present rate, it will be most difficult for any Secretary to work out clear-cut and lasting assignments of service

* See his speech at the National War College, previously cited in Chapter One.

responsibility. Without machinery for clarifying both strategic concepts and service roles and missions, the Secretary of Defense will continue to struggle against great odds in the discharge of his responsibilities. With all due respect to the views of many sincere people, the man on top in the Department of Defense, however competent, can be fully effective only if he has an effective organization to serve him—and it is increasingly obvious that this organization requires major overhaul.

THE ROLE AND FUNCTIONS OF TASK FORCE COMMANDERS

A prime move in minimizing service rivalries and in establishing more meaningful roles and missions for our fighting forces is to make better use of our various unified and specified commands. Already we have one functional task force (the North American Air Defense Command) and another (the Strategic Air Command) which is largely so except for the long-range striking forces of the Navy. In addition, we have a unified command for the entire Pacific area, one for the land area of Europe, one (almost entirely naval) for the Atlantic, and others of varying kinds in Alaska, Latin America, and the Mediterranean. It has already been suggested that these various unified and specified commands be divorced from service control and/or relationships and established in fact, as well as in theory, as instruments of the Secretary of Defense. The responsibilities of the Secretary for the direction of combat operations, now delegated to the military chiefs of each department, could and should be exercised by him directly, after receiving the advice of the Joint Chiefs of Staff.

The present responsibility of the Joint Chiefs to provide for the strategic direction of the armed forces, subject to the authority and direction of the President and the Secretary of Defense, could then be carried out through the issuance to the theater and other commanders of directives and instructions, which, according to their importance, could either be approved by, or issued in the name of, the Secretary of Defense. This would end the present confused arrangement whereby the theater commander may receive frequently conflicting instructions from three separate sources and under five different authorizations. And, finally, it would insure that the Secretary clearly bore the responsibility for the various actions—or failure to act—ostensibly taken in his behalf. In no other way can he insure the coordination and control essential either to the conduct of a general nuclear war or to the "stop-and-go" type of operation which may characterize limited war.

As a corollary to this arrangement, the unified and specified commanders, freed from the control of a given service, could present directly to the Secretary of Defense their concepts of strategic operations for the execution of their assigned missions and their requirements for numbers and types of forces. Then the Joint Chiefs of Staff could be brought directly into the problem of reconciling the various requirements and adjusting the various force levels on a command basis. At present, they enter into the picture only at a later stage, after the various theater and other requirements have been consolidated on a service basis, as prescribed by the Key West Agreement. The difference, seemingly small, is in practice tremendous, since under present procedures every force level becomes a service-developed and service-sponsored compromise, rather than one based on the total requirements and relative priorities of the various commands. To present these requirements in such a way as to divorce them from service positions would go a long way toward easing service differences and difficulties.

In their determination of requirements, the unified and specified commanders should be instructed to plan for the execution of missions by the most appropriate means. Similarly, the Joint Chiefs, in their consideration of force requirements and in their promulgation of general policies and doctrines, should stress the interchangeability both of missions and means: in other words, the formation of task forces tailored to the job at hand. There is no logical reason, whatever the wording of the Key West Agreement, why Air Force units cannot—and should not—attack a submarine pen or why Army missile units should not participate in the air defense of a United States naval base; in fact, as Admiral Radford testified last year before the Symington Committee, they can in an emergency do so. To facilitate increased planning for and use of units on a functional basis, the present Joint Chiefs of Staff responsibility for "recommending to the Secretary of Defense the assignment of primary responsibility for any function of the Armed Forces requiring such determination"[2] should be extended to include both weapons and missions at theater level. Thus the Joint Chiefs of Staff (and the Secretary of Defense) could insure both that the service developing a weapon did not necessarily acquire total control of it and that duplicating forces were not built up to perform similar missions. In other words, a step could be taken toward functional assignment of responsibilities without necessarily undertaking the perhaps desirable but impossible task of reorganizing the entire Department of Defense on a functional basis.

THE NEW ROLE OF OUR MILITARY CHIEFS

It is obvious that the steps outlined above would place important new responsibilities on the Joint Chiefs of Staff. In addition to participating directly, and far more intensively, in the determination of force levels and weapons systems for various unified and specified commands, they would also be more largely involved in guiding the planning of possible operations of these commands,* under the authority of the Secretary of Defense. As will be noted later, their responsibilities in the field of logistic planning would be similarly increased. They would serve both as a "requirements committee" in considering the requests of the various commands and as an agency of the Secretary of Defense for checking on the composition of service programs. In short, the Joint Chiefs of Staff would become, for the Secretary of Defense, the equivalent of the Operations Division of the old War Department General Staff, which dealt with the over-all strategic direction of the war and with related political-military and logistic problems, subject only to policy decisions and direction by proper civilian authority.

At the same time that the work load of the Joint Chiefs, as a corporate body, was being increased, the military chiefs of the various services would also be taking on new responsibilities. It is obvious that the measure making the military chief responsible to the service secretary for all operations† will add to his burdens, particularly in the case of the Chief of Naval Operations, who will be for the first time charged with directing the various bureaus of the Navy. In order to free the military chiefs for operations and policy implementation in all the far-flung fields of administration and for the more directly military pursuits of organizing, training, and maintaining forces in readiness for combat (as well as to conform to other proposals already made), certain changes should be made in their present functions.

First, they should not, as the Chief of the Air Force and the Chief of Naval Operations now do, exercise command control over troops, ships, and planes in forces assigned to unified and specified commanders. Their command authority should extend only to those elements in training, in reserve, or engaged in logistical and administrative activities within the United States. Second, they should no longer, for reasons already discussed, exercise authority with respect to unified and specified commands, either directly or under the executive agency concept. Third, they should not be members of the Joint Chiefs of Staff, although they must closely coordinate their activities with the plans of the latter in order to insure development of adequate service combat and logistical support capabilities.

---

* At present, the detailed contingency plans of the various commands, are noted, but not approved, by the Joint Chiefs of Staff.

† *Supra*, pp. 192 to 193.

This last recommendation may come as a shock to those who believe that planning is inextricably related to operations, or that the role of the services requires that they be represented on the Joint Chiefs of Staff. The truth is that the services themselves divorce planning from operations, both within their staff structure and, more importantly, in their organization for combat. In the larger sense, the Joint Staff and the service staffs are all "planners," and the conduct of military operations is to be carried out by the task forces of theater commanders. Aside from such powers as it derives from serving as executive agency, the service role is largely that of supplying and supporting the units actually engaged in combat according to instructions received from the Joint Chiefs or the Secretary of Defense. While the presence of the same person in both planning and executive capacities may be helpful, there is no indication that it is essential.*

Indeed, it is this very duality of assignment of the service chiefs which is the cause of most of the difficulties with strategic concepts and roles and missions. Given the dual task of both representing one of the armed forces and determining national military strategy, the service member of the Joint Chiefs of Staff almost invariably interprets strategy in terms familiar to and favorable to his service—nor can he humanly do otherwise. It is redundant to again cite the testimony to this effect of Major General Otto L. Nelson, Jr., former Secretary of the Air Force Finletter, and former Secretary of Defense Lovett; their statements are perhaps too well known. What is not so well known is that General George C. Marshall, former Army Chief of Staff and Secretary of Defense, also expressed himself as follows:

Even under the stress of war, agreement has been reached in the Joint Chiefs of Staff at times only by numerous compromises and after long delays, and coordination in material and administrative matters has largely been forced by circumstances arising out of the war and then incompletely. . . . Divorced from administrative and operating responsibilities, the Joint Chiefs of Staff would be of inestimable value to the nation in the formulation of basic military policies and the development of a balanced security establishment.[3]

If the problem, then, is caused by the introduction of service interests, the most effective way of solving it is to deprive the services, as such, from representation on the Joint Chiefs of Staff.

* In all fairness it should be noted that this view is contrary to that held by several study groups on Defense Department organization, including the task force of the Second Hoover Commission which studied the Joint Chiefs of Staff. (*Five Staff Papers*, Vol. One, p. A-74.)

Perhaps the most direct way of so doing would be to establish a single Chief of Staff of the Armed Forces. But, in addition to the political difficulties which would attend any such attempt, there is reason to believe that the armed forces have not, at this stage of unification, developed such widespread interservice knowledge and such willingness to accept unilateral direction as to make this move militarily feasible. Instead it is suggested that the members of the new Joint Chiefs of Staff should be drawn from the three services, as they now are, with the Chairman coming from any one of the armed forces.* However, all those selected for the Joint Chiefs of Staff, in addition to other qualifications, should have proven their understanding of joint and/or combined operations, preferably by service as theater commanders as well as by schooling, by duty on joint and combined staffs, and by evident aptitude for interservice and interagency work. In this way it should be possible, through the partial divorcement of these men from service ties and their definite removal from service operations, to produce a better-rounded and more objective body of staff advisors who would, in the words of Lieutenant General Elwood R. Quesada, USAF-Retired, "bring to the Joint Chiefs expert knowledge without special interest."[4]

THE ORGANIZATION AND FUNCTIONING OF THE JOINT STAFF

To be fully effective, the revised Joint Chiefs of Staff would have to be supported by a truly unified and functionally organized staff which gave representation to each of the three services (and, where desirable, to their various technical corps and bureaus) but made no effort to parcel out three ways either the top positions or the assignments to various teams. At the present time both the Joint Staff (which is limited by law to 210 members drawn equally from all three services) and the network of interlocking committees on which the members of the Joint Staff sit are organized on a triservice basis; i.e., each contains one member from Army, Air Force, and Navy (or Marine Corps). Even the top positions in the Joint Staff are divided equally among the three armed forces, and where a member of one service is in charge of a given section of the staff he has deputies from each of the other two services. Theoretically this system is designed to provide a balanced appraisal of all plans and proposals; in actuality it not only is organizationally

* There would appear to be no basis other than sentiment for continued separate representation by the Marine Corps; however, the high competence and extensive knowledge of triservice operations manifested by senior officers of the Marine Corps would appear to warrant their increased use on the Joint Staff and in multiservice command positions.

cumbersome but also tends to perpetuate service differences and rivalries.

Although the services probably will oppose reorganization of the Joint Staff on a purely functional basis, the Chairman should exercise the authority given him to "organize and manage the Joint Staff, including the committees and subcommittees pertaining thereto,"[5] to carry through such a change in the Joint Staff itself. (Among other things this will make easier the "effective, full, complete, and early collaboration" between the principal Joint Chiefs of Staff committees and the counterpart organizations of the Office of the Secretary of Defense which is also an aim of the directive.)

While the various interservice committees should be continued in order to insure better correlation between plans and resources, drastic changes should be made in their method of operation. First, the Joint Staff should be wholly responsible for the preparation of the agenda and the placement of items thereon. Any matters which the services desired to discuss should be added only with the consent of the Director, Joint Staff (or by order of the Chairman of the Joint Chiefs or the Secretary of Defense), and would be presented in the form and manner determined by the Joint Staff. Second, the Joint Staff representative, who would automatically serve as chairman of any committee, should not be required to accept views or positions advanced by the three services and/or the Marine Corps. In other words, the paper would be coordinated with the three services if that were possible, but not cleared with them. Here again, a *reclama* by the chief of each service would be possible. Thirdly, only those matters affecting coordinated and long-range planning, or requiring a correlation between resources and actions, should be handled in committee, while many others should be disposed of within the Joint Staff and by the Joint Chiefs of Staff directly.

In order to insure the competence and integrity of the Joint Staff, steps should be taken to safeguard the independent position and judgment of its members. As long as these men, upon completion of their assignment, revert completely to service control and are dependent on their particular service for promotion, their loyalty to the Joint Staff will necessarily be subject to strain. While the great majority of the officers detailed to the Joint Staff probably act without conscious consideration of personal advantage, the stress on human nature can be lessened. The Secretary of Defense should monitor their future careers to see that the assignments given them are compatible with their capabilities, that their promotions are not delayed, and that they are afforded opportunities to serve again on joint or combined staffs. While Secretary of Defense Wilson has already taken a step in this direction

by requiring that service on joint staffs or in the Office of the Secretary
of Defense be considered in the selection of general and flag officers,
much more needs to be done along the line indicated above.[6] Ultimately,
it may be necessary to consider the centralization under the Secretary of
Defense of higher-level assignments and promotions, and some will
argue for the establishment of a separate staff corps completely divorced
from the military services.

Finally, there should be integrated into the Joint Staff organization
competent and long-term civilian personnel on two bases. First, as has
been mentioned elsewhere, there should be established a liaison office
staffed on a rotating basis by outstanding representatives of the various
functional offices in the Office of the Secretary of Defense. These individuals could advise the Joint Staff on departmental policies and positions, keep their own assistant secretaries informed on Joint Chiefs of
Staff plans and recommendations, smooth the way for coordination of
papers, and serve as a nucleus for the staff needed to man an operations
room in an emergency. Secondly, there should be appointed on either a
full or a part-time basis high-level consultants including but not limited
to the scientific and technical advisers recommended by the Rockefeller
Commission. Granting the difficulty of staffing the positions mentioned
with men of the necessary caliber, and the even more ticklish business
of introducing civilians into what (save for the Weapons Systems Evaluation Group) has been almost entirely a military operation, these
measures should still pay dividends.

The steps outlined above would have the effect of reducing the workload of those engaged in Joint Staff activities, of speeding action, and of
reserving the power of military advice to a single group, the Joint
Chiefs of Staff, rather than to a series of interservice committees at all
levels of activity. That such a system would require men of the highest
integrity and judgment goes without question—but so does any important system. That the organization proposed would indeed help to
obviate interservice rivalries is at least partly self-evident, but there is
one more measure which should be taken to further this desirable goal.

RESEARCH, DEVELOPMENT, AND EVALUATION
OF WEAPONS SYSTEM

Of all the causes within recent years for service rivalries, the greatest
has probably been the rapid development of new weapons systems. Although, as Admiral Radford testified, the problem of the basic organization of the services and the possibilities of more unified effort would
exist in any event,[7] the situation has been exacerbated by the contest

for control of various weapons systems. At the same time these weapons systems have tended to make obsolete the roles and missions to which the services still cling.

In this connection it is worth requoting the statement of President James Killian of the Massachusetts Institute of Technology.

One thing is abundantly clear. The military task no longer divides up neatly into three mission areas, defined by the vehicle the fighting man rides in. . . . I suggest that in dealing with air defense, with intercontinental ballastic missiles, and with other great weapons systems we must create the organizational patterns which will make it possible, first, effectively to develop them without wastage of manpower and resources, and secondly, to manage them in terms of their wholeness as systems. So far we have not been able, in the definition of roles and missions of the services, to keep pace with evolving weapons systems technology and as a consequence we lengthen our lead time, we make more difficult our decision-making process, we needlessly increase costs, and we find it difficult to avoid friction and duplication of effort.[8]

To some extent measures to this end have been recommended above, such as the increased independence of the functional and theater commands, the granting to the Joint Chiefs of authority to recommend force levels and weapons systems for employment within given commands, and the divorcement of the services both from the various commands and from the Joint Chiefs of Staff. But these steps, however desirable in themselves, do not impartially determine the capabilities of weapons systems, speed up (or slow down) their development, and provide for their integration into the armed forces. For this, other action must be taken.

The first area of concern must be the Weapons System Evaluation Group (WSEG). At present this organization, which is charged with making "complete, objective, and independent analyses" of present and future weapons systems, their comparative cost and effect, and their influence upon strategy, organization, and tactics,[9] is jointly responsible to the Joint Chiefs of Staff and to the Assistant Secretary of Defense (Research and Engineering). Its director now, as has been the case since its formation, is an officer of one of the services. Despite the uniformly high quality and objectivity of these directors, it is extremely difficult for an organization subordinate to the Joint Chiefs of Staff, partly staffed by military professionals, and led by a service officer, to exercise maximum initiative, objectivity, and freedom of judgment. Accordingly, WSEG, and its related contract organization, the Institute for Defense Analyses, should be given greater powers of self-government. Although WSEG may continue to be administered by the Office of the Assistant Secretary of Defense (Research and Engineering), it should for obvious reasons be removed from the jurisdiction of the Joint Chiefs and should take policy direction from no one except the Secretary of Defense. The aim should be to establish an impartial advisory group of great competence and prestige whose services are available to all and will be used before major new weapons systems are introduced.

The Assistant Secretary of Defense in charge of research apparently has all the authority which he now needs. Two separate directives[10] give him the power to coordinate research projects and direct him to insure the interchange of research and development information and strategic guidance with the Joint Chiefs of Staff by actively collaborating in the development of strategic directives and estimates, by advising the Joint Chiefs of Staff on joint requirements, and by providing operations analyses to the Joint Chiefs through the Weapons Systems Evaluation Group. The major problem appears to be that, since the individual services retain responsibility for research projects, the Assistant Secretary neither directly controls their efforts nor is possessed of sufficient information concerning service missions, troop levels, and requirements to evaluate individual projects in relation to a complete whole. While it does not appear desirable to transfer all research funds and projects to the Assistant Secretary, as some have recommended, he should exercise his authority to see that complete pictures of requirements and trends are presented by the services, that these correspond to Joint Chiefs of Staff strategic guidance and directives, and that duplicate research projects are undertaken only when the best scientific analysis has indicated the necessity for such duplication. Under no circumstances should duplicating projects be assigned to different services, lest service rivalries be perpetuated and intensified.

As the number of alternative choices among weapons systems increases with growing technological knowledge, proper management will more and more require both rigorous scientific examination of projects proposed and very pronounced qualities of judgment. The arduous process of selecting among alternative avenues of exploration can be hastened, if not simplified, by analyzing relative trends in Soviet capabilities, in our own capabilities, and in those of other countries. By a study of possible innovations which may most drastically affect relative capabilities, and by operational gaming of those innovations, we can isolate out the more fruitful areas for further experimentation. In this way, through operational analysis and long-range planning, guidance can be provided not just to the research and development effort but to the whole military establishment.* Such guidance is essential if the development of our military forces is to proceed along planned and rational lines and if the services are to be prepared to utilize properly and speedily the weapons which can be provided.

Footnotes

1. Section 202(c)(1), National Security Act of 1947, as amended.
2. DOD Directive 5100.1, Section III, B, 9.
3. Quoted in *Five Staff Papers*, Vol. One, pp. A-37-38.
4. Quoted in *Five Staff Papers*, p. A-55.
5. DOD Directive 5158.1, Section III, para. 7(a) (8).
6. For similar recommendations concerning handling of Joint Staff personnel see Second Hoover Commission, *Five Staff Papers*, pp. A-64, A-72, and A-76.
7. *Symington Committee Hearings on Airpower*, pp. 1458-1459.
8. *Ibid.*, p. 1186.
9. Department of Defense Directive 5128.8, April 13, 1956, *Weapons System Evaluation Group*, Section IV, para. 1.
10. Department of Defense Directive 3200.2, *Responsibilities, Policy and Procedures for R&D Project Coordination*, dated November 5, 1954, and Department of Defense Directive 5128.7, *Responsibilities of the Assistant Secretary of Defense (Research and Development)*, dated November 12, 1953.

* This idea, in considerably expanded form, was advanced by Dr. Ellis A. Johnson, Director of the Operations Research Office, in a speech, "The Nature of War," delivered before the National War College, September 7, 1955.

Fifteen

ADMINISTRATION

Equally as important as organizational changes, even if less tangible, are those of procedure. It is for this reason that we propose to discuss budgetary and fiscal controls, cross-servicing techniques, and similar matters. Although they fall more into the procedural than the organizational side of the Defense Department, both their present impact and their potential effect are so great as to warrant their consideration. However, procedures alone will not solve problems; this is the task of the men who make the procedures work. And if men of the requisite quality and quantity are to be obtained, then both additional incentives and changes within the Defense Department are required. This also will be our concern in this chapter.

BUDGETARY AND FISCAL CONTROLS

The first Hoover Commission report established the concept of a cost and performance budget. Implicit therein was the principle that once the head of an operation was given the job to do, he would in turn develop a budget based on previously established cost data to do the work assigned. This approach was adopted by the Bureau of the Budget and thus, in effect, for all Governmental agencies. In the intervening years between the first and the second Hoover reports it became abundantly apparent that in order to exercise firm control over expenditures in a given year or month, it would be necessary to introduce into the system additional refinements, such as more uniform work standards, to serve the dual purpose of establishing "yardsticks" for measurement of achievement and providing control instruments. It is just as easy, for example, to hold down Army expenditures through the establishment of personnel ceilings as through cutting requests for funds; in fact, the personnel ceiling may well be more effective. Equally, the personnel ceiling may be used to reduce the "division slice" in the Army by cutting down on numbers and grades of personnel while approved force levels retain the same major units. Such budgetary and fiscal controls can be—and have been—used to force decisions on various matters, to change the pattern of weapons development, or to alter the relative status of readiness of various elements of the military.

In part, the use of such methods of control is an almost inevitable development. Since the questions of strategy, force levels, and weapons development have not been resolved by the normal and prescribed process of decision-making, the tendency has been to settle them indirectly through the expansion and selective use of control measures. Already there has been some talk, in and out of the Pentagon, to the effect that the United States cannot afford both nuclear weapons and delivery systems and conventionally-armed forces, and that therefore the latter must go. It is difficult to determine what part this sentiment has played in specific moves, such as those to pare down Army forces or to reduce the number of Air Force wings. Nevertheless, there can be little question that the element of cost has entered into both over-all decisions on the size and composition of the armed forces and specific programs such as for air lift. In effect, then, fiscal decisions and fiscal controls are being used to shape both the military strategy of the United States and the strength of its armed forces. And it can be expected that this process will continue.

The real difficulty is two-fold. First, under present systems, neither budgetary allocations nor reductions can be applied with surety to any specific force. The Air Force, for instance, might well apply a cut in maintenance funds to transport aircraft or to B-52's rather than to the upkeep of planes used to maintain the flying proficiency of students at the Air War College. Second, this is not the best method for maintaining civilian control over military requirements. Carried to its logical conclusion, it could mean that the recommendations of the Joint Chiefs of Staff on force levels, weapons development, and personnel and material requirements would, whatever their formal reception, become vitiated through budgetary decisions and fiscal controls. In effect, the Joint Chiefs of Staff function of providing strategic guidance for the armed forces would cease to be meaningful, and direction of our military effort would rest largely with the Defense Comptroller and the Director, Bureau of the Budget. As the Second Hoover Commission pointed out, fiscal controls, "though important, are not an effective substitute for orderly planning."[1]

The first objection to the use of fiscal controls can be largely overcome by the initiation of a true program budget.[2] As previously mentioned, each service, at least ostensibly, budgets on a program basis. Thus the Army, instead of seeking appropriations specifically for the Quartermaster Corps, the Corps of Engineers, and so on, now groups its requests for funds under such headings as personnel, procurement, and maintenance. For decision-making purposes this is not fully satisfactory, since these functional categories are not subdivided according to the roles and missions for whose support the monies are requested. To do this would require, for example, that under each heading the Army indicate what sums were being spent for air defense elements, for garrison forces (as in Korea, Japan, and Germany), for the strategic reserve, and so on.

The adoption of a true program budget would have a dual advantage. First, by marrying categories (such as Army, Air Force, and Navy expenditures for air defense) we could for the first time get an accurate picture of what we are spending for one purpose. Second, and more importantly, we could determine each year what it would cost simply to maintain air defense at the present level of capability and how much would be required to increase effectiveness to a desired level. Moreover, we could measure the projected increase in effectiveness against the projected (or actual) cost both to determine what we got for our money last year and what we are likely to get in the future. Granted that some elements of our value judgment, such as the state of operational readiness, may be esoteric, others, such as the number of NIKE batteries in position, are highly objective; by operational analysis all of these factors could be integrated into the consideration of various program alternatives.

The institution of a true program budget could have important results. It could provide for the first time a method of relating policy recommendations by the National Security Council with both specific force requirements and program costs.* The development, costing, and evaluation of similar categories, into which the elements of all services would fall, would enable better weighing of the relative merits of increases for different types of forces, although admittedly this might be difficult in the case of such diverse elements as the strategic striking force and the units being readied for anti-submarine warfare. Under the proposed system, since both appropriations and reductions could be applied against specific and pre-determined elements, relative rates of build-up or decline could be controlled, thus giving the civilian authorities a more rational and more directional control over force levels. Moreover, if the various task force commanders had to submit triservice budgets for consideration by the Defense Department as well as the respective services, this would in large measure take from the

---

* A tentative effort to group forces according to the nature of their primary mission and to determine the cost of their supporting programs by categories was initiated in 1956, but it did not progress far enough to fit the recommendation above.

hands of the military departments the control over force bases which they now have by virtue of their mandate to consider, consolidate, and budget for all force requirements of their particular service.

But would this device of the program budget, even though admittedly useful, serve automatically to solve all problems? Of course not. What it can do is provide an instrument whereby the cost of each unified command, specified command, or task force could be measured and labeled, thereby enabling specific increases or reductions in funds to be applied to specific forces. This does not obviate the necessity for a mechanism which can decide on both the strategic requirements for various types of forces and the relative priorities of program for their support, since resources plainly will never meet all demands. The first task is quite properly that of the Joint Chiefs of Staff and the Secretary of Defense, operating according to the policy guidance furnished by the National Security Council. The second task should be that of the various assistant secretaries concerned with such functions as personnel, logistics, and research and development, in direct conjunction with the Secretary of Defense or his Deputy.

This suggestion is not made in criticism either of the present Comptroller of the Defense Department or of the systems for whose institution he has been largely responsible, but rather to see that all available resources of the Department of Defense are thrown into the important task of determining defense policy and programs. As Dr. Smithies points out, the present budgetary role of the Comptroller "is a product of the fiction that budgeting merely involves translation of programs into dollars,"[3] while the real problem is that of relating programs to military estimates of requirements. Evaluation, review, the establishment of techniques and procedures, the improvement of managerial and accounting systems—all are proper functions of the Comptroller. Definitive advice on future programs is not. Within the areas mentioned there are many steps which could be taken to bring the budgetary cycle more in line with the decision-making cycle, to minimize the amount of work required in program development, to reduce the time-lag in the apportionment of funds, and to make managers at all levels more truly responsible for efficiency and costs of operation. In these directions lie opportunities for economy and for speed of decision which would well repay the additional effort required to simplify and extend budgetary and fiscal procedures.[4]

CROSS-SERVICING AS AN ORGANIZATIONAL TECHNIQUE

In the field of business operations there are two other instruments which are worth mentioning, not so much because of their ostensible utility in promoting economy as because of their adaptation to the solution of organizational problems. Both of these instruments have to do with cross-servicing but in somewhat different fashions. The first is the policy, long-adopted in theory but seldom effectively implemented, of multiple use of installations and facilities. In its minimal aspects this means, for instance, that an Air Force plane can land on and refuel at a naval air base, or that Navy personnel may be given dental care in an Army clinic. This, with appropriate cross-funding, is fairly frequent although not widespread. The meaningful extension of this program would involve the consolidation and/or common use of the facilities of one service by elements of another. To illustrate, if Army and Navy hospitals in the same area are operating at less than capacity, the Army hospital could be closed down and the Navy directed to care for all Army patients in the area. Similarly, this process could be extended to signal communications centers, depots, port facilities—and, conceivably, even to the adjacent Air Force and Navy air fields in Washington. Potentially this cross-servicing offers an opportunity to minimize duplication and to reduce cost; in practice its application has been spotty and meager, partly because of difficulties in handling funding and repayment but largely because of service opposition to the elimination or dual use of facilities whose full capacity they might need in an emergency.

The second instrument is single-service procurement. Under this system the Navy might be named to purchase, store, and distribute to user agencies and major installations all fuel oil, gasoline, and other general-use petroleum products. Similarly, the Army might be charged with wholesaling foodstuffs, the Air Force with rocket propellants, and so on. To date this effort has been applied, under the "single-manager" concept, mainly to a small number of common-use items such as petroleum products and rations but not to such relatively unstandardized objects as tanks, aircraft, and missiles, although there have been some variants of this. Thus the Air Force has procured for the Army all light aircraft and some helicopters, while Mr. Wilson's decision on responsibility for missiles of various types[5] carried with it at least an implication that one service might develop missiles for use by its colleagues.

The two instruments of cross-servicing could be used to change in some measure the allocations of roles and missions and to affect the operations of the three services. The Navy might well be directed to operate ports, docks, wharves, and similar facilities for all services, thus ending such anomalies as the Air Force-controlled Port of Manila and other and much larger-scale confusions of function and duplications of equipment and personnel. Similarly, the Army could be told to take over all depot operations, the Air Force all air transport flights, and so on as a mean of bringing about greater functionalization among the services.

In a larger vein, the freedom which a service acquires by virtue of its independent development, procurement, and use of material could be curtailed through use of a single-service procurement. For instance, the procurement by the Army of all ground combat equipment might well lead to closer coordination in tactical and technical efforts by Army and Marine Corps as well as to trends toward greater standardization of equipment. Moreover, such a step could minimize duplicatory research and development which, whatever its intrinsic merits, is bad insofar as it represents service control of particular weapons and weapons systems.* More importantly, the assignment to one service of responsibility for all development of certain types of missiles might produce salutary results as far as competition of service-sponsored rival systems is concerned—although it would admittedly create difficulties in insuring that the needs of each service for weapons of a given type were adequately considered.

Thus, entirely aside from their value in reducing costs of operations,† cross-servicing and single-service procurement could be used to promote greater functionalization among the services, to minimize duplication in research, development, and procurement of weapons systems, and to alleviate some of the interservice struggles for complete possession of various weapons. Applied abroad as well as domestically, they could go a long way toward overcoming the difficulties of the present system wherein each service is responsible for budgetary and logistic support of its own elements. Given greater power to adjust logistical operations as well as combat missions, the theater commander could better coordinate the activities of his component forces and move toward a more integrated and less service-oriented structure.

IMPACT OF FISCAL AND PROCEDURAL CONTROLS UPON DEPARTMENT OF DEFENSE ORGANIZATION

To what, then, might all this lead? First, and quite obviously, it could lead to a greater concentration of power in the hands of the

---

* This was done with respect to Army research on light aircraft by Mr. Wilson's directive. *Ibid.*, para. 1. e.

† The Second Hoover Commission, at least, had some doubt about the efficacy of the single-manager concept because of the difficulty in eliminating duplication, the probable increase in costs, and the question of insuring equitable treatment of all services in an emergency. (*Business Organization of the Department of Defense*, pp. 41-42).

civilian officials of the Department of Defense. The Defense Comptroller could well become on the "business" side of the Department of Defense the equivalent in stature and power of the Chairman of the Joint Chiefs of Staff, if not measurably his superior. This is precisely why it has been recommended that decisions concerning programs be made by the Secretary after consultation with *all* his civilian assistants, of whom the Comptroller is only one. Since the power to control force levels through approval of programs already exists, the main problem is to see that it is exercised by the sole person responsible for both the military and the civilian side of the Department of Defense, the Secretary himself.

Secondly, the task force and other unified and specified commanders would gain increased independence from both the Joint Chiefs of Staff and the military departments. Whereas now they are dependent on the Joint Chiefs of Staff for decisions on allocations of forces, and on the services for implementing deployments and subsequent budgetary support, they could to a larger degree write their own tickets. If the budget request of the North American Air Defense Commander included funds to support 100 Nike battalions, and his budget were approved, he could be sure that the Army would have money for 100 battalions. Moreover, he could be equally sure that the Army could not on its own decide that tank battalions for its forces in Europe were more important than the Nike battalions and divert the resources of the Air Defense Commander to someone else's use; the Defense Comptroller would stop that. The Secretary of Defense, in approving various elements of the program budget, could override or counteract service decisions on the forces to be assigned to given commands or the funds to be provided them, and could thus further support the approved recommendations of the theater commander or of the Joint Chiefs of Staff.*

As a third result, the military services would become increasingly divorced from decisions on strategy, force levels, and weapons, which would be more largely determined by the unified commanders, the Joint Chiefs of Staff, and the Secretary of Defense. In large measure the service departments as such would become housekeeping elements, the

---

* This system in embryo is already in effect in one area of Department of Defense operations, the military aid program. Department of Defense Directive 5132.3, dated July 1, 1955, prescribes that the theater commanders recommend to the Assistant Secretary of Defense (International Security Affairs) both the types and levels of forces to be given United States support and the programs for their support. Although the advice and assistance of the Joint Chiefs of Staff and the services are sought, the Assistant Secretary of Defense (International Security Affairs) has full knowledge of the proposals of the theater commanders against which to evaluate other recommendations.

main concern of which would be with the administrative and logistic support of unified and specified commands.* Under these circumstances, their guidance and policy direction would come largely from the "business" side of the Department of Defense. In effect, in the over-all scheme of things the services would take a position comparable to that of the various bureaus of the Navy, while the elements under the control of task force commanders would have the traditionally separate command channels of naval operating forces.

THE MEN BEHIND THE MACHINE

Nothing that has been said above should be taken to minimize the importance of quality manpower in the Department of Defense. The emphasis must be definitely upon more competent and better-qualified personnel. The essential requirement for decentralization, with all that it implies in the way of less cumbersome procedures and more responsive decisions, is loyal, motivated, and capable subordinates. It is one of the failings of the Defense Department as of all large bureaucracies that multiplication of controls and diffusion of authority tend to be substitutes for competence of personnel.

On the military side this is a problem the full impact of which has yet to be felt. To date the armed services have produced a surprisingly large number of capable and well-rounded individuals equal to the responsibilities of the highest civil and military offices in the land. However, there are indications, such as the high rate of resignations among recent graduates of the service academies,[6] that the number of such individuals may be drastically reduced in the future. Relatively low pay, poor prospects for the future, and the dislocations and discomforts suffered by service families have been cited by the departing officers as major causes for separation. When to this egress from the junior ranks is added on the part of senior officers a heavy number of voluntary retirements prior to completion of service it becomes obvious that the prospects for maintaining an officer corps of highest caliber are indeed bleak.

The failure to retain officers is partly due to the marked decline in real wages during a period when virtually all other groups are enjoying substantial advances. In part it is probably caused by the instabilities of military life already mentioned—a feeling of insecurity stemming from past and pending reductions in the size of the military forces, and a sentiment that the government has not "kept faith" with regard to the privileges and prerequistes theoretically enjoyed by military personnel.

* They would, of course, also retain certain responsibilities for the development of doctrine, for training personnel, and for administering such support and reserve elements as were not specifically assigned to a task force or command.

But in some measure at least the exodus (and the dissatisfaction of many still in service) may be occasioned by a belief that the military are no longer trusted to execute a mission on their own responsibility and by a strong feeling of frustration at the multiplicity of administrative controls exercised at all levels of command.

On the civilian side, the picture is somewhat different. First, there has been no effort to build up a corps of "senior civil servants" who could fill the higher positions in the Defense Department. Indeed, the increasing number of positions which are reserved for political appointees and the salary ceilings placed upon top civil service positions have worked positively against the development of high-level civil servants. Second, the comparatively low salaries of top political offices, the difficulties of going from civil life into and out of government jobs, and the increasingly low power and prestige of many positions have inhibited qualified and experienced people from accepting them.* In particular, there is little evidence of people gaining experience in lesser positions before moving on to top posts. Mr. Gordon Gray and Mr. Donald Quarles are the exceptions rather than the rule.

To help overcome these difficulties and problems, which have already been discussed at some length, certain steps would seem to be indicated.

First of all, the pay scales for senior military and civil service personnel should be adjusted upward to correspond more nearly with those of their foreign service contemporaries, if not with those of similar positions in business.

Second, larger numbers of high-level positions, at least up to the level of Deputy Assistant Secretary, should be opened to these individuals. The cases of Mr. McNeil in the Defense Department and of Ambassador Murphy in the State Department show that outstandingly competent individuals can be drawn from career services to fill "policy" positions.

Third, the requirements for advancement to such positions should be stiffened and the ways of qualifying for them expanded so that chance and proximity may become less important than at present. Badly needed is a schooling and selection system for senior civil servants which approaches that of the armed services.

Fourth, and perhaps most important, the positions to be filled by senior officials, whether military, civil service, or political appointees, should be of consequence, should present a challenge, and should offer

* As far back as 1953, the *Report of the Advisory Committee on Army Organization*, p. 45, noted that only two of the six persons who had held the post of Assistant Secretary of the Army for Supply had had any pertinent experience in either civilian or military life.

an opportunity to make a contribution. All too frequently, particularly at the service level, positions meet these requirements only in theory. It is extremely difficult, for example, to see why both a three-star officer and a civilian with the title or status of Assistant Secretary should be separately concerned with research and development; one or the other may well be operating at something less than full capacity. Either one could do a better job than both. And a reduction in the number of high positions may be the surest way of making the remaining ones both more important and more attractive.

The recommendations we have outlined here should help in three ways to improve the morale of those within the Department of Defense. First of all, increased compensation is a tangible indication of official concern, and in that respect also a stimulus to higher morale. Secondly, measures which reduce service bickering and service misinformation should also raise the morale of the many officers and civilians in all services who consider the national interest more important than service advancement and regard members of other services as fellow-Americans rather than competitors to be outwitted or outmaneuvered. Thirdly, the steps suggested to increase individual responsibilities, to improve and speed up operations, and to promote the smoother functioning of the Department of Defense should increase the morale of senior officials both within the Pentagon and in major commands elsewhere. That this can be done without cutting service ties, without at this time forcing "unification," and without turning the Department upside down should be a cause of gratification to all those who serve their country in the Department of Defense.

Footnotes

1. *Business Organization of the Department of Defense*, p. 18.

2. For a detailed explanation of the present budgetary cycle and process in the Department of Defense, and of the possible nature of a program budget, see pp. 229-277 of Arthur Smithies' excellent book, *The Budgetary Process in the United States, op. cit.*

3. *Ibid.*, p. 261.

4. For a discussion of both procedural problems in the budgetary field and of measures to increase economy and efficiency of procurement, see *ibid.*, pp. 257-325, and Second Hoover Commission, *Five Staff Papers*, Vol. One, Section B.

5. Association of the United States Army, *op. cit.*, Appendix C, para. 5.

6. According to the *Army-Navy-Air Force Register*, Vol. 78, No. 4052 (August 3, 1957), p. 2, 18.1 per cent of all Naval and Military Academy graduates who have entered the Air Force since 1945 have resigned. *The Army Times*, Vol. XVII, No. 51 (July 27, 1957), pp. 1 and 8, reports that over 20 per cent of the West Point classes of 1951, 1952, and 1953 have resigned their Army commissions, and estimates that the rate will rise to 25 per cent with the class of 1954.

Part IV

CONCLUSION

Sixteen

A PROGRAM FOR CONSIDERATION

The last ten years have witnessed both the formation and the development of the Department of Defense. During this decade, great progress has been made in creating a defense instrument responsive to unprecedented technological, military, and political challenges. Nevertheless, there are clear indications that this progress has been neither so fast nor so extensive as the times require. There can be little question that the fragmentation and diffusion of the decision-making power within the Pentagon, the cumberousness of our procedures, and the over-emphasis upon "sound" business practices have adversely affected our efforts to maintain a military and technological advantage over the Soviet Union. Reasonable men may differ as to the nature and importance of the continuing difficulties, but not as to their existence.

Mention has already been made of the organizational and procedural defects which, in our judgment, handicap the Department of Defense, but it may help to recapitulate them here.

1. Civilian control has been exercised primarily through budgetary decisions and processes rather than through policy decisions on the difficult strategic and organizational problems confronting us. Moreover, civilian supervision has been equated with civilian control, thereby contributing to the multiplicity of offices and the clogging of channels so characteristic of the Defense Department today. In the process, the contributions which the military can and should make to the formulation of national security policy have increasingly been ignored or slighted.

2. In part, this has been the fault of the military themselves. The Unification Act legalized the bitter service rivalries which have pervaded the entire defense establishment; and the committee system of organization established thereunder has made virtually impossible the reaching of military decisions on vital strategic issues. In many instances the military services have settled for a compromise solution to urgent prob-

lems; in other cases they have provided no solution at all. The resulting hodge-podge of irreconcilable strategies, plans, and programs has provided no basis for a rational choice of alternatives by civilian authorities and has left them no recourse except that of piecemeal and largely indiscriminate reductions in military requirements.

3. This difficulty does not spring solely from the organizational pattern of the Department of Defense. The rapid technological change so characteristic of our times has had a major impact on military strategy and tactics. Changes are occurring so rapidly that innovations in weaponry are outstripping both changes in tactics and concepts for the employment of new weapons. Partly because of the pace of change, partly because of honest differences over the efficacy of untried weapons and methods (and partly because of financial limitations), the services have found it most difficult to take full advantage of technological developments. More important, in an era when weapons transcend service boundaries they have found it virtually impossible either to organize a cohesive collective effort which can cope with the wide range of problems confronting us or to devise non-duplicatory service roles, missions, and weapons systems.

4. One result of these difficulties is that the defense dollar is not well spent. With each service developing different weapons for the same purposes, with each military department seeking to be logistically and operationally self-sustaining, duplication and overlap is inevitable. Moreover, since there is little correlation between the strategic and logistic plans of one service and those of another, gaps as well as duplications frequently appear. Worst of all, there is no way to tell, from present budget categories, either the cost of particular forces such as those preparing for anti-submarine warfare or the interrelationship among strategic concepts, forces, and programs.

5. It is noteworthy that these defects in the administration of the Defense Department have occurred despite—and in a sense because of—the preoccupation of the top officials with business management, procurement, and fiscal controls. Attention has been concentrated on installing cost accounting and control systems which, despite their necessity, cannot and will not produce large-scale economies. Attention has been distracted from the fact that the primary purpose of the Department of Defense is to provide for the security of the United States, and that real savings can result only from the more rational allocation of resources to this purpose—and from a clearer determination of strategic means to this end.

6. Finally, it must be noted that the unresolved organizational and

procedural problems within the Department of Defense have had side effects in other fields. They have made it difficult to relate national security policy either to military problems or to budgetary costs. They have complicated, confused, and slowed the decision-making process within government and hampered the control of operational military forces whether poised within the United States or deployed elsewhere. And they have caused increasing confusion among our citizens concerning the nature of our military policy and the effectiveness of our national defense programs. In view of the need for clear public understanding of the vital issues confronting us, this is perhaps the most serious criticism of all.

The judgments which have been passed are severe ones, with which other reasonable men may disagree. But it is not alone our opinion that much is wrong with the Department of Defense; it is that of history. The launching by the Soviet Union of an earth satellite is incontrovertible evidence of Soviet progress in military technology; the United States has been overtaken in its chosen field. And what makes the matter worse, if newspaper accounts can be believed, is that divided authority and interservice rivalry prevented the United States from being the first to put a "moon in the sky."[1] While it may be well that the "Sputnik" itself has no military values, its implications for the United States are obvious—and ominous.

BASES FOR IMPROVEMENT

The critical shortcomings just described cannot be resolved without changes in the organization of the Defense Department. The pressures for change within the Pentagon and the public criticisms of the Department of Defense make it inevitable that the present structure of the Department will be altered. If past trends continue, the result will be a further concentration of authority and responsibility in the Office of the Secretary of Defense, a greater centralization of operations, and a more detailed supervision of the actions and programs of the military services. We remain unconvinced that such changes by themselves will be either effective or helpful. It is our belief that changes both more radical in nature and more responsive to the problems confronting us are required.

The only brief we hold for the specific proposals which we have advanced is that they embody principles which should be followed if we seek progress rather than mere change. These basic principles are:

1. Continued and meaningful civilian control which can attain better management, economy, efficiency, and completeness in defense programs; enable a sounder approach to the political-military problems

of national security; and assume more effective political responsibility for both the objectives and the conduct of military operations.

2. Maintenance of military responsibility for the provision of meaningful professional advice and assistance, for the implementation of policy, and for the daily operations of the military departments and commands.

3. Clarification of the respective roles of military and civilian officials, of the channels of command and communication between them, and of their relationships with one another.

4. Continuation, so far as is compatible with other requirements, of the basic structure of the Defense Department and the separate existence of the military services with their special competence, proud traditions, and sense of mission.

THE PROPOSALS IN SUMMARY

From our analysis of conditions within the Department of Defense, from a consideration of the detailed criteria for effective organization, and from the basic principles which we judge should govern change, we have derived certain recommended changes. It cannot be argued that these recommendations afford the only way to achieve an efficient and effective Department of Defense, but they do, in our opinion, provide for the minimum improvements required. These recommended changes, which have been described in Chapters Thirteen through Fifteen, may be summarized as follows:

1. The status of the Joint Chiefs of Staff as advisors to the Secretary of Defense should be clarified and confirmed by ending their independent access to the National Security Council* and delineating the areas and circumstances in which they may act for the Secretary of Defense. This would permit the Joint Chiefs of Staff to concentrate on the erection of the strategic framework for our defense effort, on the development of plans for the employment of functional forces, and on the review and correlation of military requirements. Measures should be taken both to insure increased contact between top military and civilian officials and to establish a single message center for the Joint Chiefs of Staff and the Office of the Secretary of Defense which would serve as the unique and authoritative channel for orders to service departments and to the unified commands.

2. The Secretary of Defense should be provided with a staff secretariat capable not merely of keeping him informed of operations within the Department but also of assisting him in his task of relating military

---

* This would not preclude the Joint Chiefs from appearing before the NSC at the call of that body.

requirements to national policy. This secretariat should be specifically charged with coordinating long-range planning efforts in the field of national defense. In times of peace this defense secretariat would remain independent of other elements of the Office of the Secretary of Defense; in times of war or of extreme crisis it would merge with selected elements of the Joint Staff to form a defense command post.

3. Under the Secretary of Defense, the civilian service secretaries should concentrate policy-making power in their own hands, with the service chiefs assuming under their command direct administrative responsibility for the full range of departmental activities. The present number of assistant secretaries operating in the Department of Defense should be sharply reduced, and those remaining organized on a common functional basis. Every effort should be made to curtail detailed civilian supervision and to make the military authorities responsible to their civilian chiefs for policy implementation.

4. Overseas interservice commands and functional task forces such as the Strategic Air Command should be divorced from service control and make immediately responsible to the Secretary of Defense. They should present directly to him their strategic plans, their military requirements, and their budgetary needs.

5. The Joint Chiefs of Staff should serve the Secretary not only as advisors with respect to the needs of these commands but also as agents of the Secretary of Defense for guiding the planning and execution of operations by the various commands. In order that they may better carry out their role as planners, and more objectively consider strategic concepts, roles, and missions, and operational tasks, the members of the Joint Chiefs of Staff should be relieved from their operational responsibilities as military heads of the armed services.

6. The three service chiefs, although responsible to the service secretaries for all operations of their respective departments (as indicated in 3 above), would no longer sit as members of the Joint Chiefs of Staff. Moreover, although retaining command responsibilities or forces in training, in support, or in strategic reserve in the United States, they would cease to exercise direct command or control over forces assigned to particular overseas or task force commanders.

7. The Joint Staff of the Joint Chiefs of Staff should be reorganized on an integrated rather than a triservice basis and staffed by selected civilians as well as by military personnel. It should be made more largely responsible for the development and coordination of integrated strategic and logistic plans, with service cooperation but without any service power of veto.

8. The Weapons Systems Evaluation Group and its related organ-

ization, the Institute for Defense Analyses, should be divorced from the Joint Chiefs of Staff and attached directly to the Office of the Secretary of Defense. It should be used both to determine by operational analysis the most promising areas of military endeavor and to impartially assess strategic doctrine and weapons systems capabilities.

9. The Assistant Secretary of Defense (Research and Engineering) should, with the advice of the Weapons Systems Evaluation Group, actively promote research activities and foster promising developments, making these known to the Joint Chiefs of Staff, the military services, and the task force commanders, and insuring that the weapons systems requirements of these commanders are given consideration in assigning research tasks and priorities. Moreover, in those cases where duplicatory research and development projects are justified, he should, in order to minimize service rivalry and competition in weapons systems development, refrain from assigning them to different services. In general this official should more positively foster innovation and more effectively end duplication in research and development.

10. The Department of Defense should develop a true program budget based on military tasks and missions. Only in this way will it be possible to determine the actual cost of various types of forces, to relate military programs to national policy, and to establish rational priorities for the build-up or reduction of forces.

11. Increased use should be made of single-service procurement and of multi-service use of installations, both for reasons of economy and in order to blur service lines. The ultimate aim is a better-organized and more truly functional logistic system which can efficiently supply tri-service commands.

12. Finally, and going outside of organizational changes, additional inducements must be offered to qualified personnel. Better pay, increased status, and additional job openings for career personnel, civilian and military, must be paralleled by efforts to increase the opportunities for meaningful action afforded political appointees, to reduce the number of such positions (lest they be further cheapened), and to make easier the transition into and out of government service. While in the long run there is no substitute for motivation, the measures suggested will make it easier—and more rewarding—for the motivated to serve in the Department of Defense.

A LOOK INTO THE FUTURE

It should not be thought that, even if the organizational and procedural rearrangements proposed were all adopted, all of the present and

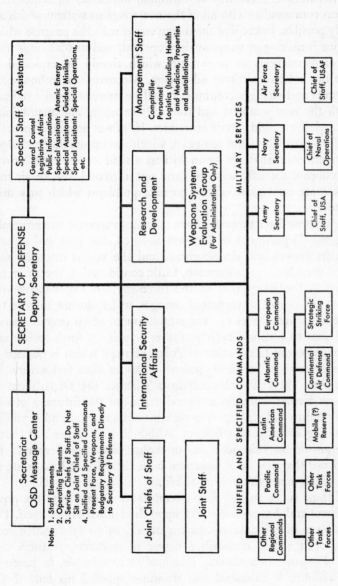

THE NEW ORGANIZATION OF THE DEPARTMENT OF DEFENSE

future problems of the Defense Department would be solved. To take just one illustration, there will be continual difficulties in acquainting the overseas commanders with all of the new weapons systems which are potentially possible, in keeping them conversant with the progress which each service is making in weapons development, and in obtaining from them recommendations as to systems which should be exploited to maximize our relative military advantage. Moreover, as technological developments and changes continue, it will be more and more difficult to fit both the new weapons and the units manning and maintaining them into relatively rigid service structures. If, as was predicted recently, space flight is possible within ten years, which service should be charged with that function? Shall we again witness a mad scramble to "prove" that spaceships essentially serve to carry out a ground, sea, or air mission? These are only some of the possible problems which may arise in the future.

The changes we have proposed have taken into account the principles on which the Department of Defense is based, the past and current trends of its growth and development, and the vested interests both within and outside of the institution. Little consideration, therefore, has been given to the integration of the three military departments; the time is not yet ripe. The suggested changes, which do not involve the merger of the armed forces nor the establishment of an overall general staff, endeavor to conform both to the principles set forth earlier and to the Congressional Declaration of Policy of 1947, which is perhaps as valid—and certainly as politically potent—today as when first written.

Nevertheless, the essential question is whether the Department of Defense can forever maintain a triservice (or, for the future, a quadri-service) structure and still operate with maximum speed and flexibility and at the highest peak of efficiency. Although it is recognized that a definitive answer to this question, on either side, would require far more evidence than has been presented here, there are at least some indications which may guide further thinking.

One of these is the entirely new circumstance arising from the possibility of direct and devastating attack upon the United States itself. The whole problem of response to nuclear attack, or to intelligence foreshadowing such attack, demands a degree of readiness, tautness, and tightness of organization scarcely imagined or imaginable. In peace or in war, flexibility is enhanced and decisions speeded up only if the decision-making apparatus within the military establishment is not subject to inherent checks and balances. The problem is to make sure that increased uniformity of organization does not lead to rash and ill-advised actions. In an age when thermonuclear destruction is only fifteen minutes away by guided missile, speed *with* judgment may be at a premium.

Finally, in an age of astronomical costs for complex weapons, the United States simply cannot afford the luxury of competing and duplicating systems. The armed forces must get the maximum results from the resources made available to them. Whatever the benefits of maintaining separate services, no one has ever justified their retention on grounds of economy. At the very least, ways in which to integrate the three military departments into one warrant urgent and extensive consideration.

Footnote

1. *The New York Times*, October 9, 1957, p. 1; *The Washington Post and Times-Herald*, October 11, 1957.

Seventeen

SHARPENING THE BLADE

There are three basic questions which should be asked concerning any reorganization:

1. Is it necessary?
2. Does it accomplish the desired results?
3. Does it have a chance of succeeding?

Some form of reorganization is clearly needed if we are rationally to operate the large and sprawling Department of Defense and enable it better to carry out its mission: the defense of the United States interests and values in the thermonuclear age. That change is necessary has been demonstrated beyond doubt—and not alone by this book.

We believe that the measures we have proposed would materially improve the effectiveness of the Department of Defense. While the organization chart of the Department might look almost the same if those measures were taken, certain changes of far-reaching importance would have been made within that vast mechanism. And while these might not enable us to cope with the increasingly complex problems of the distant future, they would appear adequate to the task immediately at hand.

This leaves, then, the question of whether the measures proposed are feasible. This is not a question which can be easily answered, since some of the alterations we have recommended do not in all respects coincide either with the present trends or with the pace of change in the Department of Defense. More importantly, the roots of some of the problems lie deep in the soil of American life. Thus we must consider the relationship of our military organization to American values and traditions, as well as the validity in today's world of the ways in which we have traditionally handled military affairs.

Chief among the factors causing difficulty are those which relate to differences between civilian and military values. In part, as has already been explained, such differences arise both from the different types of decisions with which civilians and the military are confronted and from the nature of their respective experiences with the decision-making process. In part they arise from the fact that until very recently the lives of the professional military man and the civilian were mutually isolated from one another. Only during the last generation have the military, as leaders of citizen-soldiers, members of civilian communities, and participants in scientific research, business management, and political decision-making, begun truly to integrate themselves into American life. And even more recent has been the continuing and large-scale participation of civilians in military affairs, both as temporary members of the armed forces and as co-workers in scientific, management, and political-military matters. The residue of mutual ignorance and suspicion between military and civilians makes difficult common understanding of, and joint agreement on, organizational and procedural problems.

One evidence of this suspicion and distrust is so important in itself as to warrant attention. Mention has already been made of our ingrained fear of a military dictatorship—of the rise of a "man on horseback." Whatever the rationality of such a belief, it is one of long standing. Our Founding Fathers, with a political philosophy based on the "Glorious Revolution" in England, and with recent and harsh experience with irresponsible British soldiery, wrote into the Constitution their distrust of the military. And, although our history, save for such minor, clumsy, and fruitless attempts as those of James Wilkinson, has been singularly free of any evidence of a military thirst for power, the fear still remains. It must be overcome before we can accept and use the professional soldier for what he is: a specialist in military affairs, with *mores* and attitudes neither more nor less peculiar than those of his fellow specialists who serve as doctors, lawyers, or accountants.

In part the persisting belief in the possibility of a military dictatorship derives from a still more prominent American political thesis: antipathy to the concentration of power in the hands of one individual or group. The separation and division of powers, which is enshrined in our Federal Constitution, is repeated and expanded in other political institutions— including the Department of Defense. Of the essential value of the division of power in preventing autocracy there can be no doubt; of the wisdom of its applicability to every single facet of government there is serious question. And nowhere is that question more grave than in the case of the military, whose very function in our national life requires speed of decision and precision of execution.

Accompanying our diffusion of power is a traditional belief in the desirability of reaching agreement by consensus. The development of consensus, the hammering out of compromise, is an important part of the democratic process, and one whose value with regard to the determination of public issues cannot be overestimated. However, as applied to the Department of Defense, agreement by consensus frequently means either no agreement at all or the adoption of militarily meaningless compromises. The attempt to apply the process of consensus to our military decision-making is responsible for much of the irresolution and many of the troubles which have plagued the Defense Department.

In addition to the attempt to apply *in toto* these long-held political theses to military organizational patterns, there are carry-overs of values from other areas of American life. Chief among them is the belief, derived from our experiences and policies in the field of economics, that competition is always "good." In a free enterprise economy this is generally (although not universally) true; in a military establishment it is largely nonsense. Since the services are "competing" only for the taxpayer's dollar, they tend to concentrate on, or at least to over-advertise, activities and achievements which they believe will secure them the largest number of dollars. Their "competition" does not lower prices, increase output, or result in greater efficiency; quite the contrary. If competition in government does promote efficiency, it would seem logical to establish four complete governments rather than simply to build four separate air forces. Is one any more justifiable than the other?

To these obstacles might be added another of different nature but of equally great importance: the very complexity of the issues involved and the general lack of understanding of these issues. True, our people are overwhelmed by a flood of detailed facts—such as the successes, failures, and rivalries of the different services in the development of ballistic missiles; but it is difficult for the citizen to fit these bits and pieces into a comprehensible mosaic on which he is prepared to stake his own judgment against others as he is prepared to do on issues of domestic policy. The impact on our national security of the complex organizational and operational systems of the Pentagon is difficult for experts even to understand, much less to formulate in terms meaningful to the general public. Yet only a public which clearly understands the nature and implications of our militiary policies will vigorously and intelligently support the kind of effort that will be required during the years ahead. The development of such understanding is one of the principal objectives of this book for, as George Washington stated in his farewell address, "In proportion as the structure of government gives force to public opinion, it is essential that public opinion should be enlightened."

THE ROLE OF THE PUBLIC

What, then, can the public do? What can each of us, as individuals and as citizens, do to prepare ourselves for a consideration of broad problems of military organization? It seems to us that the public has two parts to play—perhaps more important parts than those of any of the other participants.

The first of these is an individual task: that of intelligently re-examining the premises upon which accepted policies are based. Improvements in the Defense Department cannot come solely from the adoption of new organizational arrangements; indeed, these arrangements themselves may not be acceptable unless certain long-held tenets are re-evaluated. Success depends on the values held by both military and civilian participants: their attitudes and objectives, their mutual understanding, the realism with which they appraise our present problems. This in turn leads directly to the larger problem of civil-military relations in our society—the recognition by civilians of the essential roles of the professional military man in maintaining our national security, and the unqualified acceptance by the military of the principles of our political order. The foundation stone of that mutual understanding has been laid; the rest of the base must be erected. Only on such a base can we hope to build a balanced and effective defense structure.

The second task of the public at large is that of attaining and expressing a consensus with regard to the national security policy of the United States and the defense organization designed to support and to implement that policy. There are those who argue that the process of consensus does not involve the bulk of the public but only the opinion leaders and group representatives. There are others who maintain that it is impossible to obtain public consensus on issues so complex and of such little direct concern as the organization of the Defense Department. Both of these views have elements of validity, but it seems to us that their authors miss the essential point. Our political system is based upon the belief that the public can and should decide the broad principles underlying the organization and conduct of government. If democracy is to work, issues must—as they can—be formulated in such terms as to enable the generation of intelligent public opinion and the development of popular support for one proposal or another. That informed leadership may shape public opinion merely places upon those leaders a greater responsibility to help formulate and debate the issues.

In the process of formulating and forming a consensus, the greatest responsibility for leadership falls upon the elected representatives of the people—the President and the Congress. It is to them that the people turn both for a statement of the issues and for the information and argumentation which may help in developing enlightened public opinion. Improvements in defense organization, as in the whole field of national security policy, are so heavily dependent upon the quality of leadership displayed in both the Executive Branch and in the Congress that it is imperative to discuss the respective roles of these two arms of government.

THE ROLE OF THE EXECUTIVE BRANCH

Primary responsibility for the formulation of military policy, for the shaping of military forces, and for the success of the defense effort lies with the Executive Branch. The President is the Commander-in-Chief of the armed forces—and with that authority goes responsibility. While it is true that the Congress is constitutionally charged with making "rules for the government of the land and naval forces," and that the President has many concerns other than those relating to national defense, this does not relieve him of his task; it merely emphasizes the need for a concerted effort to make the necessary improvements.

The President has at his disposal four tools which uniquely enable him to take action. First, he has authority, unless overridden by Congress, to make organizational changes in the Department of Defense, as has been done on several occasions previously. Second, through his executive office he prepares the military budget, presents it to Congress, and controls, within limits, the allocation and the expenditure of the monies appropriated by the Congress. Third, he appoints, by and with the advice and consent of the Senate, the senior military and civilian officials of the Department of Defense—thus determining the type of men who will be called upon to formulate and to implement policy. Finally, he is in a unique position to exercise leadership—not just within the Department of Defense, but with the Congress and with the American people at large. There are no doubt limits beyond which Presidential leadership cannot prevail, especially on narrow issues of great local importance, but there are few cases where the American people have failed to respond to Presidential urgings on questions of vital import.

Assuming that the President and other policymaking members of the Executive Branch are convinced of the need for change, what might be their leadership responsibilities?

In the first place, it will require leadership to acknowledge the need for change and to determine impartially the limits of change. It will require even stronger leadership to overcome apathy and inertia, and to oust vested interests from their entrenched positions. It will require that judiciousness which is the essence of leadership to bring about needed alterations without doing permanent harm to the structure of the military service or the morale of those serving in the Department of Defense. And, since some of the essential changes do cut deeply, it will require the very finest of leadership to inspire others at all levels to carry out their tasks. For instance, the military services have in the past opposed the adoption of a program budget because it would all too clearly show the lack of relation between strategic plans, force levels, and programs, and could enable the application of priorities to military spending. However, such a budget would also provide the Congress—and the public—with a much better check on partisan claims with regard to the strengthening or weakening of forces and the sufficiency of programs—and could be equally anathema to some politicians. It will thus require the highest leadership to implement proposals the effect of which might be to eliminate cherished prerogatives or to expose inefficiencies on the part of the directing officials, military or civilian.

Beyond this, moreover, the Executive Branch will have to take the lead in obtaining Congressional and public support for its proposals. It should do this first of all by translating its proposals, whatever the technical complexity of the enabling legislation, into clear terms and by relating them to vital principles and issues. Second, it should take the responsibility for implementing such of the alterations as lie within its powers, especially those procedural measures which do not change existing principles of organization. This is essential to avoid extending the debate on defense organization into minor and essentially technical fields. Thirdly, since the final word on basic changes within the structure lies with Congress, the Executive Branch should provide to Congress clear and comprehensive arguments for change; and it should seek to win the support of the powerful committees which deal with the armed forces and with government organization. Undoubtedly, skillful negotiation with and cultivation of Congress will be required to win assent to some measures. Finally, the Executive Branch will have to lead the effort to create public understanding of and support for the broad changes which are recommended.

All this is said not to print a primer on Presidential handling of major issues but to point up the magnitude and the difficulty of the steps which will be required to overcome the obstacles already enumerated. The changes we have proposed, while not radical, touch upon some of the basic tenets of American life and upon the rivalries of powerful and jealous military services. It can be anticipated that both service interests and those of other pressure groups will coalesce around certain issues, such as the recommendation that the military chiefs of the services no longer sit as members of the Joint Chiefs of Staff.

In effect, the full range of security problems can be solved only by a determined effort at all levels of public life. Unless the Executive Branch acts to place its own house in order, unless it provides the essential leadership and impetus to change, the effort may well fail. Such a failure could affect adversely the fortunes of the nation.

THE ROLE OF CONGRESS

But not all of the job can be done by the Executive Branch alone. To paraphrase an old saying, the executive proposes but Congress disposes. And Congress is responsible not only for the support of the armed forces but also for the basic legislation concerning them. Meaningful improvement within the Defense Department will be forthcoming only when both the legislative and the executive branches agree on basic principles. It is not likely that these branches, with their differing responsibilities, will always see eye to eye; but the divergencies between them can be reduced. If the organizational problem can be resolved in such a way that both branches, in discharging their respective responsibilities, can utilize the same criteria, considerable improvement in the determination of national security policy is possible. It is for this reason that so much stress has been placed on certain of our proposed changes, such as the development of functional task forces and the adoption of a program budget.

The Congress has been slow to recognize that its considerations of military policy and of the defense budget might be made easier if it approved a different organizational pattern for the armed forces. Having legislatively sired an organization which is organically incapable of functioning properly, Congress does not hesitate to criticize its deficiencies—but it has ignored its own responsibility for the bastardized Department of Defense.

This situation does not spring from any inattention to the problem or lack of effort on the part of Congress, but rather from certain basic factors in Congressional thinking. These are:

1. A sincere belief that any true integration would require, or lead to, the establishment of a single military Chief of Staff and General Staff, which would constitute a threat to our American way of life.

2. The traditional fear on the part of the legislative branch that any real integration of the Defense Department under tight control of the executive would result in depriving the Congress of the information

it needs to discharge its Constitutional responsibilities and would cause a diminution of Congressional authority.

3. In the absence of forceful and meaningful Executive Branch leadership, the urge and pressure to handle defense issues on a narrow political basis—either by simply opposing Executive Branch proposals or by devoting primary attention to insuring that Congressional local interests are protected or promoted.

Whatever may be thought of these Congressional attitudes, they represent serious obstacles to Congressional cooperation in any reorganization of the Defense Department. In all fairness it must be admitted that some Congressional fears are well grounded. Successive administrations have been less than clear or candid in presenting to Congress their military plans, programs, and requirements, and have attempted to control subsequent presentations by subordinate military and civilian officials. And, although other Congressional fears, such as that of a "man on horseback," are perhaps largely emotional, this does not mean that they are any less difficult to suppress. Arguments to the effect that our proposals provide for meaningful civilian control and carefully avoid establishing a single Chief of Staff are likely to be less than fully persuasive.

What is required, then, is that Congress rise at this time to the heights which it has attained on other occasions. It must understand that, as long as the present structure of the Department of Defense is maintained, Congress will never obtain a clear and comprehensive statement of our security needs or possess effective means of insuring that its Constitutional responsibilities have been discharged. It must recognize that our pressing security problems are soluble only if the military are put in an organizational framework where they can—and are forced to—solve them. It must press for erection of such a framework to encompass the whole field of weapons development and evaluation, the strategic planning process, service roles and missions, and the nature and objectives of civilian control. And Congress must insure that any reorganization which is proposed clearly enables the presentation to its members, as the representatives of the American people, of the broad issues of national security.* It is in the forum of

---

* During the earlier debates on unification, it was suggested that the Joint Chiefs of Staff submit to the Congress a military program and budget separate from that proposed by the Department of Defense. While such a procedure is not recommended here, we do recognize that the Congress is entitled to military advice undiluted by executive branch controls, and that, since it cannot in reason establish a military staff of its own, the Congress must obtain that advice from the Joint Chiefs of Staff. Unfortunately, this still requires that the Joint Chiefs serve two masters—a fact which must be recognized and accepted by both branches of government concerned.

Congress that such issues must first be debated if the American people are to exercise a valid choice among competing strategies and policies.

Such moves will not be easy for the Congress. They will require the development of a whole new approach to the question of military organization, changes in the methods of authorizing and appropriating monies for the Defense Department, and a new confidence in and exchange of information between the Congress and the Executive Branch regardless of which party controls either. They may well require that individual Congressmen sacrifice local interests and cherished prejudices for the good of the nation. This they have done before—and can do again.

CHALLENGE AND RESPONSE

From what has been said, it might be concluded that proposals such as ours have little chance of adoption. The complexity of the issues involved, the opposition of vested interests within and outside the services, the lack of public understanding, and the fact that the changes proposed run somewhat counter to strongly-held feelings and opinions—all seem to augur ill. And yet American history is full of occasions when people rose to similar challenges. The Sherman Anti-Trust Act, the Interstate Commerce Act, and the Federal Reserve Act stand today as memorials to previous surges, as in a different and a larger sense, do such bi-partisan triumphs as the Lend-Lease Act, the Marshall Plan, and the North Atlantic Treaty Organization. In terms of military organization, we are in another period of crisis, when national survival may well depend on our ability to respond instantaneously but responsibly to enemy moves.

This is a severe judgment—but it is true. Historically, America's survival has depended on the fact that there has never arisen in Eurasia a power or combination of powers with the strength to dominate that region and the freedom to challenge an isolated America. Today this is changed. Without our support, the non-Communist nations on the rim of the Eastern Hemisphere might long since have been overrun or cowed. Although our productive capacity and technological ability, combined with the resources of the Western Hemisphere, might enable us temporarily to stabilize such a situation, it is certain that our present way of life would not survive the attempt. Nor is this all. For the first time since the Revolution, there exists the possibility not just of American defeat but of her national destruction. In time the Soviet capability to deliver nuclear weapons upon North America is sure to increase; and as yet there are no signs of a certain defense against such an attack.

What makes the danger so profound is that changes in the world balance of power, and in the military technology which is one manifestation of power, have coincided with the development of an alien and hostile ideology. In the Soviet Union and its allies we face not just an aggregation of militarily-powerful nation states but a threat to our entire political and social system. Although military strength is by no means the sole answer to that threat, it constitutes the shield behind which we and our allies can progress economically, socially, and politically. It is not an end in itself, but a means to a larger end: the preservation and ultimately the peaceful triumph throughout the world of democratic and humanitarian principles and ideas.

In sum, then, we face the very real possibility that our nation may fall, and our dream end—as did that of "Eternal Rome"; we face the fact that the nature of our response to this challenge will reveal whether or not American social and political institutions, based on the principles of constitutional democracy, can survive; and we know that, in part, our success in meeting the present test depends upon the effectiveness of our defenses.

Certain conclusions follow inevitably. It will require increasing effort and attention to shield ourselves and our allies against the protracted Communist assault. We cannot expect to counter the ambiguous threats posed by growing Communist military power while constantly decreasing the proportion of our resources which we devote to that task. And we cannot expect even additional security expenditures to maintain the precarious balance of terror unless we effectively and efficiently utilize our resources. Our defense structure must be adequate to the task confronting it.

We believe that the present structure is not adequate. This book has described many and serious shortcomings in the organization and operations of the Defense Department. Although reasonable men may well discount some of these feelings or disagree with certain of the recommendations which we have advanced, we do not believe that our over-all judgment can be lightly set aside. We are convinced that an effective American response to the Communist challenge must include major improvements in our defense establishment. We have argued that such changes can and must be accomplished within the framework of our basic political institutions and beliefs, for we have no desire to undermine from within the political system which we seek to defend. But—and we repeat—ours or similar changes are essential—as a minimum.

The problem we confront is not unique. Each people, each generation, faces a challenge to its powers. Upon the American people has devolved the awesome responsibility of maintaining a way of life and guarding a civilization which could be destroyed in an instant. Toward the discharge of this responsibility we must apply every effort. In its service we must use every instrument compatible with our moral and political principles. And we must see that the Department of Defense, a prime instrument in efforts to secure the free world, can meet the heavy and novel burdens which the future will impose. Certainly the task of preparing the Department for its role is no more difficult than that which confronted Elihu Root when he carried through Congress the radical Army Reorganization Act of 1903. Who will say that this generation cannot produce men of similar skill and determination—in the Executive Branch, in Congress, and among the public at large?

Set in Linotype Electra
Format by Joe Vesely
Manufactured by The Haddon Craftsmen, Inc.
Published by HARPER & BROTHERS, *New York*